Is Your
GOD
Too Small?

Unless otherwise specified, all Scriptures are taken from the King James Version of the Holy Bible.

IS YOUR GOD TOO SMALL?

© 2007 by Dr. Lawson L. Schroeder

Printed in the United States of America

ISBN 1-933641-26-6

Is Your GOD Too Small?

The attributes and actions of Almighty God—
Their meaning to the people of the world

Lawson L. Schroeder, D.D.S.

Contents

Preface 7

Introduction 13

False Gods Versus the True God 17

Is The Bible True? 51

Who Is the God of the Holy Bible?................................. 71

What Does God Know?.. 143

What Has God Done? What Is God Doing?
    What Will God Do? 205

What Does God Have Planned?...................................... 237

So What?... 271

The Four "Rs" That Return Us to God 283

Preface

Since the beginning of human history and continuing to the present age, almost all people have considered many monumental questions. Some of these questions are:

» Where did we come from?
» Why are we here?
» Where are we going?
» What is our significance within the grand scheme of the universe?
» What happens to us after we die?
» Is there some sort of life after death?
» Is there a God?
» Has God revealed Himself?
» What is God like?
» How big is God?
» Did God create the universe?
» Did God create life?
» Did God create plants, animals, and humans?
» Does God care how people live?
» How much does God know?
» Is God dead?

For thousands of years, philosophers and scientists, witch doctors and shamans, priests and popes, theologians and scholars, kings and queens, potentates and dictators, national leaders and community officials, merchants and military, farmers and ranchers, and, most importantly, ordinary people from all civilizations have sought answers to these very important questions.

As a matter of fact, these questions are a puzzle to many people, causing them to wonder about the meaning of life. So, are there correct answers to these questions? And if so, where can the answers be found?

Yes, there are accurate answers to these questions, and the answers are found in the Christian Bible! The Holy Bible has been preserved, read, trusted, and obeyed by Christians for almost two thousand years because they believe the Bible to be the true Word of God. Long before the completion of the twenty–seven books comprising the New Testament portion of the Christian Bible, Hebrew people preserved, honored, and cherished the ancient writings of Moses and other godly men who had received their inspiration directly from the Holy Spirit of God. The thirty–nine books that comprise the Old Testament of the Holy Bible record the origins of the earth, the universe, and mankind, and document how sin and suffering entered the perfect world that God created. The Old Testament also records a multitude of events that reveal both the nature of people and the history of the Hebrew nation.

One of the messages communicated by the Old Testament is that when people reject God's leadership they tend to become selfish, sinful, unfriendly, self–centered, mean, cruel, rebellious, greedy, dominating, inconsiderate, deceptive, violent, vile, unfaithful, prideful, degenerate, and ungodly. Interestingly, these character qualities are opposite to the nature of the Almighty Creator God as revealed in the Holy Bible. For His own reasons, God does not choose to have fellowship with people who have rejected His love and His leadership. However, God truly loves all of the people He has created. God knows that without His help, humans are unable to become acceptable to Him. For this reason, God made a way for humans to become acceptable to Him.[1]

---

1. "For God so loved the world, that he gave his only begotten Son, that whosoever believeth in him should not perish, but have everlasting life. For God sent not his Son into the world to condemn the world; but that the world through him

This "way" is often referred to as God's plan of redemption—a plan revealed in the Bible. God's plan of redemption is centered on one person, the Lord Jesus Christ. Jesus Christ is Savior! Throughout the Old Testament many prophecies concerning the Messiah are recorded so humans may look for Him, recognize Him, believe Him, trust Him, respond to Him, and follow Him.

The New Testament of the Bible presents the only true solution to the problems of mankind by revealing Messiah as promised in the Old Testament. The twenty–seven books of the New Testament document the birth, life, teachings, death, resurrection, ascension, and promises of the future return of the Lord Jesus Christ. The fulfillments of many Old Testament prophecies concerning the promised Messiah, the Lord Jesus Christ, are found in the New Testament. The remaining prophecies concerning Messiah will be fulfilled during His second coming and beyond in God's plans for the future. The New Testament also records some of the first–century history of the Christian church and reveals how God will eliminate the influence of Satan and sin from His creation.

The Christian Holy Bible is the only accurate record of God's written communication to mankind. God could have used other methods to share His message of the meaning of life. But God chose to accomplish this extraordinarily important task through the writings of men that He inspired to document His principles for living, how the end of this age would come about, and to provide a glimpse of both Heaven and Hell.

> **All scripture is given by inspiration of God, and is profitable for doctrine, for reproof, for correction, for instruction in righteousness: That the man of God may be perfect, throughly furnished unto all good works.**
> —2 Timothy 3:16–17

might be saved" (John 3:16–17).

The Holy Bible is the only totally accurate source for answers to these monumental questions and the many other great questions of people who seek to find meaning and purpose for human life and for the existence of the universe.

Sadly, however, many people have not seriously studied the Bible to learn the right answers to these questions. Because of the failure to study, understand, and believe the Holy Bible, a number of alternative and incorrect answers have been developed. A few people outright reject the existence of God and deny the possibility of any "supernatural" intervention into the origin of, or the working of, the universe. These people generally believe that the universe and life appeared by chance through a "cosmic" accident or chance occurrence. Others who do not wish to completely deny the existence of God have formulated a multitude of compromised belief systems that allow for a little, to a lot, of supernatural intervention into the creation of the universe and all of the life that it contains. Still others believe there is a "higher power" that is involved with life in the universe. Belief systems like this may include a "circle of life" concept that encompasses living things. Many people have created, carved, or invented their own gods to match their needs and desires. Additionally and unfortunately, multitudes have been deceived by religious groups and leaders who have produced their own holy book(s). These religious groups have developed procedures that people must follow in order for them to become acceptable to their false god(s). Some of these many false gods are Allah, Astarte, Aphrodite, Ashtoreth, Baal, Being, Brahma, Buddha, Goddess, Helios, infinite intelligence, Ishtar, Isis, Law, Lord Krishna, Mind, Mother Earth, Mother Nature, Principle, Shiva, Spirit, Tammuz, The Absolute, Vahiguru, Venus, Vishnu, and Zeus.[2]

Some people have chosen to serve Satan (the devil himself) and call him their god. Many moral, law–abiding, decent, kind, thoughtful,

2. *Rose Book of Bible Charts, Maps & Timelines*, Rose Publishing, Inc. Torrance CA. 2005, pp. 168–174 and 6 April 2007 <http://www.christiangay.com/he_loves/false.htm>

and wonderful people think that if their "good deeds" outweigh their "bad deeds" that at the end of their lives they will become acceptable to their god or God, and they will be rewarded in Heaven or during life after death. Seemingly, still others have chosen to not try to find answers to these questions and therefore live without any thought for the meaning and purpose of life outside of themselves and perhaps their friends and community.

Finally, there are people who call themselves Christian but who are not adequately aware of the attributes, abilities, and knowledge of the God that they love and trust. Yet, some Christians have sought God and studied Scripture sufficiently to realize that the magnitude of God is beyond human comprehension, and through Bible study have learned that God loves and cares for all of His creation in a truly extraordinary manner!

Dear reader, this book has been prepared for you so that you may begin to understand the view of God that is recorded in the Holy Bible. Regardless of your religious background or persuasion, I challenge you to compare your belief system and your god(s) or God with the unique, holy God described in the Christian Bible. When you complete this comparison, it is possible that you will find that your god or God is too small to answer your questions or meet your needs. If your God is too small, please know that it is possible for you to meet, serve, and love the true and only God of the universe. At the conclusion of this book is a section that will explain how you can have a personal relationship with God that will last for eternity. Hopefully, this book will help you realize how big Almighty God really is!

Introduction

In this book I will not try to impress you with exceptional writing skills and witty remarks. However, I do want your reading to be an interesting, insightful, and informative experience. The purpose of this book is to allow the words from the Holy Bible to introduce you to the God who by His spoken word created the entire universe from nothing—in only six twenty-four–hour days. I will try to be as honest as I can be to identify my own thoughts and assumptions in contrast to what the Bible says. In addition, to help you know the source of the information presented in this book, you will find a proven and valuable writing technique used in this book: footnotes. Footnotes will be found at the bottom of every page where the author believes there is information needing reference or explanation. This should be helpful for you—the intelligent and thoughtful reader.

Here is an example of an illustration utilizing footnotes:

Question: Is there an example from the Bible that demonstrates how much God knows?

Answer: Jesus Christ said that God knows when one sparrow falls on the ground. Jesus also stated that God does not forget a single sparrow.

Bible references:

Are not two sparrows sold for a farthing? and one of them shall not fall on the ground without your Father. But the very hairs of your head are all numbered. Fear ye not therefore, ye are of more value than many sparrows.

—Matthew 10:29-31

Are not five sparrows sold for two farthings, and not one of them is forgotten before God? But even the very hairs of your head are all numbered. Fear not therefore: ye are of more value than many sparrows.

—Luke 12:6-7

The late Dr. Henry M. Morris[3] made the following comment on the verses found in Matthew and Luke, "Jesus also said that 'five sparrows [are] sold for two farthings' (Luke 12:6). Evidently the sparrow merchants of that day had already introduced the sales method of quantity discounts!"[4]

In case you are not familiar with the term *farthing*, this is the name of a British coin worth one–quarter of a penny. Farthings were first minted in England in the thirteenth century and were used as legal tender in England until December 31, 1960.[5] It is interesting that the image of a sparrow is found on one side of a farthing minted in 1954.

So what does God know—about sparrows, other birds, and humans?

For God to know when one sparrow falls to the ground anywhere on earth, we must affirm that God has extraordinary—no, supernatural—abilities. Consider the magnitude of being able to accomplish this one task.

1. God must know a sparrow from every other bird. God says that He knows "all the fowls of the mountains."[6]

---

3. Henry M. Morris, 1918–2006, B.S. in Civil Engineering, Rice Univ., M.S. in Hydraulics, and Ph.D. in Hydraulic Engineering, Univ. of Minnesota, assisted in founding Creation Research Society and the Institute for Creation Research, widely regarded as the founder of the modern creationist movement.
4. Morris, Henry M., *The Defender's Study Bible—King James Version*, World Publishing, Inc., Iowa Falls, Iowa 50126, U.S.A., 1995, p. 1021.
5. 29 December 2006 <http://en.wikipedia.org/wiki/British_Farthing_coin>
6. "I know all the fowls of the mountains: and the wild beasts of the field are mine" (Ps. 50:11).

2. God must know the number of sparrows in the world at every moment.

3. God must know the location of every sparrow in the world at every moment.

4. God must know the position of every sparrow in every part of the world at every moment—whether the bird is in an egg, in flight, or perched on some object.

5. God must know the health status and the thoughts of every sparrow at all times. God must know if the sparrow on a perch is planning to fly, and God must know if a flying sparrow is thinking about landing.

6. God's knowledge about the status of sparrows is for this moment in time, but God's knowledge is also for every previous moment in time going back to the moment when God created the very first sparrows.[7]

7. God must truly care about sparrows and His creation to keep track of what to us may seem to be a very minor and unimportant collection of information.

8. If God knows this much about sparrows and cares this much about sparrows, it is certainly reasonable to assume that God must also care about albatrosses, bluebirds, cardinals, doves, eagles, finches, great gray owls, hummingbirds, Iceland gulls, jaybirds, king elders, larks, mallards, northern mockingbirds, oilbirds, purple martins, quail, robins, swans, turkey vultures, upland sandpipers, Virginia rails, whip-poor-wills, yellow–bellied sapsuckers, zone–tailed hawks, and every other kind of bird in the world. [8]

9. Since God tracks, knows, and cares about the movements of sparrows, it would be logical and reasonable to expect that God would extend this same care and knowledge for all birds in the world. God knows as much about all of the other birds as He does about

---

7. Genesis 1:21—On the fifth day of creation week God created "every winged fowl after his kind."

8. 29 December 2006 ‹http://www.birds.cornell.edu/AllAboutBirds/BirdGuide/›

sparrows. As incredible as it seems, God knows when any bird falls to the ground. And, God knows this about every bird since He created birds on day five of creation week.

10. God also possesses this knowledge about all of the species of birds that are now extinct.

11. If God cares for humans like He cares for birds, it is certainly reasonable to assume that God must know where every human is in every part of the world at every moment. Is it possible that God cares for humans more than He cares for birds? Yes! Jesus said, **"Ye are of more value than many sparrows."**[9] Since this is the case, God must also know what every human is doing now and what every human is thinking at every moment.[10] This knowledge would also include the movement and thoughts of every human who has ever lived. Surely, God must also know our health status and our thoughts and intentions at every moment. The Bible has much to say on these last comments, and you should find much more information on what God knows later on in this book. According to the words of Jesus, God has more knowledge than the human mind can even begin to comprehend.[11]

From this example, you can see how I plan to present the Bible's words and statements to help us as we begin to better understand the absolute knowledge possessed by the Bible's Creator God. Hopefully, this book will allow you to think more about the abilities, the nature, and the knowledge that the God of the Bible possesses.

Is it possible that your God may be too small?

May the words, the message, and the God of the Holy Bible bring light, understanding, and hope to your total eternal being.

---

9. Matthew 10:31 and Luke 12:7
10. Job 42:2 and Psalm 139:1–10
11. "But the very hairs of your head are all numbered" (Matt. 10:30). When this verse and others are applied to all of the people who have ever lived, the unfathomable knowledge of God can be sensed.

Chapter 1

False Gods Versus the True God

> I am the LORD, and there is none else, there is no God be-
> side me: I girded thee, though thou hast not known me:
> That they may know from the rising of the sun, and from
> the west, that there is none beside me. I am the LORD, and
> there is none else.
>
> —Isaiah 45:5–6

Some of the joys of travel are found in restaurants. Eating is a worldwide custom enjoyed by almost[12] everyone in every nation. According
to *The World Almanac and Book of Facts 2007*, as of mid–2006 there were
194 nations in the world.[13] Cooks from every nation use their kitch-
ens for food preparation and presentation that they hope will delight
their customers and encourage return visits to their establishment.
For some, cooking is a matter of survival, while for others culinary
creativity is a matter of pride, enjoyment, tradition, heritage, or even
deception. You may wonder why a cook would practice deception. Keep
reading. Regardless of their menu or motivation, the fare chefs prepare
is a way to savor the flavor of a community or even a country. In the
process of dining in various restaurants you may also learn some of

---

12. Unfortunately some people experience pain or difficulty in chewing due to oral
disease or missing teeth, and they do not enjoy eating.
13. *The World Almanac and Book of Facts 2007*, World Almanac Books, A division
of World Almanac Education Group, Inc., New York, New York, p. 745. [The
United Nations has 192 member nations. Two of the 194 nations are not
members of the U.N. They are Taiwan and Vatican City, or the Holy See.]

the customs, culture, and history of the people in an area.

In a restaurant in Stuttgart, Germany, my family and I discovered a delightful ravioli–like food called maultaschen. This is a Swabian specialty made of pasta dough with a filling traditionally made of minced meat, spinach, bread crumbs, and onions with parsley flavoring.[14] Our waiter told us that maultaschen have been enjoyed in southern Germany for hundreds of years. Reportedly, it is especially popular during the Lenten season because some Christians have a custom of not eating meat during Lent. According to legend, maultaschen were invented during Lent by bored cooks, possibly monks of the Maulbronn monastery,[15] who missed eating meat during the lengthy Lenten season. They found a way to hide ground pork within the spinach and doughy shell.[16] Supposedly this deception allowed Swabians to eat meat during Lent by concealing it in this way. Apparently some believed this deception hid the meat from the watchful eye of the parish priest and possibly from their omniscient deity Himself.[17] Perhaps the origin of maultaschen is more of a tradition than actual fact, but the point remains that there are times when people think that they can conceal their thoughts, their motives, their decisions, and even their actions from God.

Some people imagine that they can hide from God. Others think that God does not know or notice what they do, or that God does not care what they do. Actually, only a small percentage of people think that God does not exist. A recent Gallup poll says that only three percent of the people in the United States are certain that God does

---

14. 20 March 2007 <http://en.wikipedia.org/wiki/maultasche>
15. The Maulbronn monastery, located in Maulbronn, Baden–Wurttemberg, Germany, began in 1147 as an abbey for the Cistercian order. The monastery was dissolved after the Reformation. Its buildings now house a Protestant theological seminary. 5 January 2008 <http://home.bawue.de/~wmwerner/english/maulbron.htm>
16. 20 March 2007 <http://www.chemengsoftware.com/germany/maultaschen.htm>
17. 20 March 2007 <http://www.recipezaar.com/2758>

not exist.[18] People who do not believe that God or supernatural beings exist are called atheists.[19] People who believe that God is unknowable or incoherent and thus meaningless and irrelevant to life are called agnostics.[20] Some atheists and agnostics have developed a website to explain their non-belief system. This website is called "About: Agnosticism/Atheism."[21] The Barna Group has said that ten percent of the adults in the United States are either atheists or agnostics. In addition, ten percent of the U.S. population identify with a faith other than Christianity. However, seventy-one percent of the people in the USA believe in God when described as the all-powerful, all-knowing, perfect Creator of the universe who rules the world today.[22]

It is very sad that people who reject the existence of God have apparently made their determination based on limited information. Through *their* reasoning, *they* have come to the conclusion that there is no God at all. These people have used their truly amazing three-pound brain—which was designed and created by God—to discern that *they* know without a doubt that throughout the entire universe there is no God. Some people believe that all we see is a cosmic accident. Others have developed some other naturalistic explanation for the existence of such a finely-tuned and amazingly complex universe. To believe that there is no God may be the epitome of arrogance, ignorance, or despair.

I cannot speak for atheists since I believe in the existence of the eternal God of the Holy Bible. However, I have met some reliable and respectable people who claim to be atheistic and some reliable and respectable people who claim to be agnostic in their belief system. It

18. Frank Newport, "Who Believes in God and Who Doesn't?", The Gallup Poll, 23 June 2006, p. 1., 6 April 2006 <http://www.galluppoll.com/content/?ci=234708pg=1>.
19. 29 December 2006 <http://dictionary.reference.com/browse/atheist>.
20. 29 December 2006 <http://en.wikipedia.org/wiki/Agnostic>.
21. 29 December 2006 <http://atheism.about.com>.
22. The Barna Group, "Beliefs: General Religious, Faith groups," 27 March 2007 <http://www.barna.org>.

appears that individuals who reject the existence of God do so based on their own personal observations. These personal observations may be numerous, and they may be significant, but they are terribly inadequate to prove that God does not exist or is unknowable. The Bible speaks regarding the concept of disbelief in the existence of God.

> **The fool hath said in his heart, There is no God. They are corrupt, they have done abominable works, there is none that doeth good.**
>
> —Psalm 14:1

Some people have said that if God existed, certain bad experiences would not have happened to them or someone they know, and bad experiences would not have happened in history. Bad experiences do not mean that God does not exist. If anything, bad experiences mean that Satan, the devil, exists. It is much more reasonable that bad experiences would be caused by Satan, a rebellious angel—and ultimate cause of evil—than by the loving Creator God of the universe. The Bible records how Satan deceived Adam and Eve in the Garden of Eden.[23] Because of the work of Satan and the rebellion of Adam and Eve, there is a curse on mankind, a curse on the earth,[24] and a curse on the universe.[25] The suffering, sorrow, and pain in the world today are the result of human rebellion and sin which at times may be combined with the deception of Satan, who is still deceiving people today.

Satan deceives individuals, families, and groups of people. Satan deceives respectable and intelligent people who refer to themselves as atheists and agnostics. Satan deceives good, respectable, friendly, involved, committed, honest, loving, giving, moral, and even church-going people. Some of these deceived people are Christians who live throughout the world.

---

23. Genesis 3:1–7
24. Genesis 3:16–19
25. Romans 8:22

One way people are deceived is by believing that if during their lifetime they do more good deeds than bad deeds then they will become acceptable to God. By earning God's approval, they will receive His eternal "reward." Satan has even deceived some fine Christian people by making them "work for their salvation." This "working for their salvation" means that throughout life, even up to the time of their death, they do not know if they will be allowed to be with God forever in Heaven. Sadly, these individuals think that they must keep doing more good things than bad things so that at the end of their lives their good deeds will "outweigh" their bad deeds or sins, and they will be acceptable to God.

George Barna has a name for people who believe that their salvation is dependent on their demonstrating that they are Christians. He refers to them as "notional" Christians. According to Barna, notional Christians describe themselves as Christians, but they don't believe they will have eternal life through their reliance upon the death and resurrection of Jesus Christ and the grace extended to people through a relationship with the Lord Jesus Christ. A large majority of notional Christians believe they will have eternal life only because of their good works and not because of a grace-based relationship with Jesus Christ.[26]

Some may find these next sentences quite shocking. George Barna reports that fifty percent of all adults who attend Protestant churches on a typical Sunday morning are notional Christians or non-Christian. Reportedly, the late Dr. Bill Bright, founder of Campus Crusade for Christ, also considered fifty percent to accurately identify the number of non-Christians attending Protestant churches on typical Sunday mornings. In an October 2003 study, Barna revealed that fifty percent of professing born-again Christians contend that a person can earn their salvation based upon their good works. This clearly contradicts

---

26. 26 December 2007 <http://barna.org/FlexPage.
aspx?Page=Topic&TopicID=46>.

the biblical teaching that salvation is by grace alone and not by works.[27] Here are some passages from the Bible that speak directly to this situation:

> *Not by works of righteousness which we have done,* but according to his mercy he saved us, by the washing of regeneration, and renewing of the Holy Ghost; Which he shed on us abundantly through Jesus Christ our Saviour; That being justified by his grace, we should be made heirs according to the hope of eternal life.
>
> —Titus 3:5–7

> But God, who is rich in mercy, for his great love wherewith he loved us, Even when we were dead in sins, hath quickened us together with Christ, (by grace ye are saved;) And hath raised us up together, and made us sit together in heavenly places in Christ Jesus: That in the ages to come he might shew the exceeding riches of his grace in his kindness toward us through Christ Jesus. For by grace are ye saved through faith; and that not of yourselves: it is the gift of God: *Not of works, lest any man should boast.*
>
> —Ephesians 2:4–9

Unfortunately, Satan has deceived many people by causing them to believe that they do not need to repent of their sins and call upon the Lord Jesus Christ to be their Lord and Savior. Satan is also deceiving large groups of people by uniting them in religious groups or religions that require sacrifices similar to those found in Scripture. Certainly, Satan uses many methods to deceive, but his primary deception is that good deeds or sacrifices can make people acceptable to their idol, god, or God. Satan has told people practicing the religions of the world that

---

27. 27 March 2007 <http://www.facingforever.org/html/lost.asp>.

if they do more "good" things or more "good" works than "bad" things then they may be acceptable to their god and may earn the right to go to a Heaven–like place at the end of their lives.

The biblical process of becoming acceptable to God, not by works but by faith alone, is often referred to by Christians as "The Good News" or "The Gospel." The gospel and salvation will be discussed in more detail later in this book.

Hurricanes, hail storms, ice storms, blizzards, floods, earthquakes, tornados, tsunamis, bolts of lightning, meteors that strike the earth, and other "natural" events which for some reason are referred to as "acts of God" by insurance companies are part of the curse on the earth that was brought about because of the deceptive work of Satan and the rebellion of Adam and Eve.[28]

In 1915, W. S. Hottel, who was then the pastor of the Mennonite Brethren in Christ Church in Bethlehem, Pennsylvania, made this clear and concise statement: "God's supreme and only test for mankind during this age is their acceptance or rejection of Jesus Christ as their Savior and Lord."[29] God allows everyone, not just atheists and agnostics, to make their choice of where they want to spend eternity. Everyone either chooses to love and obey God or to rebel against God and do what they want to do. The rejection of the existence of God has eternal consequences. Everyone who rejects God and His love has selected a course that, unless changed, will lead them to eternal separation from God! They will, by their own choice, determine their eternal destiny.

In 1918, Frederick Speakman, a British novelist, made the statement, "The roads we take are more important than the goals we announce. Decisions determine destiny."[30] The three words, "Decisions determine destiny," are certainly appropriate when people decide if

---

28. Genesis 3:17–18
29. W. S. Hottel, "What the Mennonite Brethren in Christ Stand For" 28 December 2006 <http://www.bfchistory.org/Hottelarticle.htm>.
30. 6 April 2007 <http://www.allmyquotes.com/quote/frederick_speakman/>.

they will accept or reject Jesus Christ as their Lord and Savior.

Consider this . . .

The questions, "Why do bad things happen?" and "Why do bad things happen to good people?" are certainly significant. These questions have been discussed in detail for decades by philosophers, skeptics, theologians, non–Christians, and Christians. David Fairchild, pastor of Kaleo Church in San Diego, California, recently created a blog on the topic "The problems of evil and suffering—answering it with the gospel."[31] In this discussion, Pastor Fairchild shared two arguments that have been made against the existence of God. They are outlined below.

The Scottish skeptic and philosopher David Hume (1711–1776) argued against the existence of God with these statements and conclusion:

1. A good God would destroy evil.
2. An all powerful God could destroy evil.
3. Evil is not destroyed.
4. Therefore, there cannot be such a God who is both good and powerful.

John Leslie Mackie (1917–1981), an Oxford University professor, stated these observations and conclusion regarding the existence of God:

1. If God exists, there couldn't be evil unless he would have a reason for justifying His permitting it. (When people say they don't see why God would allow evil, what they are saying is that they can't think of a reason why God would allow evil and suffering.)
2. Evil exists all around.

---

31. 22 March, 2007, <http://www.pastorfairchild.com/2007-07/24/the-problem-of-evil-and-suffering--answering-it-with-the-gospel/>.

3. There is no reason we can discern for God's justifying His permitting of evil.
4. Therefore God must not exist.

Perhaps the following list will help address the conclusions of Hume, Mackie, and others concerning the existence of God and the situation of bad things and evil existing in the world. This list was presented by John Stonestreet[32] while on the faculty of Bryan College[33] in Dayton, Tennessee. He summarizes four common reasons that people often give to explain why God allows bad things to happen:

1. God is all-powerful, but He doesn't care that much about the people in His Creation.
2. God cares about people, but He does not have the power to "fix all situations."
3. God is not all-powerful and He does not care about His creation, or He is so feeble that He cannot or does not care about how people live.
4. God is all-powerful and He does care about His creation, but Almighty God chooses to allow certain events to happen for specific reasons known only to Him.[34]

I believe that the correct answer to the question, "Why do bad things happen?" is found in Mr. Stonestreet's fourth point. God does have the power to eliminate bad experiences and evil from the world, but for His own purposes He has not chosen to remove these undesirable events from the world at this time. In addition, Pastor David Fairchild

---

32. John Stonestreet has a B.A. in Bible, Bryan College, and an M.A. in Christian Thought from Trinity Evangelical Divinity School.
33. Bryan College is a four-year liberal arts, non-affiliated Christian college with an enrollment of approximately 1,000 students. It is located in Dayton, Tennessee.
34. Stonestreet, John, *Why Does God Let Me Hurt?*, a lecture given during the Summit Conference held at Bryan College in Dayton, Tennessee, on 31 July 2006.

concluded his blog discussion on the presence of evil and suffering in the world by saying that God may have reasons for evil and suffering which we cannot discern at this time.[35]

As you consider Mr. Stonestreet's four reasons that may explain why God allows bad things to happen in the universe He created, it would certainly be prudent to see what God has to say about this subject in the Holy Bible. As you read this book, you will find many Bible passages that reveal some of God's reasons for allowing bad things to happen. You will have the opportunity to decide for yourself why bad things happen.

If a person truly believes that there is no God, how would he or she answer the question, "Why do so many good things happen?" You may learn in the Bible if God plans to allow bad things to continue happening in His universe. You may also consider if God has plans for more good things to happen at some time in the future. According to the Bible, there is going to be a time in the future that will be peaceful, beautiful, and wonderful! This glorious time will be experienced by all people who have asked God to forgive their sins and who have placed their trust in the salvation and redemption provided through the Lord Jesus Christ![36] Near the conclusion of the last book in the Bible, God promises a time when there will be no more pain, no more suffering, no more death, no more sorrow, and no more tears.[37] This is a promise that only the God of the Bible can make and keep.

You are entitled to your opinion. Whether your decision is right or wrong, it's yours! God is gracious and He will not force you to change your opinion about Him. However, the Bible says that if you seek Him with all of your heart, you will find Him. Here is a verse from the

---

35. 25 March 2007 <http://www.pastorfairchild.com/2007-02/24/the-problem-of-evil-and-suffering--answering-it-with-the-gospel/>.
36. Since God is immutable, His method of redemption never changes. During the Old Testament era and the New Testament/church age, the forgiveness of sins was and is based on a substitutionary blood sacrifice using the exchanged life principle. 28 December 2007 <http://www.bible.org/page.php?page_id=377>.
37. Revelation 21:4

Bible that makes it possible for the author to confidently make the preceding statement.

> **But if from thence thou shalt seek the LORD thy God, thou shalt find him, if thou seek him with all thy heart and with all thy soul.**
>
> —Deuteronomy 4:29

The next section of this chapter will address some very good questions that have been asked by many good people. Following each question is an answer that may add to your understanding. The answers include information from various sources. And most of the answers include some of the Bible's comments on these questions.

Aren't there many gods?

Yes, there certainly are many gods that are fervently venerated, respected, and worshiped by the religions of the world. God, the author of the Bible, definitely recognized the existence of gods and idols that are made by men. He made many comments about their harmful influence. Here are a few passages from the Bible that state what the God of the Bible thinks about the gods of the world's religions.

> **... and against all the gods of Egypt I will execute judgment: I am the LORD.**
>
> —Exodus 12:12b

> **For great is the LORD, and greatly to be praised: he also is to be feared above all gods. For all the gods of the people are idols: but the LORD made the heavens.**
>
> —1 Chronicles 16:25–26

> **For all the gods of the nations are idols: but the LORD made the heavens.**
>
> —Psalm 96:5

In the following two verses God says that there are no other gods:

Tell ye, and bring them near; yea, let them take counsel together: who hath declared this from ancient time? who hath told it from that time? have not I the LORD? and there is no God else beside me; a just God and a Saviour; there is none beside me. Look unto me, and be ye saved, all the ends of the earth: for I am God, and there is none else.

—Isaiah 45:21–22

Remember the former things of old: for I am God, and there is none else; I am God, and there is none like me.

—Isaiah 46:9

What is a false god or an idol?

The term idol is routinely used in the Bible to refer to a false god or the object of worship by individuals or groups of people. Here are two definitions of the word "idol."

» idol—The specific term that denotes the image of a god when such is the object of worship, but any material symbol of the supernatural which is the object of worship may be called an idol.[38]

» idol—(1) an image of divinity, a symbol or representative of a deity or any other being or thing made or used as an object of worship; broadly: a false god: a heathen deity (2) an effigy, a statue (3) a pretender, an impostor (4) something or someone on which affections are strongly and often excessively set: an object of passionate devotion.[39]

38. *The Interpreter's Dictionary of the Bible—An Illustrated Encyclopedia*, George Arthur Buttrick—Dictionary Editor, Abingdon Press, Nashville, New York, 1962, Vol. 2, E–J, p. 673.

39. *Webster's Third New International Dictionary of the English Language—Unabridged*, Editor in Chief Philip Babcock Gove, Ph.D., Merriam–Webster Inc. Publishers, Springfield, Massachusetts, 1993, p. 1124.

Here are a few passages from the Bible that state what God thinks or says about idols or false gods:

> **Turn ye not unto idols, nor make to yourselves molten gods: I am the LORD your God.**
>
> —Leviticus 19:4

> **Ye shall make you no idols nor graven image, neither rear you up a standing image, neither shall ye set up any image of stone in your land, to bow down unto it: for I am the LORD your God.**
>
> —Leviticus 26:1

> **. . . For he is an holy God; he is a jealous God; he will not forgive your transgressions nor your sins. If ye forsake the LORD, and serve strange gods, then he will turn and do you hurt, and consume you, after that he hath done you good.**
>
> —Joshua 24:19–20

> **For the LORD is a great God, and a great King above all gods.**
>
> —Psalm 95:3

> **And the idols he shall utterly abolish.**
>
> —Isaiah 2:18

> **Therefore say unto the house of Israel, Thus saith the Lord GOD; Repent, and turn yourselves from your idols; and turn away your faces from all your abominations.**
>
> —Ezekiel 14:6

> **And it shall come to pass in that day, saith the LORD of hosts, that I will cut off the names of the idols out of the land, and they shall no more be remembered: and also I will cause the**

prophets and the unclean spirit to pass out of the land.

—Zechariah 13:2

As concerning therefore the eating of those things that are offered in sacrifice unto idols, we know that an idol is nothing in the world, and that there is none other God but one.

—1 Corinthians 8:4

Yes, God is well aware of the existence of idols, imposter gods, fake gods, and false gods and their prophets. The first of the Ten Commandments says, "Thou shalt have no other gods before me."[40] The Ten Commandments were written in stone by God Himself.[41]

God also knows that humans can be deceived and tricked by false gods. He has warned people to watch out for the deception that comes with false gods and false prophets. Joshua stated that God "will not forgive your transgressions nor your sins. If ye forsake the LORD, and serve strange gods, then he will turn and do you hurt, and consume you, after that he hath done you good."[42]

The second commandment[43] speaks against worshiping false gods such as is done by animists. The belief system known as animism says that the earth is a spiritual world where individual spirits may inhabit ordinary animals and objects. These animals could be bears or birds and the objects could be mountains or the moon. Any animals or any objects apparently can become the home of a personalized spirit. Any of these animals or objects could be idols or false gods. Whether the spirits are gods or not is apparently determined by the belief of the individual or group.[44]

---

40. Exodus 20:3
41. Exodus 34:1
42. Joshua 24:19–20
43. "Thou shalt not make unto thee any graven image, or any likeness of any thing that is in heaven above, or that is in the earth beneath, or that is in the water under the earth" (Exod. 20:4).
44. 29 December 2006 <http://en.wikipedia.org/wiki/Animism>.

Don't most religions have some sort of a god?

Historians say that most Egyptians who lived from two thousand to four thousand years ago believed that there were many gods. Here is a brief list of ancient Egyptian gods and their areas of influence. [45]

» Amen—"The Hidden One," a primordial creation deity
» Bast—Egyptian cat goddess
» Chons—Egyptian moon god
» Geb—god of the earth
» Min—Egyptian fertility god
» Osiris—Egyptian god of the underworld and of vegetation
» Re—Egyptian sun god
» Shu—Egyptian god of the air
» Thoth—Egyptian moon god

What are the major religions of the world?

The following is a list of religions and religious preferences of the peoples of the world. This information has been compiled by the Central Intelligence Agency of the United States government in their World Fact Book. The percentages are estimates from 2004. [46]

»	Christians	33.03 %
»	Muslims	20.12 %
»	Hindus	13.34 %
»	Buddhists	5.89 %
»	Sikhs	0.39 %
»	Jews	0.23 %
»	other religions	12.61 %
»	non religious	12.03 %
»	atheists	2.36 %

45. 29 December 2006 <http://socsci.colorado.edu/LAB/GODS/>.
46. 29 December 2006 <https://www.cia.gov/cia/publications/factbook/print/xx.htm>.

The following Bible verse shares a strong statement about non–Christians being involved in the worship of false gods:

> **But I say, that the things which the Gentiles sacrifice, they sacrifice to devils, and not to God: and I would not that ye should have fellowship with devils.**
>
> —1 Corinthians 10:20

What is a religion?

With all due respect to the Central Intelligence Agency, Christianity is not a religion. A religion is mankind's process of trying to attain goodness, perfection, and possibly even acceptance with God through human efforts. But in true Christianity, God takes the initiative and reaches for man. Christianity is God saying that man can only approach Him through individual acceptance of His Son, the Lord Jesus Christ.[47]

Do Christians have a God?

Yes! The existence and the attributes of Almighty God are revealed in the Holy Bible. The Christian God is the Creator of the entire universe. The God of the Bible exists as the Father, His Son Jesus Christ, and the Holy Spirit.

Do Muslims have a god?

Yes, the Muslim god is Allah. Allah is the god of the Qur'an (Koran), but Allah is not the God of the Bible because Allah's attributes and teachings are quite different from the God of the Bible. Mohammed's teachings and writings deny that the Lord Jesus Christ is God. However, many Muslims believe Jesus Christ was a great prophet, and, because He lived such a good life, He is in Heaven at this time. The

---

47. Lindsey, Hal and Carlson, C.C., *The Late Great Planet Earth*, Zondervan Publishing House, Grand Rapids, Michigan, 1970, p. 115.

Qur'an alleges that Allah is the God of Abraham and hence the God of the Bible. But there are a number of passages in the Qur'an that describe Allah as a deceiver, the author of evil, the author of historical errors found in the Qur'an, and the author of carnal pleasures. There are multiple major differences in the attributes of the God of the Bible and the character of Allah recorded in the Qur'an. One of them is: "And [the unbelievers] *schemed* and planned, and Allah *schemed also, and the best of schemers is Allah*" (S. 3:54).[48] However, the following passages from the Bible describe God as not being a deceiver, a tempter, and not looking upon evil:

> **For thou art not a God that hath pleasure in wickedness: neither shall evil dwell with thee.**
>
> —Psalm 5:4

> **Thou art of purer eyes than to behold evil, and canst not look on iniquity. . . .**
>
> —Habakkuk 1:13a

> **Let no man say when he is tempted, I am tempted of God: for God cannot be tempted with evil, neither tempteth he any man.**
>
> —James 1:13

The character and nature of Allah is definitely not the same as the God of the Bible. Since Allah is not the God of the Holy Bible, then according to the Bible, Allah is a false god.[49]

Do Hindus have a god?

Yes, Hindus declare that there is only one supreme being or god, the personal form of ultimate reality. This being has various aspects

---

48. Shamoun, Sam, "Is Allah the God of the Bible?" 28 December 2007 <http://www.answering-islam.org/Shamoun/god.htm>.
49. 29 December 2006 <www.truthandgrace.com/allah.htm>.

or many minor gods that are all part of the one supreme being. The Hindu worship of many deities is considered *monotheistic polytheism* and not simple *polytheism*. Hindus believe that their god is the god of all religions. They also believe that there are three gods, Brahma, Vishnu, and Shiva, who are considered the Hindu trinity and are responsible for the cosmic activity of creation, preservation, dissolution, and recreation. Since the Hindu god is not the God of the Holy Bible, according to the Bible, the Hindu god is a false god.[50]

Do Buddhists have a god?

Buddhism is generally viewed as a religion without a Creator God or a supreme being. Some Buddhists greatly revere their founder Buddha as a god, but at best he would be considered a false god because Buddha is not the God of the Holy Bible.[51]

Do Sikhs have a god?

Yes, the god of Sikhism is called Vahiguru. In this religion a full understanding of their god is beyond human understanding. Vahiguru is formless, eternal, and unobserved, a personal transcendental creator who is omnipresent and infinite. Sikhism began as a religion in northern India during the sixteenth century. Most Sikhs live in the Punjab in India. The god of the Sikhs is a false god because Vahiguru is not the God of the Holy Bible.[52]

Do Hare Krishnas have a god?

Yes, the International Society for Krishna Consciousness was founded by A. C. Bhaktivedanta Swami Prabhupada in 1965 in New York City. This religion is based on Hindu teachings from the sixteenth century A.D. The Krishna god is called Lord Krishna. He is a personal creator and the souls of all living things are part of him.

---

50. 29 December 2006 <www.koausa.org/Gods/index.html>.
51. 29 December 2006 <http://en.wikipedia.org/wiki/God_in_Buddhism>.
52. 29 December 2006 <http://en.wikipedia.org/wiki/Sikhism>.

Do Jews have a God?

Yes, the God of Jewish people is called Yahweh. Adonai or "My Lord" is another of the many names given to the Creator God of the Bible. The Jewish God is revealed in the Old Testament of the Bible. The Jewish God is the true God of the Holy Bible.[53]

Is there a god in pantheism or in the New Age religion?

Not in the sense of a unique being, the religion of pantheism generally refers to all matter as being interconnected. Most adherents to this belief system seem to believe that everything in the universe is god.[54] The belief statement of the World Pantheism Movement says that the universe is self–organizing and ever–evolving. They believe that people should strive to live in harmony with nature both locally and globally, and they should treat all living beings with compassion and respect. Pantheists do not believe in any supernatural powers and a creator God is therefore not necessary.[55]

The New Age religion seems to believe that just about everything in the universe is spiritually interconnected with an energy that may be referred to as god. Since the universe was created by the God of the Holy Bible, the New Age god is certainly not the God of the Holy Bible and, therefore, is a false god.

Can humans become God?

Some religions, including Buddhism and Mormonism, include the possibility of human beings elevating themselves to the level of a god. In these religions there is apparently a very low opinion or a very serious misunderstanding of the nature and the abilities of Almighty God. Any human who would seriously consider elevating himself to become an equal to the God of the Bible is an example of a person whose God is too small.

---

53. 29 December 2006 <www.faqs.org/faqs/judaism/FAQ/05-Worshp/section-12. html>.

54. 29 December 2006 <www.pantheist.net/society/god_of_pantheism.html>.

55. 29 December 2006 <www.pantheism.net/manifest.htm>.

What about false gods or idols?

» Do false gods or idols exist? Yes
» Is it possible for people to have a holy book or books that tell of a false god? Yes
» Is it possible for people to be deceived or tricked into serving a false god? Yes
» Is it possible for people to pray to a false god? Yes
» Is it possible for people to worship a false god? Yes
» Is it possible for people to construct idols that represent a false god? Yes
» Is it possible for people to build elaborate temples to honor a false god? Yes
» Is it possible for people to sacrifice something to a false god? Yes
» Is it possible for people to serve a false god? Yes
» Is it possible for people to give money to a false god? Yes
» Is it possible for people to act as priests to serve a false god? Yes
» Is it possible for people to make lots of money while serving a false god? Yes
» Is it possible for people to force others to serve their false god? Yes
» Is it possible for people to think that they are right in serving a false god? Yes
» Is it possible for people to participate in pilgrimages for a false god? Yes
» Is it possible for people to perform elaborate rituals for a false god? Yes
» Is it possible for people to give their possessions to a false god? Yes
» Is it possible for people to trust their eternal destiny to a false god? Yes
» Is it possible for people to die for a false god? Yes
» Is it possible for millions of people to do any of these activities? Yes

» Is it possible for millions of people to be deceived by a false god? Yes
» Is it possible for generations of people to follow a false god? Yes
» Is it possible for people to spend eternity in Hell because they served a false god? Yes
» Is it possible for a false god to fail to deliver the promises it makes? Yes!
» Is it possible for a false god to enable anyone access to Heaven? No
» Is it possible for anyone who has not made Jesus Christ his or her Lord to do enough good works to earn their entrance into Heaven? Absolutely no!

God directed the following statements about idols or false gods to be written by Moses and to be included in the Bible:

Ye shall not go after other gods, of the gods of the people which are round about you.

—Deuteronomy 6:14

They provoked him to jealousy with strange gods, with abominations provoked they him to anger. They sacrificed unto devils, not to God; to gods whom they knew not, to new gods that came newly up, whom your fathers feared not.

—Deuteronomy 32:16–17

Can false gods or idols have false prophets?

Yes, false gods or idols can and do have false prophets. The heathen god known as Baal is a false god that was served by King Ahab of Israel and at least four hundred fifty prophets. There were also four hundred prophets of the groves. This is reported in the following passage:

Now therefore send, and gather to me all Israel unto mount Carmel, and the prophets of Baal four hundred and fifty,

and the prophets of the groves four hundred, which eat at Jezebel's table.

—1 Kings 18:19

This is what Jesus said about false prophets:

Beware of false prophets, which come to you in sheep's clothing, but inwardly they are ravening wolves. Ye shall know them by their fruits....

—Matthew 7:15–16a

Yes, false prophets do exist and false prophets do deceive people, and yes, God knows that people are deceived by idols and false gods. The following statement says what people should do when they realize that they are serving a false god.

I have sent also unto you all my servants the prophets, rising up early and sending them, saying, Return ye now every man from his evil way, and amend your doings, and go not after other gods to serve them, and ye shall dwell in the land which I have given to you and to your fathers: but ye have not inclined your ear, nor hearkened unto me.

—Jeremiah 35:15

Is God dead?

On April 8, 1966, the front cover of *Time* magazine asked the question, "Is God Dead?"[56] This question was posed because of the writings of Christian theologians Gabriel Vahanian, Paul van Buren, William Hamilton, Thomas J. J. Altizer, and the Jewish rabbi Richard Rubenstein. These men were following the progression of thought initiated by Friedrich Nietzsche.[57]

---

56. 29 December 2006 <www.time.com/time/covers/0,16641,19660408, 00.html>.
57. 29 December 2006 <http://en.wikipedia.org/wiki/God_is_dead>.

Friedrich Wilhelm Nietzsche was a German–born philosopher who lived from 1844 to 1900. Nietzsche produced critiques of religion, morality, culture, and philosophy. In 1882 he wrote the book *The Gay Science*, where he introduced the concept that "God is dead."[58]

There was a range in the meaning of "dead" in these men's minds— from the belief that God's influence and moral teachings are no longer applicable in their world, to the total and true death of God. In 1961, Vahanian published the book *The Death of God*, where he proposed that modern secular culture had lost all sense of the sacred. He concluded that for the modern mind "God is dead," but he did not mean that God did not exist; instead he proposed a post–Christian and a post-modern culture. At the other extreme of thought, Altizer supported the true death of God. Altizer no longer supported the existence of a transcendent and eternal God.[59]

Thomas Altizer believed that the death of God was actually a self–extinction process that began at the world's creation and was completed with the death of Jesus Christ. Supposedly at the crucifix-ion of Jesus Christ, the Spirit of God was poured out onto the whole world and this is what we experience today.[60]

How should we answer the question, "Is God dead?" We can an-swer the question with one word—No! We can expand this answer by saying, "No, God is not dead!" The death of God would negate the attributes of God. A. W. Tozer[61] wrote that no tenant of the Christian creed could retain its significance if the idea of eternity were removed from it.[62] Tozer made this statement before the "Is God dead?" ques-tion was brought before the public. One of thousands of passages of Scripture that would certainly lose their meaning if God were dead is

58. 29 December 2006 <http://en.wikipedia.org/wiki/Friedrich_Nietzsche>.
59. 29 December 2006 <http://en.wikipedia.org/wiki/God_is_dead>.
60. 29 December 2006 <http://en.wikipedia.org/wiki/Thomas_J._J._Altizer>.
61. Aiden Wison Tozer (1897–1963) was a Christian and Missionary Alliance minister.
62. Tozer, A. W., *The Knowledge of the Holy*, HarperSanFrancisco, HarperCollins Publishers, Inc., 1961, p. 39.

listed here:

> **Behold, the LORD's hand is not shortened, that it cannot
> save; neither his ear heavy, that it cannot hear.**
> —Isaiah 59:1

The "death of God" concept is an excellent example of the thinking of well–educated people who have a God that is too small. If the God of the Bible were not alive, there would be no universe, there would be no earth, and there would definitely be no us. There would be absolutely nothing. The God of the Bible made everything and sustains everything.

> **All things were made by him; and without him was not any
> thing made that was made.**
> —John 1: 3

God is holding everything together.

> **For by him were all things created, that are in heaven,
> and that are in earth, visible and invisible, whether they
> be thrones, or dominions, or principalities, or powers: all
> things were created by him, and for him: And he is before all
> things, and by him all things consist.**
> —Colossians 1:16–17

According to the Bible it is not possible for God to die because He is eternal. Here are two references that share this truth.

> **The eternal God is thy refuge, and underneath are the ever-
> lasting arms: and he shall thrust out the enemy from before
> thee; and shall say, Destroy them.**
> —Deuteronomy 33:27

**Now unto the King eternal, immortal, invisible, the only
wise God, be honour and glory for ever and ever. Amen.**

—1 Timothy 1:17

But for the sake of discussion, if somehow God did die, everything that
He has made would also cease to exist. Actually, God could destroy
everything that He has created, and God would still be alive and well.
God does not "need" the universe that He created in order for Him to
have meaning and purpose for His existence. God created the universe,
and humans, for His own special reasons. God has given and preserved
the Holy Bible in order that we may have a more accurate understanding of His nature, His creation, and His plans for the future.

The more that is learned about the earth, the solar system, and the
universe, the more it appears that God created the universe for human
beings. This concept has been described in the Anthropic Principle
that was first presented in a 1973 paper by the astrophysicist and cos-
mologist Brandon Carter from Cambridge University. The Anthropic
Principle attempts to explain the observed fact that the fundamental
constants of physics and chemistry are *just right* or *fine-tuned* to allow
the universe and life as we know it to exist. The universe gives the appearance that it was designed to support life on earth.[63] In addition,
"Simply stated, the conditions allowing for intelligent life on Earth also
make our planet strangely well suited for viewing and analyzing the
universe."[64] The existence of such a perfectly positioned and prepared
planet called Earth is definitely consistent with the creation account
presented in the Bible. The Bible clearly states that God created the
heavens and the earth.[65]

---

63. 29 December 2006 <ourworld.compuserve.com/homepages/rossuk/c-anthro.
htm>.
64. Gonzalez, Guillermo and Richards, Jay W., *The Privileged Planet—How Our
Place in the Cosmos Is Designed for Discovery*, Regnery Publishing, Inc., Washington, D.C., 2004, page x in introduction.
65. "In the beginning God created the heaven and the earth" (Gen. 1:1).

So who is God?

There are many false gods, but there is only one true God. God is the Creator God, the God of the Jewish Bible, the God of the Christian Holy Bible, the Lord God Almighty.

The Apostle's Creed is the oldest creed in the Christian faith and has been the basis for most other Christian creeds and doctrinal statements. The Apostle's Creed has its roots in the earliest period of church history and is a concise summary of who God is and of God's involvement with mankind.[66]

The Apostle's Creed

I believe in God, the Father Almighty, the Creator of heaven and earth, and in Jesus Christ, His only Son, our Lord: Who was conceived of the Holy Spirit, born of the Virgin Mary, suffered under Pontius Pilate, and was crucified, died, and was buried.

He descended into hell. The third day He arose again from the dead. He ascended into heaven and sits at the right hand of God the Father Almighty, whence He shall come to judge the living and the dead.

I believe in the Holy Spirit, the holy catholic church, the communion of saints, the forgiveness of sins, the resurrection of the body, and life everlasting. Amen.

The Nicene Creed of 381 is an ecumenical statement of faith accepted by the Catholic Church, the Eastern Orthodox Church, Oriental Orthodoxy, the Assyrian, the Anglican Communion, Lutheranism, the Reformed churches, Methodism, and many other Protestant denominations.[67] This statement or creed provides a description of God and some of His involvement with mankind. Listed below is the Nicene Creed of A.D. 381.

---

66. 8 December 2007 <www.reformed.org/documents/index. html?mainframe=http://reformed.org/documents/apostles_creed.html>.
67. 8 December 2007 <http://en.wikipedia.org/wiki/Nicene_Creed>.

The Nicene Creed

We believe in one God the Father Almighty, Maker of heaven and earth, and of all things visible and invisible. And in one Lord Jesus Christ, the only–begotten Son of God, begotten of the Father before all worlds, God of God, Light of Light, Very God of Very God, begotten, not made, being of one substance with the Father, by whom all things were made; who for us men, and for our salvation, came down from heaven, and was incarnate by the Holy Spirit of the Virgin Mary, and was made man, and was crucified also for us under Pontius Pilate. He suffered and was buried, and the third day he rose again according to the Scriptures, and ascended into heaven, and sitteth on the right hand of the Father. And he shall come again with glory to judge both the quick and the dead, whose kingdom shall have no end.

And we believe in the Holy Spirit, the Lord and Giver of Life, who proceedeth from the Father and the son, who with the Father and the Son together is worshipped and glorified, who spoke by the prophets. And we believe one holy catholic and apostolic Church. We acknowledge one baptism for the remission of sins. And we look for the resurrection of the dead, and the life of the world to come. Amen.[68]

The following sentences from the Baptist Faith and Message statement provide another description of the nature of the Lord God Almighty:

There is one and only one living and true God. He is an intelligent, spiritual, and personal Being, the Creator, Redeemer, Preserver, and Ruler of the universe. God is infinite in holiness and all other perfections. God is all powerful and all knowing; and His perfect knowledge extends to all things, past, present, and future, includ-

---

68. 8 December 2007 <http://creeds.net/ancient/nicene.htm>.

ing the future decisions of His free creatures. To Him we owe the highest love, reverence, and obedience. The eternal triune God reveals Himself to us as Father, Son, and Holy Spirit, with distinct personal attributes, but without division of nature, essence, or being.[69]

These words and the words of the Apostle's and Nicene creeds give an excellent answer to the question, "Who is God?"

Additionally, we see more about God in the following historical account. In chapter eighteen of First Kings, a tremendous illustration of God's intervention into the affairs of men is documented. This event took place between 918 and 897 B.C. during the twenty-two–year reign of Ahab, king of Israel.[70] The following statement summarizes the deeds of Ahab.

And Ahab the son Omri did evil in the sight of the LORD above all that were before him.

—1 Kings 16:30

A prophet of Almighty God named Elijah challenged King Ahab and a group of four hundred fifty false prophets who worshiped and served a god they called Baal and a group of four hundred prophets of the groves to a contest that would demonstrate if their god or the Lord God of the Bible is superior. Elijah said that the true God would send fire down from Heaven to incinerate an offering placed on an altar prepared specifically for this contest. For almost an entire day at least four hundred and fifty men summoned Baal to send down fire from Heaven to consume the bullock that they had prepared and placed on their altar. But even after all of their effort, the prophets of

---

69. 30 December 2006 <http://sbc.net/bfm/bfm2000.asp#ii>.
70. Jones, Floyd Nolen, *Chronology of the Old Testament—A Return to Basics*, Kingswood Press, The Woodlands, Texas 77393-0220, 1999, Chart #5a—Kings of the Divided Monarchy Simplified.

Baal received no answer and no fire from their god to consume their sacrificial offering. Then Elijah repaired the altar of the Lord that was broken down, using twelve stones. He then dug a trench around the altar. Wood was placed on the altar along with the sacrificial bullock, which was placed on top of the wood. After these preparations were completed, twelve barrels of water were poured over the offering, the wood, and the altar. The water ran round about the altar and filled the trench with water. Then Elijah prayed, "LORD God of Abraham, Isaac, and of Israel, let it be known this day that thou art God in Israel, and that I am thy servant, and that I have done all these things at thy word. Hear me, O LORD, hear me, that this people may know that thou art the LORD God, and that thou hast turned their heart back again."[71] Then the God of the Bible demonstrated His power by sending fire from Heaven that consumed not only the sacrifice laid on the altar, but the entire altar including the water that had been poured over the sacrifice and the altar!

Dear friend, if your god or God is one of those mentioned in the preceding questions or perhaps your god was not mentioned in this section, I lovingly encourage you to continue reading so that you may consider and appreciate the awesome nature and supernatural abilities of the God of the Holy Bible. If you consider yourself a Christian, I challenge you to read this book and see if your concept of God is too small. I will be honest with you, when I became a Christian over fifty years ago, my concept of God was way too small. Over the last half century I have learned so much more about the Creator God described in the Bible, and yet I know that I have just started to appreciate how big God really is. I believe that there may well be many others who will receive an eternal benefit by starting now to realize how big God really is!

Here are a few statements from the Bible that identify and describe God:

---

71. 1 Kings 18:36b–37

For the LORD thy God is a consuming fire, even a jealous God.

—Deuteronomy 4:24

(For the LORD thy God is a merciful God ;) he will not forsake thee, neither destroy thee, nor forget the covenant of thy fathers which he sware unto them.

—Deuteronomy 4:31

Hear, O Israel: The LORD our God is one LORD.

—Deuteronomy 6:4

Turn ye not unto idols, nor make to yourselves molten gods: I am the LORD your God.

—Leviticus 19:4

Just balances, just weights, a just ephah, and a just hin, shall ye have: I am the LORD your God, which brought you out of the land of Egypt.

—Leviticus 19:36

. . . For he is an holy God; he is a jealous God; he will not forgive your transgressions nor your sins. If ye forsake the LORD, and serve strange gods, then he will turn and do you hurt, and consume you, after that he had done you good.

—Joshua 24:19b-20

God is our refuge and strength, a very present help in trouble. Therefore will not we fear, though the earth be removed, and though the mountains be carried into the midst of the sea.

—Psalm 46:1-2

Hast thou not known? hast thou not heard, that the everlasting God, the LORD, the Creator of the ends of the earth, fainteth not, neither is weary? there is no searching of his understanding.

—Isaiah 40:28

In the beginning was the Word, and the Word was with God, and the Word was God. The same was in the beginning with God. All things were made by him; and without him was not any thing made that was made. In him was life; and the life was the light of men. And the light shineth in darkness; and the darkness comprehended it not.

—John 1:1–5

And I saw, and bare record that this is the Son of God.

—John 1:34

There was a man of the Pharisees, named Nicodemus, a ruler of the Jews: The same came to Jesus by night, and said unto him, Rabbi, we know that thou art a teacher come from God: for no man can do these miracles that thou doest, except God be with him.

—John 3:1–2

The woman saith unto him, I know that Messias cometh, which is called Christ: when he is come, he will tell us all things. Jesus saith unto her, I that speak unto thee am he.

—John 4:25–26

Search the scriptures; for in them ye think ye have eternal life: and they are they which testify of me.

—John 5:39

Then cried Jesus in the temple as he taught, saying, Ye both know me, and ye know whence I am: and I am not come of myself, but he that sent me is true, whom ye know not. But I know him: for I am from him, and he hath sent me.

—John 7:28–29

Jesus therefore, knowing all things that should come upon him, went forth, and said unto them, Whom seek ye? They answered him, Jesus of Nazareth. Jesus saith unto them, I am he. And Judas also, which betrayed him, stood with them. As soon then as he had said unto them, I am he, they went backward, and fell to the ground. Then asked he them again, Whom seek ye? And they said, Jesus of Nazareth. Jesus answered, I have told you that I am he: if therefore ye seek me, let these go their way.

—John 18:4–8

And, behold, I come quickly; and my reward is with me, to give every man according as his work shall be. I am Alpha and Omega, the beginning and the end, the first and the last.

—Revelation 22:12–13

I Jesus have sent mine angel to testify unto you these things in the churches. I am the root and the offspring of David, and the bright and morning star.

—Revelation 22:16

This first chapter has begun our humble study of the God of the Bible. In the following chapters I sincerely hope that you will obtain a good look at the nature, the attributes, and the abilities of the God of the Bible. Then you can have a more informed answer to the important question "Is your God too small?" Also, as we consider additional information about the holy Creator God of the universe, the truly awesome nature of God should become more apparent to you. This will, hopefully, be a blessing that you do not want to miss.

The Lord God Almighty is preeminent!

Chapter 2

Is The Bible True?

Thy word is true from the beginning: and every one of thy righteous judgments endureth for ever.

—Psalm 119:160

Sanctify them through thy truth: thy word is truth.

—John 17:17

Jesus saith unto him, I am the way, the truth, and the life: no man cometh unto the Father, but by me.

—John 14:6

Why can we trust the Bible to be totally and completely true?

This is an excellent question and an adequate answer includes a broad range of material. So our answer will be shared in increments.

The truthfulness or trustworthiness and total accuracy of the Bible is dependent upon the nature of its author, who is the Creator God of the universe. The inerrant Holy Bible is the result of God's Holy Spirit providing divine inspiration to a diversity of people that wrote as they were inspired, using different writing styles and different perspectives. God knew that a completely accurate document would be essential to clearly and effectively communicate His message to the people of the world.

We are unable to understand the complete nature of God. In this book we will refer extensively to the attributes of God. A. W. Tozer said an attribute of God is whatever God has in any way revealed as being true of Himself.[72] It is possible that God has attributes that He chose not to reveal to us in the Bible. However, the Holy Bible certainly reveals quite a lot of information about God's nature and His character. Definitely God has a number of attributes! Many of these will be listed, and some will be discussed later in this book. For now we will focus on the attribute that God is Truth.

God being Truth means that God will never lie and God will never mislead or deceive. God invented words, language, and the ability of people to communicate. God also made it possible for animals to communicate, but we will not pursue that arena of interest in this book. Certainly, God is capable of creating and preserving the Bible so that it accurately and clearly communicates His message to mankind. Since God is Truth and He inspired and directed the writing of all of the Holy Bible, the Bible can be trusted completely. This means that we can believe what God says in the Bible.[73] Mike Viccary[74] said, "The Scriptures are trustworthy because God does not lie."[75] Don Landis[76] made the following statement about the Bible being truthful. "The fact that God gave us the Scripture is the reason we know that it is accurate and that it is exactly what He wants us to have. And because God has spoken it, we can be confident in the Scripture's authority."[77]

72. Tozer, A.W., *The Knowledge of the Holy*, HarperSanFrancisco, HarperCollins Publishers, Inc., New York, 1961, p. 12.
73. "All scripture is given by inspiration of God, and is profitable for doctrine, for reproof, for correction, for instruction in righteousness" (2 Tim. 3:16).
74. Mike Viccary received a Ph.D. in solid state chemistry/electron microscopy from Radford University. He also earned a diploma in biblical and pastoral studies at the London Reformed Baptist Seminary. He is now a science teacher at a Christian school in the United Kingdom.
75. Viccary, Mike, "Biblical chronology—our times are in His hands," *Journal of Creation*, 21(1):62, 2007.
76. Don Landis is pastor of Community Bible Church in Jackson, Wyoming, and the founder and president of Jackson Hole Bible College <www.jhbc.edu>, a one-year program with emphasis on the earth's creation.
77. Landis, Don, "And God Said", *Answers Magazine*, October–December 2007, p. 89.

The Bible has perfect unity and a consistent message, which was written by forty authors in sixty-six books over a two thousand-year time span.[78] This amazing and unique structure was made possible because its writers were inspired by an omniscient God to write His message in His manner.

It should be noted that some Bibles contain information in addition to the actual text of the Bible. The added information is intended to be helpful to the Bible reader. This supplementary material includes chapter[79] and verse[80] designations, commentary on passages, explanatory remarks, and colorful maps that attempt to locate places mentioned in the Bible. While this additional material may be interesting and it may be enlightening, it may not always be accurate. Some honest and sincere Bible scholars on occasion may err in their observations, their opinions, and their statements. Bible map makers may fail to position accurately every biblical area or community on the maps they create. Bible scholars and Bible map makers are human, and humans do make mistakes—even when they have the very best intentions. However, the text of the Bible can be trusted completely because God knows everything, and God does not make mistakes!

The Bible makes many statements about the accuracy and trustworthiness of its message and uses different words and terms to describe itself. Some of these terms are "word," "words," "word of God," "word of truth," "truth," "word of the Lord," "words of the Lord," "book of the Lord," and "scriptures." You will see most of these terms used in latter passages.

According to *Strong's Concordance of the King James Bible*, the word "Bible" is not found in the text of the King James Bible. But we do know that the word Bible comes from the Greek word *byblos*, which

---

78. Edwards, Brian H., "How Can We Be Sure Which Books Belong in Our Bible?", *Answers Magazine*, October–December 2007, p. 32
79. Stephen Langton, Archbishop of Canterbury, introduced modern Bible chapter divisions in 1227.
80. Robert Estienne's Greek Testament introduced modern verse divisions in 1551.

originally meant "papyrus."[81] Papyrus was the paper used in recording some of the earliest writing of mankind. *Byblos* then came to mean "books" and eventually it meant "The Bible."

Interestingly, Bible passages reveal some of the things God says about the Bible and His message contained in the Bible.

And Moses wrote all the words of the LORD, and rose up early in the morning, and builded an altar under the hill, and twelve pillars, according to the twelve tribes of Israel.

—Exodus 24:4

If I were hungry, I would not tell thee: for the world is mine, and the fulness thereof.

—Psalm 50:12

For ever, O LORD, thy word is settled in heaven.

—Psalm 119:89

Thy word is very pure: therefore thy servant loveth it.

—Psalm 119:140

Thy word is true from the beginning: and every one of thy righteous judgments endureth for ever.

—Psalm 119:160

Every word of God is pure: he is a shield unto them that put their trust in him. Add thou not unto his words, lest he reprove thee, and thou be found a liar.

—Proverbs 30:5–6

---

81. Papyrus was made from a plant which is called the bulrush in the Bible. The ark which carried the baby Moses was made of bulrushes. "And when she could not longer hide him, she took for him an ark of bulrushes . . ." (Exod. 2:3a).

Hear, O heavens, and give ear, O earth: for the LORD hath spoken, I have nourished and brought up children, and they have rebelled against me.

—Isaiah 1:2

Seek ye out of the book of the LORD, and read: no one of these shall fail, none shall want her mate: for my mouth it hath commanded, and his spirit it hath gathered them.

—Isaiah 34:16

The grass withereth, the flower fadeth: but the word of our God shall stand for ever.

—Isaiah 40:8

Heaven and earth shall pass away: but my words shall not pass away.

—Mark 13:31

And he said unto them, These are the words which I spake unto you, while I was yet with you, that all things must be fulfilled, which were written in the law of Moses, and in the prophets, and in the psalms, concerning me.

—Luke 24:44

He that hath received his testimony hath set to his seal that God is true.

—John 3:33

Search the scriptures; for in them ye think ye have eternal life: and they are they which testify of me.

—John 5:39

Sanctify them through thy truth: thy word is truth.

—John 17:17

For whatsoever things were written aforetime were written for our learning, that we through patience and comfort of the scriptures might have hope.

—Romans 15:4

Study to shew thyself approved unto God, a workman that needeth not to be ashamed, rightly dividing the word of truth.

—2 Timothy 2:15

And that from a child thou hast known the holy scriptures, which are able to make thee wise unto salvation through faith which is in Christ Jesus. All scripture is given by inspiration of God, and is profitable for doctrine, for reproof, for correction, for instruction in righteousness: That the man of God may be perfect, throughly furnished unto all good works.

—2 Timothy 3:15–17

God, who at sundry times and in divers manners spake in time past unto the fathers by the prophets, Hath in these last days spoken unto us by his Son, whom he hath appointed heir of all things, by whom also he made the worlds.

—Hebrews 1:1–2

But the word of the Lord endureth for ever. And this is the word which by the gospel is preached unto you.

—1 Peter 1:25

Knowing this first, that no prophecy of the scripture is of any private interpretation. For the prophecy came not in old time by the will of man: but holy men of God spake as they were moved by the Holy Ghost.

—2 Peter 1:20–21

And he that sat upon the throne said, Behold, I make all things new. And he said unto me, Write: for these words are true and faithful.

—Revelation 21:5

And he said unto me, These sayings are faithful and true: and the Lord God of the holy prophets sent his angel to shew unto his servants the things which must shortly be done.

—Revelation 22:6

The following is a statement on the significance of the Holy Bible that was approved in 1932 by the Lutheran Church Missouri Synod:

We teach that the Holy Scriptures differ from all other books in the world in that they are the Word of God. They are the Word of God because the holy men of God who wrote the Scriptures wrote only that which the Holy Ghost communicated to them by inspiration, 2 Timothy 3:16, 2 Peter 1:21. We teach also that the verbal inspiration of the Scriptures is not a so-called (theological deduction), but that it is taught by direct statements of the Scriptures, 2 Timothy 3:16, John 10:35, Romans 3:2, 1 Corinthians 2:13. Since the Holy Scriptures are the Word of God, it goes without saying that they contain no errors or contradictions, but they are in all their parts and words the infallible truth, also in those parts which treat of historical, geographical, and other secular matters, John 10:35.[82]

All of the hundreds of prophetic statements made by the writers of the Bible have either been accurately fulfilled or they will be accurately fulfilled in the future. The prophecies in the Bible are all accurate because God is omniscient—He possesses all knowledge. It is extraordinarily difficult for humans to understand what omniscient truly means. The omniscient God knows all of the past history of the world. The

---

82. 29 December 2006 <www.lcms.org/pages/internal.asp?NavID=563>.

omniscient God knows everything that is happening in the present. And yes, the omniscient God knows all of the future events that will take place in the world. The real reason the prophecies in the Bible are always accurate is that the author of the Bible is truthful, faithful, and knows all of the events of history even before they occur. Moreover, the author inspired all of the Bible's writers to write just as He wanted them to write.[83]

Errors have been found in other ancient books that document the history of the world. However, the history recorded in the Bible is completely accurate because the author of the Bible knows all of the history of the world.

Scientific information recorded in the Bible is totally accurate even though much of this information was documented by the Bible's human writers long before this information was experimentally confirmed by the scientists of the world. The scientific information found in the Bible is true because God, who inspired the writers of the Bible, created all of the scientific information that is recorded in the Bible. God also created all of the scientific information that is not included in the Bible.

Neither science, history, nor any other discipline has ever demonstrated a mistake in the Bible.[84] There is always the possibility that translators or printers could make an error in completing their work, but this would not be a mistake in the Bible originally provided by God. Henry M. Morris made an important comment about errors in the Bible:

> It is important to remember that the doctrine of inspiration and inerrancy applies only to the original autographs, rather than to any

---

83. Wise, Kurt P., *Faith, Form, and Time—What the Bible teaches and science confirms about creation and the age of the universe,* Broadman & Holman Publishers, Nashville, TN, 2002, p.26.
84. Lutzer, Erwin W., *Seven Reasons Why You Can Trust the Bible,* Moody Press, Chicago, 1998, p. 68.

particular copy or translation. Nevertheless, the ancient scribes were very meticulous, and any copyist errors are few and far between. We can have confidence that Chronicles, as well as all other books of the Bible, have been preserved substantially intact.[85]

Some scholars and skeptics have claimed that there are mistakes in the Bible. But because the Bible was written by the God who knows everything, it has no mistakes or errors! There are almost certainly passages that we do not yet fully understand, but these are not errors.[86]

Erwin W. Lutzer[87] made the following statement about errors in the Bible:

> Even when we allow for the errors copyists made; even when we take into account that the various manuscripts do have minor variations, we have a reliable biblical text upon which our faith is based. No doctrine is affected by differences in spelling, word order, or the addition of an explanatory word or phrase.[88]

Dr. Lutzer also says that there are fifteen hundred statements in the Bible that claim, directly or indirectly, its divine origin. The Bible's sixty–six books speak with a consistent voice that these are the words of God.

To say that the writers were either deceived or lying just does not wash. If so, the Bible is surely the most fraudulent book that has ever been written! It would be a matter of incomprehensible

85. Morris, Henry M., *The Defender's Study Bible—King James Version*, World Publishing, Inc., Iowa Falls, Iowa 50126, USA, 1995, p. 487.
86. 29 December 2006 <http://christiananswers.net/q-eden/edn-t003.html>.
87. Erwin W. Lutzer (B.A., Winnipeg Bible College; Th.M., Dallas Theological Seminary; M.A., Loyola University; and L.L.D., Simon Greenleaf School of Law) in 1998 was senior pastor of Moody Church in Chicago, Illinois.
88. Lutzer, Erwin W., *Seven Reasons Why You Can Trust the Bible*, Moody Press, Chicago, 1998, p. 77.

irony that the very book that has inspired the highest standard of morality, the book that has given the world the most coherent worldview, the book that has given us a Christ who is admired even by skeptics—that this book is based on multiplied deceptions is beyond belief.[89]

The Bible is the all–time best seller of books. It has had a profound and beneficial effect on people from all walks of life in every generation and in every location where it has been read. No other book has had such universal appeal nor has produced such lasting effects. All of this is true because the Bible was written by God, who knows the needs of all of mankind and has provided the necessary information in the Bible to allow anyone to receive forgiveness for their sins and hope for their future.

There are over twenty thousand ancient manuscripts that document the New Testament text. These manuscripts vary in size from a part of a page to an entire Bible. The earliest New Testament manuscripts date from A.D. 100 to A.D. 199. The manuscripts of the New Testament were written by people from different nationalities, different cultures, and different backgrounds. In spite of all the differences in their origins, the message is consistent. It has been said that this consistency makes the New Testament the most reliable document of antiquity. The real reason that over twenty thousand ancient manuscripts documenting the New Testament text exist today is that the manuscripts were written by men inspired by God, and that people from different nations recognized the extraordinary value of these writings and therefore preserved them as the Word of God.[90]

True Christianity rests only on a completely accurate Bible. J. B. Phillips[91] referred to true Christianity as "The Real Thing" years before a

---

89. Ibid., p. 43.

90. 29 December 2006 <www.clarifyingchristianity.com/b_proof.shtml>.

91. John Bertram Phillips, 16 September 1906–21 July 1982, was one of Britain's most famous Bible communicators. He translated some books of the Old Tes-

widely distributed carbonated soft drink or cola beverage manufacturer used this term in its advertising. True Christianity changes people on a personal level and is not to be judged by its success or failure to reform the world which rejects it. The same could be said for the Holy Bible. If the Bible or Christianity fail where they are accepted, there might be grounds for complaint. But the Bible and Christianity do not fail. The Bible reveals the true way of living, the way to know God, and the way to live life of eternal quality. If the Bible fails or if real Christianity fails, the failure is for the same reasons that Jesus Christ failed—any condemnation rightly falls on the world which rejects both the Bible and Jesus Christ.[92]

The following quotation explains more fully the importance of a totally accurate Bible:

> The Bible contains statements that are figures of speech, non–technical descriptions, and sections that are difficult to understand. If there are any errors in Scripture, no matter how small, the book can no longer be our standard of truth, as I determine which Bible statements are right and which are wrong. And if I can't trust God to get the facts straight on things like dates and measurements (where I can check on Him), why should I expect Him to be more accurate in areas like sin and salvation (where I can't check on him)?[93]

Because God's Word is Truth and Jesus is Truth we can live in complete confidence that God will keep His word and His promises. "The Chicago Statement on Biblical Inerrancy" produced in 1978 by nearly three hundred evangelical scholars during an international summit conference held in Chicago, Illinois, stated:

tament and all of the New Testament.

92. Phillips, J. B., *Your God Is Too Small*, Macmillian Publishing Co. Inc., New York, 16th Printing, 1976, p. 123–124.
93. 29 December 2006 <www.christiananswers.net/q-acb/acb-t001.html>.

(1) God, who is Himself Truth and speaks truth only, has inspired Holy Scripture in order to reveal Himself to lost mankind through Jesus Christ as Creator and Lord, Redeemer and Judge. Holy Scripture is God's witness to Himself.

(2) Holy Scripture being God's own Word, written by men prepared and superintended by His Spirit, is of infallible divine authority in all matters upon which it touches: it is to be believed, as God's instruction, in all that it affirms: obeyed, as God's command, in all that it requires; embraced, as God's pledge, in all that it promises.

(3) The Holy Spirit, Scripture's divine Author, both authenticates it to us by His inward witness and opens our minds to understanding its meaning.

(4) Being wholly and verbally God–given, Scripture is without error or fault in all its teaching, no less in what it states about God's acts in creation, about the events of world history, and about its own literary origins under God, than in its witness to God's saving grace in individual lives.

(5) The authority of Scripture is inescapably impaired if this total divine inerrancy is in any way limited or disregarded, or made relative to a view of truth contrary to the Bible's own; and such lapses bring serious loss to both the individual and the church.[94]

Dr. Kurt Wise[95] has made a number of superb statements regarding the trustworthiness of the Bible. He points out, for example, that Chris-

---

94. 29 December 2006 <www.bible-researcher.com/chicago1.html>.

95. Kurt P. Wise received a B.A. from the Department of Geophysical Sciences at the University of Chicago and an M.A. and a Ph.D. in paleontology from Harvard University under Stephen Jay Gould. He has lectured and written widely on the subject of young–age creationism. He was an associate professor of science and director of the Center for Origins Research and Education (C.O.R.E.) at Bryan College in Dayton, Tennessee. Dr. Wise is now a professor of science and theology and director of the Center for Theology and Science at the Southern Baptist Theological Seminary in Louisville, Kentucky.

tians say they believe that the Bible is true for a number of reasons. He then enumerates some of the more common reasons that are given:

1. The Bible is well substantiated by many manuscripts. There are definitely many more partial and complete ancient manuscripts of the Bible than any other ancient documents. One example is Julius Caesar's *Gaulic Wars,* composed 50–58 B.C., which has several manuscripts in existence, but only nine or ten of which are good; the oldest is some nine hundred years later than Caesar's day. Another example is seen in the one hundred forty–two books of the Roman history of Livy, composed 59 B.C.–A.D. 17, where only thirty–five survive and only one dates from as early as the fourth century.[96] Therefore, since the Bible has more references, we can believe that the Bible is true because of the larger number of partial and complete ancient manuscripts of the Bible that have similar or identical words in their text.

2. The Bible has a consistent message in all of its sixty–six books. These books were written over a period of two thousand years[97] by forty different writers from a variety of backgrounds. Such consistency in message would not be expected unless the writers were all inspired by a single Author. So, since there is such a consistent message in the Bible, we can rightly conclude that God is the "single/sole Author" of the Bible.

3. The Bible's dietary and sanitary laws were written about three thousand years ago. These laws in general are accurate for promoting better health in humans and seemingly were quite "advanced" for the time they were documented. This means that these "laws" were inspired by God, which helps prove that the Bible is totally trustworthy.

---

96. McDowell, Josh, *Evidence That Demands a Verdict— historical evidences for the Christian faith,* Campus Crusade for Christ, Inc., San Bernardino, CA, 1972, p. 47.
97. The book of Job was probably written between 2000–1800 B.C.

4. There are a large number of prophecies in the Bible. Many of these prophecies have been accurately fulfilled according to history. Fulfilled prophecies therefore argue strongly and correctly that the inspired writers received their insight from God.

5. The Bible makes hundreds of verifiable cultural, artifactual, and architectural claims. Biblical archaeology, especially in the last one hundred fifty years, has confirmed the accuracy of the accounts in the Bible. Therefore because many of the Bible's claims and statements have recently been found to be true, all of the Bible can be assumed or trusted to be true.

6. The Dead Sea Scrolls, first discovered in 1947 by a Bedouin shepherd in Israel,[98] show that the Bible has been transmitted with great accuracy over hundreds of years. The few differences between the oldest known manuscripts of the Bible and the Dead Sea Scrolls demonstrate that there seems to be supernatural intervention which preserves the accuracy and reliability of the Bible.[99] Therefore, we can believe that the entire Bible is trustworthy because of the confirmation of accuracy provided by the Dead Sea Scrolls.

Each of these arguments suggest that we should believe the Bible because of evidence that the Bible is truthful and reliable. This type of argument provides an unbeliever reason to place initial trust in the Bible. However, this is not sufficient reason for a Christian to continue to believe the Bible is true. We should understand the Bible is true by faith. The Bible was true as originally given because its Author is truth. The Bible was preserved supernaturally because God is unchanging and just.[100]

98. 27 June 2007 <www.gnosis.org/library/dss/dss_timeline.htm>.
99. Wise, Kurt P., *Faith, Form, and Time—What the Bible teaches and science confirms about creation and the age of the universe*, Broadman & Holman Publishers, Nashville, TN, 2002, p.24–26.
100. Ibid., p.25.

The following six reasons for believing the Bible is true are valid because of the nature of God—not because of evidence found in the world. This line of reasoning is a paradigm shift in the way some people look at the credibility of the Bible.

1. It is because the Bible is true, trusted, and valued by so many people for so many generations that so many manuscripts of the Bible survive to the twenty-first century.
2. It is because the Bible was authored by one unchanging God with one purpose that perfect consistency can be found within all of its sixty-six books.
3. It is because the Bible was written by a caring God with all knowledge that the laws therein were so wholesome, so accurate, and so far ahead of their time.
4. It is because the Bible was authored by an all-knowing, truthful, and faithful God that the Bible contains so many fulfilled prophecies.
5. It is because the Bible is true that its archaeological claims are dependable and verifiable.
6. It is because the Bible is preserved by an all-powerful, just, unchanging God that the Bible's manuscripts, which are separated by multiple centuries, are so similar.

Dr. Wise says the Bible's reliability is not based on evidence that makes it look reliable; evidence exists because the Bible is reliable. The Bible is not proven to be totally accurate because of historical and archaeological evidence. Evidence exists because the Bible is 100 percent accurate! The Bible has been preserved, is reliable, and is true because of the nature and the character of its Author. The words and the message of the Bible should be believed over observation and evidence.[101]

The Bible is not true because of archaeological evidence that agrees with what the Bible says. The Bible is true regardless of what archaeo-

---

101. Ibid., p.26.

logical evidence says or does not say or what men think it says. The Bible is true because God gave it to us, and God cannot lie. You will find that the Bible is unique in its human authors, unique in content, unique in the history that it documents, and unique in the foretelling of future events. God does not deceive, and He does not mislead. God made it possible for us to have the Bible because He knew we would need this information to make sense of the world. God gave us the Bible so that we can know that He loves all people. God gave us the Bible so we can know how sin entered the world and what impact sin has on our relationship with God. God gave us the Bible so we can know that humans are sinful by nature and by decision. God gave us the Bible so that we can know that He has made a way for everyone to have their sins forgiven. God gave us the Bible so we can know that Messiah would come to earth. God gave us the Bible so we can know that it is possible for all humans to receive forgiveness for all of the sins that they commit during their lifetime. God gave us the Bible so we can know that this Messiah is the Lord Jesus Christ.

Is it possible for the Bible to provide accurate history and to be accurate in all areas where it speaks? Absolutely, in the original manuscripts! However, it is possible that some translations of the Bible have accidentally or purposely altered the meaning of words. Unfortunately, some scholars have changed the meanings of words in the Bible to fit their point of view. The Bible makes a statement with an obvious meaning, but if translators change the meanings of certain words in the Bible, the meaning of the original biblical statement will be altered. Through this practice, messages conveyed by the Bible have been altered and readers of the Bible may miss the initial and authentic message that God intended to be conveyed through the Bible. This would, of course, include those who do not read the passage but only hear it read to them. The practice of altering the meaning of words in the Bible has unfortunately caused confusion and has created a lack of confidence in the Bible's accuracy and authority.

A classic example of changing the meaning of words is found in the very first chapter of the Bible. Some theologians say that the six days of the creation week are actually very long periods of time that encompass perhaps millions of years per day. Apparently, these theologians are trying to change the meaning of the word *day* to be compatible with the popular concept that the earth is over four billion years old. Dr. James Barr[102] has said: "So far as I know, there is no professor of Hebrew or Old Testament at any world–class university who does not believe that the writer(s) of Genesis 1–11 intended to convey to their readers the ideas that creation took place in a series of six days which were the same as the days of twenty–four hours we now experience."[103] Dr. Barr also said that the figures contained in the Genesis genealogies provide, by simple addition, a chronology from the beginning of the world up to later stages in the biblical story. He also believes that the Hebrew text says Noah's flood was understood to be worldwide and it extinguished all human and animal life except for those in the ark.[104]

The late Dr. Bernard Ramm[105] was a representative of other theologians[106] who have entirely given up a literal interpretation of the early chapters of Genesis. These men say that the "days" in the first chapters of Genesis are intended to be topical rather than chronological, serving as a mere literary framework without intending to convey any historical information to the reader.[107] However, Dr. Edward Young,[108]

---

102. Dr. James Barr is regius professor of Hebrew at Oxford University who does not believe Genesis is true history.
103. James Barr, Letter to David C. C. Watson, April 23, 1984.
104. Ibid.
105. Bernard Ramm (1916–1992) was a Baptist theologian and apologist within the broad evangelical tradition. He received his M.A. and Ph.D. from the University of Southern California. He maintained that, apart from faith, God was unknowable.
106. Herrmann, Giersch, and Barth.
107. Whitcomb, John C. Jr., *The Early Earth*, Baker Book House, Grand Rapids, MI, 1972, p. 63–64.
108. Edward J. Young (1907–1968) was an ordained minister in the Presbyterian

in his work entitled, *Studies in Genesis One,* has shown that the early chapters of Genesis bear none of the style marks of poetry or saga or myth, but must be interpreted as literally as any other "straightforward, trustworthy history" recorded in Scripture.[109]

Some scholars and scientists say that the origin of the universe, the sun, and the earth with the subsequent evolution of all plant and animal life took place gradually over billions of years. The changing of the meaning of the word "day" as it is used to describe the days described in the creation week challenges both the accuracy and the integrity of the Bible at its very beginning. "If the Bible is wrong in the beginning, about origins, then why should they consider what else the Bible has to say?"[110]

The King James Version of the Bible was completed in 1611. It is surely the most widely read version of the Bible in the English language. According to the *Global Language Monitor,* there are 783,187 words in the King James Version of the Bible. And there are 12,143 different words in the Bible.[111] As of 2001, the Bible had been translated into more than twelve hundred languages. More than 168,000 Bibles were sold or given away in the United States of America every day in 2001. In 2006, the United Bible Societies[112] distributed 393 million Scriptures.[113] The Bible claims to be "The Word of God." It records the interaction of God with historical people and nations. It

Church of America (1935–1936) and in the Orthodox Presbyterian Church until his death. He was a reformed theologian and an Old Testament scholar at Westminster Theological Seminary in Philadelphia, Pennsylvania, from 1936 until his death.

109. Young, Edward J., *Studies in Genesis One*, Presbyterian and Reformed Publishing Co., Nutley, NJ, 1964, p. 105.

110. Dolezal, Larry, "What's in a name?," *Creation Ministries International Prayer News* {the newsletter for Creation Ministries International (USA)}, October–December 2006, p. 1.

111. 6 April 2007 <www.languagemonitor.com/wst_page7.html>.

112. United Bible Societies includes Wycliffe Bible Translators, American Bible Society, International Bible Society, and United Bible Society.

113. Sheppard, Pam S., "Declaring God's Glory Among The Nations," *Answers Magazine*, October–December 2007, p. 65.

reveals the meaning of life and the responsibility of human beings to their Creator.[114] The words of the Bible reveal the nature and the attributes of God. In addition, the words of the Bible reveal the nature and the actions of humans. Words in the Bible tell about supernatural events that are a part of eternity—past, present, and future. The Bible records hundreds of statements that tell us how much God knows, what God has done, what God is doing now, and what God is going to do in the future.

Words have meaning. If words have no meaning, then the communication of ideas becomes ineffective. "When words lose their meaning, people lose their lives."[115] All of the words of the Bible have meaning, and all of the words of the Bible communicate a message that God wants people to understand and, hopefully, accept. If the words of the Bible lose their true meaning, people may lose both their lives and a loving, eternal relationship with their Creator God.

Truly the Holy Bible is unique in all of the world's literature. "The Bible is indeed the very Word of the living God. Its histories are authentic, its science is accurate and far in advance of its times, its practical wisdom for daily living is unexcelled, and its insights into the human heart are profoundly perfect for every need.[116] The bottom line of this discussion is that the Bible reflects the character of God. Therefore, the descriptions of the Bible also apply to the Almighty Himself.[117] God will never lie nor deceive because for God to do this would be totally against His nature. We can trust the Bible to be truthful because God is the author of the Bible and He is Truth. God's words have always been true and God's words will always be true!

---

114. 30 December 2006 <www.christiananswers.net/bible/about.html>.
115. Stonestreet, John, Summit Conference at Bryan College in Dayton, Tennessee, 3 August 2006.
116. Morris, Henry M., *The Defender's Study Bible—King James Version,* Introduction, p. 1.
117. Lutzer, Erwin W., *Seven Reasons Why You Can Trust the Bible,* p. 208.

Chapter 3

Who Is the God of the Holy Bible?

Fear ye not, neither be afraid: have not I told thee from that time, and have declared it? ye are even my witnesses. Is there a God beside me? yea, there is no God; I know not any.

—Isaiah 44:8

As concerning therefore the eating of those things that are offered in sacrifice unto idols, we know that an idol is nothing in the world, and that there is none other God but one.

—1 Corinthians 8:4

» What is God like?
» What is God's nature?
» What are God's attributes?
» What are God's abilities?
» What does God say about Himself in the Bible?
» Who is the God of the Holy Bible?

It is a sad thought, but it is possible that millions of Christians have lived their entire lives without having tried to think seriously about the being of God. A basic knowledge of the Creator God's nature is indispensable to a sound philosophy of life and the development of a biblical world view.[118] The Holy Bible is the best resource to learn about

---

118. Tozer, A. W., *The Knowledge of the Holy*, p. 26–27.

God because it provides a tremendous picture of the nature of God. God's nature is at least partially revealed in His attributes, which are described in the Bible. Attributes are defined as "qualities or characteristics inherent in or ascribed to someone or something."[119] Many Bible scholars have documented God's attributes. Three different lists of God's attributes are provided below to help us begin to appreciate what God is really like. All three lists communicate a partial picture of the nature of God. However, even with the combined lists there remains much about God that humans cannot fathom or understand, but the Bible's introduction to Almighty God provides more information about Him than we can fully appreciate.

According to *The Forerunner,*[120] the following are attributes of God.[121]

» God is infinite.
» God is personal.
» God is Triune
» God is transcendent.
» God is omnipresent.
» God is omnipotent.
» God is omniscient.
» God is sovereign.
» God is love.
» God is holy.

According to the Parent Company, the following are God's attributes:[122]

119. 19 June 2007 <http://dictionary_reference.com/search?q=attributes>.
120. *The Forerunner* is a nationally distributed campus newspaper published by Maranatha Ministries in Gainesville, Florida.
121. 19 June 2007 <www.forerunner.com/orthodoxy/X0002_1._Names__Attributes.html>.
122. 19 June 2007 <www.parentcompany.com/awareness_of_god/aogtoc.htm>.

- » God is Spirit
- » God ls Life
- » God is Infinite
- » God is Immutable
- » God is Truth
- » God is Love
- » God is Eternal
- » God is Holy
- » God is Immortal
- » God is Invisible
- » God is Omnipresent
- » God is Omniscient
- » God is Omnipotent

According to Precept Ministries, the following are God's attributes:[123]

- » God is Omniscient
- » God is Omnipotent
- » God is Omnipresent
- » God is Eternal
- » God is Immutable
- » God is Incomprehensible
- » God is Self–existent
- » God is Self–sufficient
- » God is Infinite
- » God is Transcendent
- » God is Sovereign
- » God is Holy
- » God is Gracious
- » God is Righteous

---

123. Genesis Part 5: *Keeping Your Focus When Your Dreams Are Shattered—A Study on Joseph*—Chapters 37–50, Precept Ministries, 1999, pp. 23–27.

» God is Just
» God is Merciful
» God is Longsuffering
» God is Wise
» God is Loving
» God is Good
» God is Wrathful
» God is Truthful
» God is Faithful
» God is Jealous

Surely a complete study of the nature and attributes of God would require a lifetime of study. To organize and effectively share the results of this study with others would require the writing of many books, which would probably still be inadequate to explain the full nature of God, since He is incomprehensible. Therefore, I will not attempt to take the task of explaining the nature of God in its totality, but will leave it to those more competent than myself. However, for the scope of this book, I will attempt to highlight some of God's attributes as they relate to my perception of the magnitude of God's knowledge and His abilities.

The next section contains a number of biblical references and some explanatory information on the attributes of God from the preceding three lists.

God is omniscient

Omniscient is an absolute word that is defined as having total knowledge, knowing everything: for example, *an omniscient deity.*[124] A second and similar definition for omniscient is having infinite knowledge; knowing all things; universal or complete knowledge.[125] God knows

---

124. 19 June 2007 <http://dictionary.reference.com/browse/omniscient>.
125. *Webster's Third New International Dictionary of the English Language—Unabridged*, p. 1574.

all things perfectly. This means God has total knowledge. He is never surprised and never amazed.[126] It is easy enough to say that God knows everything, but have you stopped to seriously consider all that God knows and what this means? The following passages from the Bible describe God as being omniscient.

Behold, the former things are come to pass, and new things do I declare: before they spring forth I tell you of them.

—Isaiah 42:9

For truly my words shall not be false: he that is perfect in knowledge is with thee.

—Job 36:4

Dost thou know the balancings of the clouds, the wondrous works of him which is perfect in knowledge?

—Job 37:16

I know that thou canst do every thing, and that no thought can be withholden from thee.

—Job 42:2

O LORD, thou hast searched me, and known me. Thou knowest my downsitting and mine uprising, thou understandest my thought afar off. Thou compassest my path and my lying down, and art acquainted with all my ways. For there is not a word in my tongue, but, lo, O LORD, thou knowest it altogether. Thou hast beset me behind and before, and laid thine hand upon me.

—Psalm 139:1–6

Great is our Lord, and of great power: his understanding is infinite.

—Psalm 147:5

---

126. Tozer, A.W., *The Knowledge of the Holy*, p. 56.

The LORD by wisdom hath founded the earth; by understanding hath he established the heavens. By his knowledge the depths are broken up, and the clouds drop down the dew.

—Proverbs 3:19–20

For the earth shall be filled with the knowledge of the glory of the LORD, as the waters cover the sea.

—Habakkuk 2:14

In whom are hid all the treasures of wisdom and knowledge.

—Colossians 2:3

Neither is there any creature that is not manifest in his sight: but all things are naked and opened unto the eyes of him with whom we have to do.

—Hebrews 4:13

There are many more passages from the Bible that reveal the magnitude of God's knowledge. Some of these passages are included in this and other chapters. To attempt to understand the extent of God's knowledge will quickly bring us to the limits of the human brain's abilities. Here are some examples of God's knowledge:

Genesis 1:1 records one of the most profound statements in all of the literature of the world: "In the beginning God created the heaven and the earth." This sentence concisely says that God has created everything in the universe. God's words brought the entire universe into existence out of nothing.[127] Later in this book we will consider the order in which God created. But for now it is sufficient to realize that everything in the universe exists because God spoke and "things" ap-

---

127. "By the word of the LORD were the heavens made; and all the host of them by the breath of his mouth" (Ps. 33:6) "For he spake, and it was done; he commanded, and it stood fast" (Ps. 33:9).

peared out of nothing. "He took nothing, and out of nothing He made something. When He stopped, creation itself froze in its tracks. No more. The universe became thermodynamically closed. In a very real sense, nothing more has since appeared or disappeared. Everything that changes is simply rearranging itself." [128] The preceding statement is closely related to the First Law of Thermodynamics that basically says that energy cannot be created or destroyed.

So how much matter did God create when He created the universe? Astronomers tell us that the universe contains approximately 100 billion galaxies. All of the galaxies in the universe are estimated to equal a trillion, trillion, trillion, trillion tons of matter. This is a lot of star dust. The galaxies also include stars, rocks, minerals, ice, gas, and other forms of matter. The First Law of Thermodynamics states that energy cannot be created or destroyed. This law is demonstrated in Albert Einstein's formula $E = mc^2$. In this formula E = energy, m = mass, and c^2 = the speed of light [129] that is squared or multiplied by itself. In this formula we realize that the amount of energy in the universe is incomprehensibly large. "This is what God created, from nothing. And since the time of creation, nothing more has been added to it." [130]

All matter and all energy in the universe was created by God. Have you considered how much matter and how much energy have been created out of nothing by humans? Dr. Richard Swenson[131] answers the question in the following statement. "In all of the laboratories, all the universities, all the military installations, by all the scientists with all their sophisticated, expensive equipment and Ph.D. degrees—how much mass–energy have they created out of nothing? Zero. Not one

128. Swenson, Richard A., *More Than Meets the Eye—Fascinating Glimpses of God's Power and Design*, Navpress, Colorado Springs, CO, 2000, p. 123–124.
129. The speed of light is 186,000 miles per second.
130. Swenson, Richard A., *More Than Meets the Eye*, p. 124.
131. Richard A. Swenson, M.D., is a physician and a futurist, with a B.S. in physics Phi Beta Kappa from Denison University. For fifteen years he taught at the University of Wisconsin Medical School. Currently he is conducting research and writes about the intersection of culture, health, faith, and the future.

joule, not one gram."[132]

On day four of creation week God spoke and created from nothing 100,000,000,000 galaxies containing billions and billions of stars.[133] Scientists have "split" atoms using elaborate equipment, but humans have not actually created a single atom.[134]

The emphasis on what God has created is a prelude to realizing what God knows when we describe Him as being omniscient. God knows precisely what He has created, how He created, where His creations are now, and what His creations are doing at any and every moment in time.

Dr. Swenson says the universe reveals the following information about God:

1. God is powerful at a level beyond human comprehension.
2. God alone has the ability to create mass–energy out of nothing.
3. God formed us with the ability to observe mass–energy—but not to create it.
4. If we need a source of energy, it is better to connect to God's energy source, which is infinite, than to connect with humanity's energy source, which is nonexistent.[135]

I received a tiny glimpse into the meaning of the word omniscient while attending a number of performances of *The Mousetrap*, a classic murder mystery play by Agatha Christie.[136] My family saw *The Mouse-trap* on stage in London, England, where it has been recognized as the longest continually–running play in the history of modern theater.

---

132. Swenson, Richard A., *More Than Meets the Eye*, p. 125

133. "And God made two great lights; the greater light to rule the day, and the lesser light to rule the night: he made the stars also" (Gen. 1:16).

134. Swenson, Richard A., *More Than Meets the Eye*, p. 125.

135. Ibid., p. 125–126.

136. 5 January 2008 <http://us.agathachristie.com/site/about_christie/>. Agatha Christie is the most popular novelist in history, with over two billion of her books sold. She has been called the undisputed "Queen of Crime."

The play began its run in London on 25 November 1952. As of April 2007, *The Mousetrap* had clocked 22,627 performances.[137] Recently, *The Mousetrap* was performed by the Hilltop Players at Bryan College in Dayton, Tennessee. My son was in the play, so being a supportive dad I attended five performances in a row. After seeing the play five times in a small theater where the audience was very close to the action on the stage, I knew exactly what the actors were going to say, where they were going to stand, and what they were going to do at any given moment. I also knew which actor would be murdered in the play, and I knew who would commit this cruel deed. During the play I felt like I should stand up and warn the actor who was about to be attacked. But obviously my shouting out a warning to the actor would spoil the play for the rest of the audience and would be very disruptive. But I knew that a very bad thing was about to happen! In a miniscule way, this is the knowledge that the omniscient God possesses about our entire lives. God can certainly intervene in the action of life if He chooses. However, God may choose to allow us to reap the consequences of our decisions and actions. God has not made us robots or puppets. God respects us enough to allow us to make our own decisions.

The fourth chapter will emphasize verses from the Bible that reveal what God knows. But for now let's continue learning about God by considering several more of His attributes.

God is omnipotent

Omnipotent is another absolute word, like omniscient. Omnipotent is defined as "Almighty, unlimited power/all-powerful."[138] It is easy enough to say that God has all power in the universe, but have you seriously considered what this means? The following passages from the Bible describe God as being omnipotent:

---

137. 19 June 2007 <http://en.wikipedia.org/wiki/The_Mousetrap >.
138. *Webster's Third New International Dictionary of the English Language—Unabridged,* p. 1574.

And when Abram was ninety years old and nine, the LORD appeared to Abram, and said unto him, I am the Almighty God; walk before me, and be thou perfect.

—Genesis 17:1

Is any thing too hard for the LORD? At the time appointed I will return unto thee, according to the time of life, and Sarah shall have a son.

—Genesis 18:14

Thine, O LORD, is the greatness, and the power, and the glory, and the victory, and the majesty: for all that is in the heaven and in the earth is thine; thine is the kingdom, O LORD, and thou art exalted as head above all.

—1 Chronicles 29:11

Where wast thou when I laid the foundations of the earth? declare, if thou hast understanding.

—Job 38:4

Hast thou entered into the treasures of the snow? or hast thou seen the treasures of the hail, Which I have reserved against the time of trouble, against the day of battle and war?

—Job 38:22–23

I know that thou canst do every thing, and that no thought can be withholden from thee.

—Job 42:2

For the word of the LORD is right; and all his works are done in truth. He loveth righteousness and judgment: the earth is full of the goodness of the LORD. By the word of the

LORD were the heavens made; and all the host of them by the breath of his mouth. He gathereth the waters of the sea together as an heap: he layeth up the depth in storehouses. Let all the earth fear the LORD: let all the inhabitants of the world stand in awe of him. For he spake, and it was done; he commanded, and it stood fast.

—Psalm 33:4–9

For thou hast possessed my reins: thou hast covered me in my mother's womb. I will praise thee; for I am fearfully and wonderfully made: marvellous are thy works; and that my soul knoweth right well. My substance was not hid from thee, when I was made in secret, and curiously wrought in the lowest parts of the earth. Thine eyes did see my substance, yet being unperfect; and in thy book all my members were written, which in continuance were fashioned, when as yet there was none of them. How precious also are thy thoughts unto me, O God! how great is the sum of them! If I should count them, they are more in number than the sand: when I awake, I am still with thee.

—Psalm 139:13–18

Great is our Lord, and of great power: his understanding is infinite.

—Psalm 147:5

Lift up your eyes on high, and behold who hath created these things [stars], that bringeth out their host by number: he calleth them all by names by the greatness of his might, for that he is strong in power; not one faileth.

—Isaiah 40:26

And Jesus came and spake unto them, saying, All power is given unto me in heaven and in earth.

—Matthew 28:18

And I heard as it were the voice of a great multitude, and as the voice of many waters, and as the voice of mighty thunderings, saying, Alleluia: for the Lord God omnipotent reigneth.

—Revelation 19:6

Until recently, physicists, who study subatomic particles, atoms, elements, and molecules, have said that there are only four fundamental forces in the universe that hold everything together. This concept is summarized with the statement, "each bit of matter in the universe is influenced by four forces—no more, no less." [139] The four fundamental forces are:

1. Gravity
2. Electromagnetic force
3. Weak nuclear force
4. Strong nuclear force

Gravity is the most familiar of the four universal forces; however, it is the weakest. It is a very important force controlling the balance of power in the entire macroscopic universe. Albert Einstein's general theory of relativity is the best–known theory of gravity. According to the general relativity theory, gravity affects or distorts time. Scientific experiments have demonstrated that the higher we ascend from the earth or the further we move away from the surface of this planet, the faster time passes in relation to time on the surface of the earth. [140]

---

139. Swenson, Richard A., *More Than Meets the Eye*, p. 113.
140. An atomic clock at the Royal Observatory in Greenwich, England, which is close to sea level, ticks five microseconds per year slower than an identical clock at the National Bureau of Standards in Boulder, Colorado, located about one mile above sea level. Humphreys, D. Russell, *Starlight and Time-Solving the Puzzle of Distant Starlight in a Young Universe*, Master Books Inc., Green Forest, AR, 1994, p. 11–12.

Another way of saying this is that clocks tick faster in locations far from the earth than identical clocks tick on the surface of the earth. The rate in which time passes becomes significant in galaxies located at extreme distances from the earth, as time may be moving more rapidly in remote locations than time is passing on the earth.

In 1994 Russell Humphreys[141] published a book proposing a new creationist cosmology[142] based on the variation in the rate in which time passes in different locations. Humphrey's new cosmology explains how gravitational time distortion in the early universe would have meant that while a few days were passing on earth, billions of years would have been available for light to travel from distant galaxies to earth. This explanation shows how God could have made the earth in six ordinary days only a few thousand years ago while the entire universe was brought into existence on day four of creation week as is documented in the Bible.[143] In 2007 John Hartnett[144] published a book[145] that suggests how light from the most distant stars would have reached the earth in a very short time. Both authors have presented convincing evidence that explains how light from exceedingly distant galaxies has been able to reach the surface of this planet in a very short time according to "earth clocks." Their explanations are based on the influence of gravity on the passing of time.

How gravity works remains a mystery to scientists. Gravity is invisible to the human eye as it passes through the air, but it has a profound effect on objects. A heavenly body larger than an asteroid, with a diameter of three hundred miles or more, is round because the

---

141. D. Russell Humphreys was awarded his Ph.D. in physics from Louisiana State University in 1972.
142. The word "cosmology" deals with the general structure and the origin of the universe.
143. Humphreys, D. Russell, *Starlight and Time—Solving the Puzzle of Distant Starlight in a Young Universe*, p. 13.
144. John Hartnett, Ph.D., is an associate professor at the University of Western Australia.
145. *Starlight, Time and the New Physics* by John Hartnett, published by Creation Book Publishers, Georgia, USA, 2007.

pull of gravity toward its center crushes that object into the shape of a sphere.[146]

An electromagnetic force, or electromagnetism, is also a familiar force. It is seen in electricity and in lightning during thunderstorms. Electromagnetism is essential in the operation of the bodies of all animals and humans as it is involved in cellular function, in the bonding of bones, in the contraction of muscles, in the transmission of signals by nerves, and in the function of the brain. Electromagnetic forces are involved with the orbiting of electrons, the charges of particles, and the binding together of molecules and chemicals. Electromagnetism is literally seen in light, where there are streaming photons.[147]

The weak nuclear force has a very limited range. It is active only within atoms. It is the force responsible for the radioactive decay of elements like uranium.[148]

The strong nuclear force has an exceptionally short range of effectiveness, but it is incredibly powerful. It is the force that keeps the nucleus of an atom from flying apart. Neutrons are found in the nucleus, and they have no electrical charge.[149] The nucleus also contains protons that have a positive charge and naturally repel each other. The strong nuclear force holds the positively charged protons together in the nucleus of an atom.[150]

The incredibly small components of atoms are not solid like tiny marbles. Electrons move so rapidly and change locations so quickly that they are almost "ghost–like" in their existence.[151] In the last fifty years scientists have found particles and parts of atoms that are much smaller than protons and neutrons. These exceedingly small "critters" are called subatomic particles. They have been given some neat and unusual names like quarks, neutrinos, photons, boson, fermion,

---

146. Swenson, Richard A., *More Than Meets the Eye*, p. 114–115.
147. Ibid., p. 115.
148. Ibid., p. 116.
149. Ibid., p. 108.
150. Ibid., p. 116.
151. Ibid., p. 106.

gluon, lepton, muon, and pion. Some subatomic particles are only in existence for a few microseconds.[152]

During creation week, God made an unbelievably large number of atoms with their neutrons, protons, electrons, and subatomic particles by His speaking them into existence.

God used these atoms and subatomic particles to create the molecules that became light, water, earth, sun, moon, and all of the stars of the universe. God used other atoms and subatomic particles to create plants, birds, fishes, whales, land animals, and Adam and Eve. God also created angels. Some of God's creative activity is recorded in the following passages from the first chapter of Genesis. The italicized words are keys to understanding God's abilities.

In the beginning *God created* the heaven and the earth.

—Genesis 1:1

And *God said*, Let there be light: and there was light.

—Genesis 1:3

And *God said*, Let there be a firmament in the midst of the waters, and let it divide the waters from the waters. And *God made* the firmament, and divided the waters which were under the firmament from the waters which were above the firmament: and it was so.

—Genesis 1:6–7

And *God said*, Let the waters under the heaven be gathered together unto one place, and let the dry land appear: and it was so.

—Genesis 1:9

---

152. Ibid., p. 108–111.

And *God said,* Let the earth bring forth grass, the herb yield-ing seed, and the fruit tree yielding fruit after his kind, whose seed is in itself, upon the earth: and it was so.

—Genesis 1:11

And *God said,* Let there be lights in the firmament of the heaven to divide the day from the night; and let them be for signs, and for seasons, and for days, and years.

—Genesis 1:14

And *God made* two great lights; the greater light to rule the day, and the lesser light to rule the night: *he made* the stars also.

—Genesis 1:16

And *God said,* Let the waters bring forth abundantly the moving creature that hath life, and fowl that may fly above the earth in the open firmament of heaven. And *God created* great whales, and every living creature that moveth, which the waters brought forth abundantly, after their kind, and every winged fowl after his kind: and God saw that it was good.

—Genesis 1:20–21

And *God said,* Let the earth bring forth the living creature after his kind, cattle, and creeping thing, and beast of the earth after his kind: and it was so.

—Genesis 1:24

So *God created* man in his own image, in the image of *God created* he him; male and female *created he* them.

—Genesis 1:27

> And *God saw every thing that he had made,* and, behold, it
> was very good. And the evening and the morning were the
> sixth day.
>
> —Genesis 1:31

In past years, scientists described what they believed were the only four fundamental forces in the universe. Recently scientists have identified a repulsive dark or vacuum energy that is often called the cosmological constant. This energy is theorized to be the result of a nonzero vacuum energy detectable at cosmological scales. This energy is believed to aid in determining the dynamics of the universe as a whole.[153]

With all due respect to the scientists of our world, is it possible that there is an additional force in the universe that is more powerful than all of the forces identified by the highly educated scientists of the world? This force is employed only by Almighty God when and where He chooses. Amazingly, humans can petition Almighty God to use this force. May I suggest that there is the power of prayer that changes things, people, and situations? These changes occur because of the response of God to prayer. The meaning of the word "prayer" is "a solemn and humble approach to Divinity in word or thought, usually involving beseeching, petition, confession, praise, or thanksgiving."[154] Prayer is a human request for God to use His power in the universe He created. According to Richard Swenson, if necessary, prayer can travel faster than the speed of light. "Prayer is an instantaneous phenomenon."[155] Prayers can request God to work miracles. When God hears a prayer, He has the right to respond in any manner He chooses. God's power certainly includes all of the four or more fundamental forces in the universe, but God can also work miracles by using, altering, or "overrid-

153. Gonzalez, Guillermo and Richards, Jay W., *The Privileged Planet, How Our Place In The Cosmos Is Designed for Discovery*, Regnery Publishing, Inc., Washington, D.C., 2004, p. 205.
154. *Webster's Third New International Dictionary of the English Language—Unabridged*, p. 1782.
155. Swenson, Richard A., *More Than Meets the Eye*, p. 177.

ing" these forces. God can alter any or all of the forces in the universe at any time He chooses because the Almighty God is omnipotent.

As was recently mentioned, one of the universe's four fundamental forces, as identified by scientists, is the strong nuclear force that holds the nuclei of atoms together. However, the Bible tells us that Jesus Christ is the Creator, and it is His power that holds everything together.[156] This holding power includes what scientists call the strong nuclear force. For the record, we should realize and understand that at all times the omnipotent God controls each of the other three fundamental forces in the universe. If there are any other forces in the universe, God is in total control of them as well. Here are some passages from the Bible that communicate the creative and sustaining work of the Lord Jesus Christ.

Of old hast thou laid the foundation of the earth: and the heavens are the work of thy hands.

—Psalm 102:25

For of him, and through him, and to him, are all things: to whom be glory for ever. Amen.

—Romans 11:36

Who is the image of the invisible God, the firstborn of every creature: For by him were all things created, that are in heaven, and that are in earth, visible and invisible, whether they be thrones, or dominions, or principalities, or powers: all things were created by him, and for him: And he is before all things, and *by him all things consist.*

—Colossians 1:15–17

God, who at sundry times and in divers manners spake in

---

156. "And he is before all things, and by him all things consist" (Col. 1:17).

time past unto the fathers by the prophets, Hath in these
last days spoken unto us by his Son, whom he hath appointed heir of all things, by whom also he made the worlds; Who
being the brightness of his glory, and the express image of
his person, and *upholding all things by the word of his power,*
when he had by himself purged our sins, sat down on the
right hand of the Majesty on high.

—Hebrews 1:1–3

And, Thou, Lord, in the beginning hast laid the foundation
of the earth; and the heavens are the works of thine hands.

—Hebrews 1:10

God is omnipresent

Omnipresent is another absolute word like omniscient and omnipotent. Omnipresent is defined as "present in all places at all times:
ubiquitous."[157] It is easy enough to say that God is everywhere in the
universe, but have you seriously considered what this means? Here
are a few passages from the Bible that refer to God as being omnipresent:

Is not God in the height of heaven? and behold the height of
the stars, how high they are!

—Job 22:12

Whither shall I go from thy spirit? or whither shall I flee
from thy presence? If I ascend up into heaven, thou art
there: if I make my bed in hell, behold, thou art there. If I
take the wings of the morning, and dwell in the uttermost
parts of the sea; Even there shall thy hand lead me, and thy
right hand shall hold me. If I say, Surely the darkness shall

---

157. *Webster's Third New International Dictionary of the English Language—Unabridged,* p. 1574.

cover me; even the night shall be light about me. Yea, the darkness hideth not from thee; but the night shineth as the day: the darkness and the light are both alike to thee.

—Psalm 139:7–12

He telleth the number of the stars; he calleth them all by their names.

—Psalm 147:4

The eyes of the LORD are in every place, beholding the evil and the good.

—Proverbs 15:3

And one cried unto another, and said, Holy, holy, holy, is the LORD of hosts: the whole earth is full of his glory.

—Isaiah 6:3

Am I a God at hand, saith the LORD, and not a God afar off? Can any hide himself in secret places that I shall not see him? saith the LORD. Do not I fill heaven and earth? saith the LORD.

—Jeremiah 23:23–24

The omnipresent God fills the universe that He created, and He is also outside of the universe that He created.

God is eternal (immortal)

The concept of eternity exceeds human comprehension. The word *eternal* means "having infinite duration: having no beginning or end."[158] The Bible tells us that God is eternal. This means that God has always existed and God will always exist. It is very difficult—it is

---

158. Ibid., p. 780.

impossible—for the human mind to comprehend God's being eternal. Said another way, God had no beginning, and God will never die, nor will He cease to exist.

Dr. Henry M. Morris penned the following ideas, and they are certainly worth considering. God is eternal and self-existent. One can reject God if he chooses, believing that the finely tuned universe itself is self–existent and that it somehow organized itself into its present degree of infinite complexity. One can create a false god or a weak god that has little or no influence on the lives of individuals or civilization as a whole. Or one can choose to believe in the eternal, transcendent, omnipotent, omniscient, all–holy, self–existent God. Belief in the eternal, Almighty God is an act of faith, since complete understanding of such a Being is beyond the capacity of mortal minds. The Lord Jesus Christ identified Himself as God when he said in John 8:58, "Before Abraham was, I am."[159]

Here are some biblical references that tell us that God is eternal:

In the beginning God created the heaven and the earth.

—Genesis 1:1

See now that I, even I, am he, and there is no god with me: I kill, and I make alive; I wound, and I heal: neither is there any that can deliver out of my hand. For I lift up my hand to heaven, and say, I live for ever.

—Deuteronomy 32:39–40

The eternal God is thy refuge, and underneath are the everlasting arms: and he shall thrust out the enemy from before thee; and shall say, Destroy them.

—Deuteronomy 33:27

159. Morris, Henry M., *The Defender's Study Bible—King James Version*, p. 1567.

O give thanks unto the LORD; for he is good; for his mercy endureth for ever.

—1 Chronicles 16:34

Before the mountains were brought forth, or ever thou hadst formed the earth and the world, even from everlasting to everlasting, thou art God.

—Psalm 90:2

But thou art the same, and thy years shall have no end.

—Psalm 102:27

For ever, O LORD, thy word is settled in heaven.

—Psalm 119:89

O give thanks to the Lord of lords: for his mercy endureth for ever.

—Psalm 136:3

Hast thou not known? hast thou not heard, that the everlasting God, the LORD, the Creator of the ends of the earth, fainteth not, neither is weary? there is no searching of his understanding.

—Isaiah 40:28

For thus saith the high and lofty One that inhabiteth eternity, whose name is Holy; I dwell in the high and holy place, with him also that is of a contrite and humble spirit, to revive the spirit of the humble, and to revive the heart of the contrite ones.

—Isaiah 57:15

And at the end of the days I Nebuchadnezzar lifted up mine eyes unto heaven, and mine understanding returned unto

me, and I blessed the most High, and I praised and honoured him that liveth for ever, whose dominion is an everlasting dominion, and his kingdom is from generation to generation.

—Daniel 4:34

In the beginning was the Word, and the Word was with God, and the Word was God. The same was in the beginning with God.

—John 1:1–2

For the invisible things of him from the creation of the world are clearly seen, being understood by the things that are made, even his eternal power and Godhead; so that they are without excuse.

—Romans 1:20

Now unto the King eternal, immortal, invisible, the only wise God, be honour and glory for ever and ever. Amen

—1 Timothy 1:17

Who only hath immortality, dwelling in the light which no man can approach unto; whom no man hath seen, nor can see: to whom be honour and power everlasting. Amen.

—1 Timothy 6:16

I am Alpha and Omega, the beginning and the ending, saith the Lord, which is, and which was, and which is to come, the Almighty.

—Revelation 1:8

I am Alpha and Omega, the beginning and the end, the first and the last.

—Revelation 22:13

God is immutable

This is difficult for humans to truly comprehend. The word "immutable" means "not capable or susceptible of change: invariable, unalterable."[160] Succinctly stated, the immutable God never changes. Since God is immutable, all of God's attributes are constant, continual, and eternal. Since God does not change, He upholds the universe in a consistent and uniform way throughout time. Since God does not change, He will never ever lose His knowledge, and God will never ever lose His power!

Here are some biblical references that tell us that God is immutable:

> **Of old hast thou laid the foundation of the earth: and the heavens are the work of thy hands. They shall perish, but thou shalt endure: yea, all of them shall wax old like a garment; as a vesture shalt thou change them, and they shall be changed: But thou art the same, and thy years shall have no end.**
>
> —Psalm 102:25–27

> **For his merciful kindness is great toward us: and the truth of the LORD endureth for ever. Praise ye the LORD.**
>
> —Psalm 117:2

> **Thy righteousness is an everlasting righteousness, and thy law is the truth.**
>
> —Psalm 119:142

> **O give thanks unto the LORD; for he is good: for his mercy endureth for ever.**
>
> —Psalm 136:1

---

160. *Webster's Third New International Dictionary of the English Language—Unabridged*, p. 1131.

For I am the LORD, I change not; therefore ye sons of Jacob are not consumed.

—Malachi 3:6

Jesus Christ the same yesterday, and to day, and for ever.

—Hebrews 13:8

God is incomprehensible

The word "incomprehensible" means "impossible to comprehend: lying above and beyond the reach of the human mind (as in the incomprehensible mysteries of creation), being beyond the powers of comprehension of a particular mind: unintelligible, being beyond ordinary comprehension: unfathomable. An older meaning for incomprehensible is having or subject to no limits."[161] God is certainly beyond human understanding. It is interesting that Albert Einstein said, "The most incomprehensible thing about the universe is that it's incomprehensible."[162] Can we say that the attribute of incomprehensibility is incomprehensible? In one sense the answer could be yes, because of the complex nature of God. In another sense the answer could be no, because we can understand that God is beyond our ability to understand Him.

Here are a few passages from the Bible that tell us that God is beyond our understanding.

Canst thou by searching find out God? canst thou find out the Almighty unto perfection?

—Job 11:7

Touching the Almighty, we cannot find him out: he is excellent in power, and in judgment, and in plenty of justice: he will not afflict.

—Job 37:23

161. *Webster's Third New International Dictionary of the English Language—Unabridged*, p. 1144.
162. 26 December 2007 <www.myhero.com/myhero/hero.asp?hero=einstein>.

Hast thou an arm like God? or canst thou thunder with a voice like him?

—Job 40:9

Hast thou not known? hast thou not heard, that the everlasting God, the LORD, the Creator of the ends of the earth, fainteth not, neither is weary? there is no searching of his understanding.

—Isaiah 40:28

For as the Father hath life in himself; so hath he given to the Son to have life in himself.

—John 5:26

For the invisible things of him from the creation of the world are clearly seen, being understood by the things that are made, even his eternal power and Godhead; so that they are without excuse.

—Romans 1:20

O the depth of the riches both of the wisdom and knowledge of God! how unsearchable are his judgments, and his ways past finding out!

—Romans 11:33

God is self–existent

The term "self-existent" means "existing of or by oneself or itself: independent of any other being or cause."[163] God's self–existence means God depends upon nothing other than Himself. God has no origin. He has always existed. God is responsible to no one.

Here are some passages from the Bible that tell us that God is self–existent:

---

163. *Webster's Third New International Dictionary of the English Language—Unabridged*, p. 2060.

In the beginning God created the heaven and the earth.

—Genesis 1:1

And God said unto Moses, I AM THAT I AM: and he said, Thus shalt thou say unto the children of Israel, I AM hath sent me unto you.

—Exodus 3:14

The counsel of the LORD standeth for ever, the thoughts of his heart to all generations.

—Psalm 33:11

But our God is in the heavens: he hath done whatsoever he hath pleased.

—Psalm 115:3

To whom then will ye liken God? or what likeness will ye compare unto him?

—Isaiah 40:18

And all the inhabitants of the earth are reputed as nothing: and he doeth according to his will in the army of heaven, and among the inhabitants of the earth: and none can stay his hand, or say unto him, What doest thou?

—Daniel 4:35

In the beginning was the Word, and the Word was with God, and the Word was God. The same was in the beginning with God. All things were made by him; and without him was not any thing made that was made.

—John 1:1–3

For as the Father hath life in himself; so hath he given to the Son to have life in himself.

—John 5:26

> **For by him were all things created, that are in heaven, and that are in earth, visible and invisible, whether they be thrones, or dominions, or principalities, or powers: all things were created by him, and for him: And he is before all things, and by him all things consist.**
>
> —Colossians 1:16–17

God is self–sufficient

The term or phrase "self-sufficient" refers to someone's or something's being "able to maintain oneself or itself without outside aid: capable of providing for one's or its own needs, sufficient in or to itself, self–contained."[164] God does not need any help from the human beings that He created, and God needs no help from any other part of His creation. Yes, God has established a voluntary relation to everything He has made, but He has no necessary relation to any part of His creation outside Himself.[165]

Here are some passages that tell us God is self–sufficient.

> **Hear, O my people, and I will speak; O Israel, and I will testify against thee: I am God, even thy God. I will not reprove thee for thy sacrifices or thy burnt offerings, to have been continually before me. I will take no bullock out of thy house, nor he goats out of thy folds. For every beast of the forest is mine, and the cattle upon a thousand hills. I know all the fowls of the mountains: and the wild beasts of the field are mine. If I were hungry, I would not tell thee: for the world is mine, and the fulness thereof.**
>
> —Psalm 50:7–12

> **Who hath directed the Spirit of the LORD, or being his counsellor hath taught him?**
>
> —Isaiah 40:13

---

164. Ibid., p. 2061.
165. Tozer, A.W., *The Knowledge of the Holy,* p. 32.

Hast thou not known? hast thou not heard, that the ever-lasting God, the LORD, the Creator of the ends of the earth, fainteth not, neither is weary? there is no searching of his understanding.

—Isaiah 40:28

For as the Father hath life in himself; so hath he given to the Son to have life in himself.

—John 5:26

God that made the world and all things therein, seeing that he is Lord of heaven and earth, dwelleth not in temples made with hands; Neither is worshipped with men's hands, as though he needed any thing, seeing he giveth to all life, and breath, and all things.

—Acts 17:24–25

For of him, and through him, and to him, are all things: to whom be glory for ever. Amen.

—Romans 11:36

Now unto him that is able to do exceeding abundantly above all that we ask or think, according to the power that worketh in us.

—Ephesians 3:20

God is infinite

The word "infinite" means "without limits of any kind: subject to no limitation or external determination, having no end: extending indefinitely, having no limit in power, capacity, knowledge or excellence, extending to infinity."[166] That God is infinite means He has no limits.

---

166. *Webster's Third New International Dictionary of the English Language—Unabridged*, p. 1159.

Here are some passages from the Bible that tell us God is infinite:

> But will God indeed dwell on the earth? behold, the heaven and heaven of heavens cannot contain thee; how much less this house that I have builded?
>
> —1 Kings 8:27

> But will God in very deed dwell with men on the earth? behold, heaven and the heaven of heavens cannot contain thee; how much less this house which I have built!
>
> —2 Chronicles 6:18

> Great is our Lord, and of great power: his understanding is infinite.
>
> —Psalm 147:5

> Thus saith the LORD, The heaven is my throne, and the earth is my footstool: where is the house that ye build unto me? and where is the place of my rest?
>
> —Isaiah 66:1

> Howbeit the most High dwelleth not in temples made with hands; as saith the prophet, Heaven is my throne, and earth is my footstool: what house will ye build me? saith the Lord: or what is the place of my rest?
>
> —Acts 7:48–49

God is transcendent

The word "transcendent" means "going beyond or exceeding usual limits, being beyond comprehension, being above material existence or apart from the universe."[167] God is above His creation. Another way

---

167. Ibid., p. 2426.

of describing this attribute of God is to understand that God exists outside of both time and the universe that He created. Because God is transcendent, He can listen to the prayers of billions of people at the same time and give personal attention to each individual prayer.

Here are a few passages from the Bible that tell us God is transcendent:

In the beginning God created the heaven and the earth.

—Genesis 1:1

Before the mountains were brought forth, or ever thou hadst formed the earth and the world, even from everlasting to everlasting, thou art God.

—Psalm 90:2

Yea, the darkness hideth not from thee; but the night shineth as the day: the darkness and the light are both alike to thee.

—Psalm 139:12

Hast thou not known? hast thou not heard, that the everlasting God, the LORD, the Creator of the ends of the earth, fainteth not, neither is weary? there is no searching of his understanding.

—Isaiah 40:28

Ye are my witnesses, saith the LORD, and my servant whom I have chosen; that ye may know and believe me, and understand that I am he: before me there was no God formed, neither shall there be after me.

—Isaiah 43:10

For my thoughts are not your thoughts, neither are your

ways my ways, saith the LORD. For as the heavens are higher than the earth, so are my ways higher than your ways, and my thoughts than your thoughts.

—Isaiah 55: 8–9

Thou art worthy, O Lord, to receive glory and honour and power: for thou hast created all things, and for thy pleasure they are and were created.

—Revelation 4:11

God is sovereign

The word "sovereign" designates "the supreme repository of power in a political state, the person wielding or exercising supreme political power, one that exercises supreme authority."[168] That God is sovereign means He is supreme over creation. God has total control of the universe that He created.

Here are some passages that refer to God's sovereignty:

Turn ye not unto idols, nor make to yourselves molten gods: I am the LORD your God.

—Leviticus 19:4

For great is the LORD, and greatly to be praised: he also is to be feared above all gods.

—1 Chronicles 16:25

For who in the heaven can be compared unto the LORD? who among the sons of the mighty can be likened unto the LORD? God is greatly to be feared in the assembly of the saints, and to be had in reverence of all them that are about him.

—Psalm 89:6–7

168. Ibid., p. 2179.

For the LORD is great, and greatly to be praised: he is to be feared above all gods.

—Psalm 96:4

The LORD hath prepared his throne in the heavens; and his kingdom ruleth over all.

—Psalm 103:19

That bringeth the princes to nothing; he maketh the judges of the earth as vanity.

—Isaiah 40:23

And at the end of the days I Nebuchadnezzar lifted up mine eyes unto heaven, and mine understanding returned unto me, and I blessed the most High, and I praised and honoured him that liveth for ever, whose dominion is an everlasting dominion, and his kingdom is from generation to generation.

—Daniel 4:34

Now unto the King eternal, immortal, invisible, the only wise God, be honour and glory for ever and ever. Amen.

—1 Timothy 1:17

Which in his times he shall shew, who is the blessed and only Potentate, the King of kings, and Lord of lords.

—1 Timothy 6:15

God is holy

The word "holy" means "perfect in righteousness and divine love: infinitely good: worthy of complete devotion and trust: commanding one's fullest powers of adoration and reverence as to the holy Lord God Almighty."[169] This is another attribute that is difficult for humans

---

169. Ibid., p. 1081.

to grasp. We as humans know that we are not perfect. We know that we have limitations and flaws in our personalities and character. We know that we have thought and done things that are not right, honest, and correct. We know that we have been deceptive and less than truthful at all times. On the other hand, God is a totally perfect Being. Simply said, God has never done anything wrong, and He never will do anything wrong.

Here are a few passages from the Bible that tell us God is holy:

Speak unto all the congregation of the children of Israel, and say unto them, Ye shall be holy: for I the LORD your God am holy.

—Leviticus 19:2

And Joshua said unto the people, Ye cannot serve the LORD: for he is an holy God; he is a jealous God; he will not forgive your transgressions nor your sins. If ye forsake the LORD, and serve strange gods, then he will turn and do you hurt, and consume you, after that he hath done you good.

—Joshua 24:19–20

There is none holy as the LORD: for there is none beside thee: neither is there any rock like our God.

—1 Samuel 2:2

Therefore hearken unto me, ye men of understanding: far be it from God, that he should do wickedness; and from the Almighty, that he should commit iniquity.

—Job 34:10

But thou art holy, O thou that inhabitest the praises of Israel.

—Psalm 22:3

The LORD is righteous in all his ways, and holy in all his works.

—Psalm 145:17

And one cried unto another, and said, Holy, holy, holy, is the LORD of hosts: the whole earth is full of his glory.

—Isaiah 6:3

As for our redeemer, the LORD of hosts is his name, the Holy One of Israel.

—Isaiah 47:4

For thus saith the high and lofty One that inhabiteth eternity, whose name is Holy; I dwell in the high and holy place, with him also that is of a contrite and humble spirit, to revive the spirit of the humble, and to revive the heart of the contrite ones.

—Isaiah 57:15

God is gracious

The word "gracious" means "marked by or having divine grace: marked by kindness and courtesy, abounding in grace or mercy." "Grace" means "beneficence or generosity shown by God to man: divine favor unmerited by man: the mercy of God as distinguished from His justice, a free gift of God to man for his regeneration or sanctification: an influence emanating from God and acting for his spiritual well–being of the recipient. God is the source of grace."[170] That God is gracious means that God always operates with grace.

Here are some passages from the Bible that describe God's graciousness:

And he said, I will make all my goodness pass before thee,

---

170. Ibid., p. 984.

and I will proclaim the name of the LORD before thee; and will be gracious to whom I will be gracious, and will shew mercy on whom I will shew mercy.

—Exodus 33:19

And the LORD passed by before him, and proclaimed, The LORD, The LORD God, merciful and gracious, longsuffering, and abundant in goodness and truth, Keeping mercy for thousands, forgiving iniquity and transgression and sin, and that will by no means clear the guilty; visiting the iniquity of the fathers upon the children, and upon the children's children, unto the third and to the fourth generation.

—Exodus 34:6–7

The LORD is gracious, and full of compassion; slow to anger, and of great mercy.

—Psalm 145:8

And refused to obey, neither were mindful of thy wonders that thou didst among them; but hardened their necks, and in their rebellion appointed a captain to return to their bondage: but thou art a God ready to pardon, gracious and merciful, slow to anger, and of great kindness, and forsookest them not.

—Nehemiah 9:17

Nevertheless for thy great mercies' sake thou didst not utterly consume them, nor forsake them; for thou art a gracious and merciful God.

—Nehemiah 9:31

And therefore will the LORD wait, that he may be gracious unto you, and therefore will he be exalted, that he may have mercy upon you: for the LORD is a God of judgment: blessed are all they that wait for him.

—Isaiah 30:18

He giveth power to the faint; and to them that have no might he increaseth strength.

—Isaiah 40:29

And the child grew, and waxed strong in spirit, filled with wisdom: and the grace of God was upon him.

—Luke 2:40

And the Word was made flesh, and dwelt among us, (and we beheld his glory, the glory as of the only begotten of the Father,) full of grace and truth.

—John 1:14

And he said unto me, My grace is sufficient for thee: for my strength is made perfect in weakness. Most gladly therefore will I rather glory in my infirmities, that the power of Christ may rest upon me.

—2 Corinthians 12:9

For by grace are ye saved through faith; and that not of yourselves: it is the gift of God.

—Ephesians 2:8

I can do all things through Christ which strengtheneth me.

—Philippians 4:13

The Lord knoweth how to deliver the godly out of temptations, and to reserve the unjust unto the day of judgment to be punished.

—2 Peter 2:9

God is righteous

The word "righteous" means "doing that which is right: acting rightly or justly: conforming to the standard of the divine or the moral law: free from guilt or sin, morally right or justifiable: free from wrong."[171] This attribute of God means God's character reveals His nature, which is always right, just, and fair.

Here are some passages that describe God as being righteous:

He is the Rock, his work is perfect: for all his ways are judgment: a God of truth and without iniquity, just and right is he.

—Deuteronomy 32:4

Thy righteousness is an everlasting righteousness, and thy law is the truth.

—Psalm 119:142

Thy word is true from the beginning: and every one of thy righteous judgments endureth for ever.

—Psalm 119:160

Seven times a day do I praise thee because of thy righteous judgments.

—Psalm 119:164

My tongue shall speak of thy word: for all thy commandments are righteousness.

—Psalm 119:172

The LORD is righteous in all his ways, and holy in all his works.

—Psalm 145:17

---

171. Ibid., p. 1956.

> **But now the righteousness of God without the law is mani-fested, being witnessed by the law and the prophets; Even the righteousness of God which is by faith of Jesus Christ unto all and upon all them that believe: for there is no dif-ference: For all have sinned, and come short of the glory of God.**
>
> —Romans 3:21–23

> **And I heard another out of the altar say, Even so, Lord God Almighty, true and righteous are thy judgments.**
>
> —Revelation 16:7

God is just

The word "just" means "reasonable, well–founded, justified, not false, right, true, accurate, faithful, constant, uniform, correct, proper, fit-ting, acting or being in conformity with what is morally right or good, righteous, equitable, conforming to what is legal or lawful: legally right."[172] This attribute of God means He is always fair and correct in His decisions concerning sinful people, because being just is His nature, and because of the redemptive work of the Lord Jesus Christ. God forgives the sins of every person who accepts the Lord Jesus Christ as his or her Savior.

Here are some passages from the Bible that describe God as be-ing just:

> **O LORD, thou hast seen my wrong: judge thou my cause.**
>
> —Lamentations 3:59

> **Justice and judgment are the habitation of thy throne: mer-cy and truth shall go before thy face.**
>
> —Psalm 89:14

---

172. Ibid., p. 1228.

The LORD is longsuffering, and of great mercy, forgiving iniquity and transgression, and by no means clearing the guilty, visiting the iniquity of the fathers upon the children unto the third and fourth generation.

—Numbers 14:18

God is not a man, that he should lie; neither the son of man, that he should repent: hath he said, and shall he not do it? or hath he spoken, and shall he not make it good?

—Numbers 23:19

What shall we say then? Is there unrighteousness with God? God forbid. For he saith to Moses, I will have mercy on whom I will have mercy, and I will have compassion on whom I will have compassion.

—Romans 9:14–15

If we confess our sins, he is faithful and just to forgive us our sins, and to cleanse us from all unrighteousness.

—1 John 1:9

God is merciful

The word "merciful" means "full of mercy: marked, exercising, or disposed to mercy; clement, compassionate, lenient. While the word mercy means compassion or forbearance shown to an offender or subject: clemency or kindness extended to someone instead of strictness or severity: leniency—act of divine favor or compassion."[173] God is merciful; this means God is always full of mercy and is always compassionate.

Here are some passages describing God as being merciful:

---

173. Ibid, p. 1413.

And shewing mercy unto thousands of them that love me, and keep my commandments.

—Exodus 20:6

And he said, I will make all my goodness pass before thee, and I will proclaim the name of the LORD before thee; and will be gracious to whom I will be gracious, and will shew mercy on whom I will shew mercy.

—Exodus 33:19

O give thanks unto the LORD; for he is good; for his mercy endureth for ever.

—1 Chronicles 16:34

And refused to obey, neither were mindful of thy wonders that thou didst among them; but hardened their necks, and in their rebellion appointed a captain to return to their bondage: but thou art a God ready to pardon, gracious and merciful, slow to anger, and of great kindness, and forsookest them not.

—Nehemiah 9:17

Nevertheless for thy great mercies' sake thou didst not utterly consume them, nor forsake them; for thou art a gracious and merciful God.

—Nehemiah 9:31

Also unto thee, O Lord, belongeth mercy: for thou renderest to every man according to his work.

—Psalm 62:12

For thou, Lord, art good, and ready to forgive; and plenteous in mercy unto all them that call upon thee.

—Psalm 86:5

But thou, O Lord, art a God full of compassion, and gracious, longsuffering, and plenteous in mercy and truth.

—Psalm 86:15

But the mercy of the LORD is from everlasting to everlasting upon them that fear him, and his righteousness unto children's children.

—Psalm 103:17

Nevertheless he regarded their affliction, when he heard their cry: And he remembered for them his covenant, and repented according to the multitude of his mercies.

—Psalm 106:44–45

O give thanks to the Lord of lords: for his mercy endureth for ever.

—Psalm 136:3

The LORD is gracious, and full of compassion; slow to anger, and of great mercy. The LORD is good to all: and his tender mercies are over all his works.

—Psalm 145:8–9

It is of the LORD's mercies that we are not consumed, because his compassions fail not.

—Lamentations 3:22

But though he cause grief, yet will he have compassion according to the multitude of his mercies.

—Lamentations 3:32

But when Jesus heard that, he said unto them, They that be whole need not a physician, but they that are sick. But go

> ye and learn what that meaneth, I will have mercy, and not
> sacrifice: for I am not come to call the righteous, but sinners
> to repentance.
>
> —Matthew 9:12–13

> What shall we say then? Is there unrighteousness with God?
> God forbid. For he saith to Moses, I will have mercy on whom
> I will have mercy, and I will have compassion on whom I will
> have compassion.
>
> —Romans 9:14–15

> Not by works of righteousness which we have done, but ac-
> cording to his mercy he saved us, by the washing of regen-
> eration, and renewing of the Holy Ghost.
>
> —Titus 3:5

God is longsuffering

The word "longsuffering" means "showing patience under long provoca-
tion."[174] Certainly God is longsuffering to put up with the sinful rebellion of the human race. Inherent in the attribute of longsuffering is
the fact that God is slow to anger.

Here are a few passages from the Bible that describe God as being
longsuffering:

> The LORD is longsuffering, and of great mercy, forgiving
> iniquity and transgression, and by no means clearing the
> guilty, visiting the iniquity of the fathers upon the children
> unto the third and fourth generation.
>
> —Numbers 14:18

> The Lord is not slack concerning his promise, as some men

---

174. Ibid., p. 1334.

count slackness; but is longsuffering to us-ward, not willing that any should perish, but that all should come to repentance.

—2 Peter 3:9

And account that the longsuffering of our Lord is salvation; even as our beloved brother Paul also according to the wisdom given unto him hath written unto you.

—2 Peter 3:15

When sometime were disobedient, when once the longsuffering of God waited in the days of Noah, while the ark was a preparing, wherein few, that is, eight souls were saved by water.

—1 Peter 3:20

God is wise

The word "wise" means "characterized by wisdom, well informed, knowledgeable; exercising sound judgment."[175] Certainly God is wise, because He is omniscient, and therefore, He possesses all knowledge. Since God knows everything, He always makes sound and well–informed decisions. God's wisdom is perfect!

Here are some passages that describe God as being wise:

With him is wisdom and strength, he hath counsel and understanding.

—Job 12:13

The law of the LORD is perfect, converting the soul: the testimony of the LORD is sure, making wise the simple.

—Psalm 19:7

---

175. Ibid., p. 2624.

I will instruct thee and teach thee in the way which thou shalt go: I will guide thee with mine eye.

—Psalm 32:8

Behold, thou desirest truth in the inward parts: and in the hidden part thou shalt make me to know wisdom.

—Psalm 51:6

And the fear of the LORD is the beginning of wisdom: a good understanding have all they that do his commandments: his praise endureth for ever.

—Psalm 111:10

Great is our Lord, and of great power: his understanding is infinite.

—Psalm 147:5

For the LORD giveth wisdom: out of his mouth cometh knowledge and understanding.

—Proverbs 2:6

Hast thou not known? hast thou not heard, that the everlasting God, the LORD, the Creator of the ends of the earth, fainteth not, neither is weary? there is no searching of his understanding.

—Isaiah 40:28

Daniel answered and said, Blessed be the name of God for ever and ever: for wisdom and might are his.

—Daniel 2:20

To God only wise, be glory through Jesus Christ for ever. Amen.

—Romans 16:27

That the God of our Lord Jesus Christ, the Father of glory, may give unto you the spirit of wisdom and revelation in the knowledge of him.

—Ephesians 1:17

In whom are hid all the treasures of wisdom and knowledge.

—Colossians 2:3

If any of you lack wisdom, let him ask of God, that giveth to all men liberally, and upbraideth not; and it shall be given him.

—James 1:5

God is loving

The word "loving" means "feeling or expressing love: affectionate."[176] "The Love of God"[177] is a Christian hymn written in 1917 by Frederick Martin Lehman.[178] This hymn shares a simple and sincere expression of God's love. Here are the words to the hymn:

The Love of God

The love of God is greater far
Than tongue or pen can ever tell;
It goes beyond the highest star,
And reaches to the lowest hell.
The guilty pair, bowed down with care,
God gave His Son to win;
His erring child He reconciled,
And pardoned from his sin.

---

176. Ibid., p.1340.
177. *The Love of God* is a hymn in public domain according to 5 January 2008 <www.hymnal.net/>.
178. Frederick Martin Lehman (1868–1953) is the author and the composer of *The Love of God.*

Chorus:
> O love of God, how rich and pure!
> How measureless and strong!
> It shall forevermore endure -
> The saints' and angels' song.

When hoary time shall pass away,
And earthly thrones and kingdoms fall;
When men who here refuse to pray,
On rocks and hills and mountains call;
God's love, so sure, shall endure,
All measureless and strong;
Redeeming grace to Adam's race,
The saints' and angels' song.
(chorus)

Could we with ink the ocean fill,
And were the skies of parchment made;
Were ev'ry stalk on earth a quill,
And ev'ry man a scribe by trade;
To write the love of God above
Would drain the ocean dry;
Nor could the scroll contain the
Whole, though stretched from sky to sky.
(chorus)

God loves all people so much that He sent His Son, Jesus Christ, to be born of the virgin Mary, to live a perfect life, to die for all of mankind's sins on the cross, and to defeat death through His resurrection. The ministry of Jesus Christ is the ultimate demonstration of God's great love for us.

Here are some references from the Bible that describe the loving God:

For the mountains shall depart, and the hills be removed; but my kindness shall not depart from thee, neither shall the covenant of my peace be removed, saith the LORD that hath mercy on thee.

—Isaiah 54:10

For God so loved the world, that he gave his only begotten Son, that whosoever believeth in him should not perish, but have everlasting life.

—John 3:16

Jesus answered and said unto him, If a man love me, he will keep my words: and my Father will love him, and we will come unto him, and make our abode with him.

—John 14:23

But God commendeth his love toward us, in that, while we were yet sinners, Christ died for us.

—Romans 5:8

That Christ may dwell in your hearts by faith; that ye, being rooted and grounded in love, May be able to comprehend with all saints what is the breadth, and length, and depth, and height; And to know the love of Christ, which passeth knowledge, that ye might be filled with all the fulness of God.

—Ephesians 3:17–19

He that loveth not knoweth not God; for God is love.

—1 John 4:8

God is good

The word "good" means "genuine, true, wholly commendable, virtuous, pure; possessing absolute or intrinsic value, right, desirable, wise, benevolent, friendly, amiable, being without stain, faithful to."[179] That God is good means He continually demonstrates both goodwill and kindness to mankind. It is certainly true that God is good all of the time.

Here are some passages from the Bible describing God as being good:

> **And he said, I will make all my goodness pass before thee, and I will proclaim the name of the LORD before thee; and will be gracious to whom I will be gracious, and will shew mercy on whom I will shew mercy.**
>
> —Exodus 33:19

> **O give thanks unto the LORD; for he is good; for his mercy endureth for ever.**
>
> —1 Chronicles 16:34

> **It came even to pass, as the trumpeters and singers were as one, to make one sound to be heard in praising and thanking the LORD; and when they lifted up their voice with the trumpets and cymbals and instruments of musick, and praised the LORD, saying, For he is good; for his mercy endureth for ever: that then the house was filled with a cloud, even the house of the LORD.**
>
> —2 Chronicles 5:13

> **O taste and see that the LORD is good: blessed is the man that trusteth in him.**
>
> —Psalm 34:8

179. *Webster's Third New International Dictionary of the English Language—Unabridged*, p. 978.

Praise ye the LORD. O give thanks unto the LORD; for he is good: for his mercy endureth for ever.

—Psalm 106:1

O give thanks unto the LORD, for he is good: for his mercy endureth for ever.

—Psalm 107:1

O give thanks unto the LORD; for he is good: for his mercy endureth for ever.

—Psalm 136:1

The LORD is good to all: and his tender mercies are over all his works.

—Psalm 145:9

God is wrathful

The word "wrathful" means "feeling wrath, which is described as righteous indignation and condemnation especially of a deity or sovereign: justified punishment." An additional meaning of wrathful is "vehemently incensed and condemnatory, bitter or vindictive with a threatening, ominous, or violent appearance."[180] The attribute of God being wrathful sends a very strong message to every person who has ever committed one or more sins. It would definitely be wise to avoid the wrath of God who hates unrighteousness. God reserves His wrath for His enemies.[181] Indeed, it is very comforting to all those who have realized that they are sinners, repented, and asked God to forgive them through the sacrificial death of the Lord Jesus Christ. The blood of Jesus Christ cleanses sin and makes a person righteous in God's sight.[182]

---

180. Ibid., p. 2639.
181. ". . . And he reserveth wrath for his enemies" (Nah. 1:2b).
182. ". . . And the blood of Jesus Christ his Son cleanseth us from all sin" (1 John

Here are some passages from the Bible that describe God as wrathful:

For we are consumed by thine anger, and by thy wrath are we troubled.

—Psalm 90:7

God is jealous, and the LORD revengeth; the LORD revengeth, and is furious; the LORD will take vengeance on his adversaries, and he reserveth wrath for his enemies.

—Nahum 1:2

But when he saw many of the Pharisees and Sadducees come to his baptism, he said unto them, O generation of vipers, who hath warned you to flee from the wrath to come?

—Matthew 3:7

For the wrath of God is revealed from heaven against all ungodliness and unrighteousness of men, who hold the truth in unrighteousness.

—Romans 1:18

He that believeth on the Son hath everlasting life: and he that believeth not the Son shall not see life; but the wrath of God abideth on him.

—John 3:36

Mortify therefore your members which are upon the earth; fornication, uncleanness, inordinate affection, evil concupiscence, and covetousness, which is idolatry: For which

---

1:7b). "If we confess our sins, he is faithful and just to forgive us our sins, and to cleanse us from all unrighteousness" (1 John 1:9).

things' sake the wrath of God cometh on the children of dis-obedience.

—Colossians 3:5–6

God is truthful (God is truth)

The word "truthful" means "telling or disposed to tell the truth: accurate and sincere in describing reality."[183] Another way of defining the attribute that God is truth is to say that God has not, does not, and will not ever lie or deceive. From a positive position we can know that since God is truthful, He is honest and all that He says is reality. In addition, since God is the author of the Bible, it can be trusted as being totally true! God cannot lie because it would contradict His truthful nature.

Note: Since God invented language and vocabulary, He is certainly capable of using the appropriate words to describe what constituted the length of a day during creation week. God made it quite clear that the seven days of creation week were seven twenty-four–hour–long days. In the book of Genesis, God documented the length of days with the following statements: "And God called the light Day, and the darkness he called Night. And the evening and the morning were the first day."[184] "And God called the firmament Heaven, And the evening and the morning were the second day."[185] "And the evening and the morning were the third day."[186] "And the evening and the morning were the fourth day."[187] "And the evening and the morning were the fifth day."[188] "And God saw every thing that he had made, and, behold, it was very good. And the evening and the morning were the sixth day."[189] "And

183. *Webster's Third New International Dictionary of the English Language—Unabridged*, p. 2457.
184. Genesis 1:5
185. Genesis 1:8
186. Genesis 1:13
187. Genesis 1:19
188. Genesis 1:23
189. Genesis 1:31

on the seventh day God ended his work which he had made; and he rested on the seventh day from all his work which he had made."[190] In the book of Exodus, God again refers to the length of days in a week as being seven twenty-four–hour–long days.[191] Because God caused and was present during the creation of the earth and the universe, the history that He recorded in the Bible should be trusted from the very first of Genesis. The following statement is included in the Ten Commandments: "For in six days the LORD made heaven and earth, the sea, and all that in them is, and rested the seventh day: wherefore the LORD blessed the sabbath day, and hallowed it."[192]

Here are some passages from the Bible demonstrating that God is truth:

God is not a man, that he should lie; neither the son of man, that he should repent: hath he said, and shall he not do it? or hath he spoken, and shall he not make it good?

—Numbers 23:19

He is the Rock, his work is perfect: for all his ways are judgment: a God of truth and without iniquity, just and right is he.

—Deuteronomy 32:4

The law of the LORD is perfect, converting the soul: the testimony of the LORD is sure, making wise the simple.

—Psalm 19:7

Surely he shall deliver thee from the snare of the fowler,

---

190. Genesis 2:2
191. "It is a sign between me and the children of Israel for ever: for in six days the LORD made heaven and earth, and on the seventh day he rested, and was refreshed" (Exod. 31:17).
192. Exodus 20:11

and from the noisome pestilence. He shall cover thee with his feathers, and under his wings shalt thou trust: his truth shall be thy shield and buckler. Thou shalt not be afraid for the terror by night; nor for the arrow that flieth by day; Nor for the pestilence that walketh in darkness; nor for the destruction that wasteth at noonday.

—Psalm 91:3–7

For his merciful kindness is great toward us: and the truth of the LORD endureth for ever. Praise ye the LORD.

—Psalm 117:2

Thy word is true from the beginning: and every one of thy righteous judgments endureth for ever.

—Ps. 119:160

Every word of God is pure: he is a shield unto them that put their trust in him. Add thou not unto his words, lest he reprove thee, and thou be found a liar.

—Proverbs 30:5–6

And the Word was made flesh, and dwelt among us, (and we beheld his glory, the glory as of the only begotten of the Father,) full of grace and truth.

—John 1:14

Jesus saith unto him, I am the way, the truth, and the life: no man cometh unto the Father, but by me.

—John 14:6

Sanctify them through thy truth: thy word is truth.

—John 17:17

Study to shew thyself approved unto God, a workman that needeth not to be ashamed, rightly dividing the word of truth.

—2 Timothy 2:15

In hope of eternal life, which God, that cannot lie, promised before the world began.

—Titus 1:2

That by two immutable things, in which it was impossible for God to lie, we might have a strong consolation, who have fled for refuge to lay hold upon the hope set before us.

—Hebrews 6:18

God is faithful

The word "faithful" means "true and constant in affection or allegiance: loyal, firm in adherence to promises, oaths, or undertakings, conscientious. Some synonyms for the word faithful are loyal, true, constant, staunch, and steadfast."[193] The faithfulness of God is very comforting to the people who trust Him and His Word. The Bible contains hundreds of promises that God has made to humanity.[194] Perhaps one of the greatest promises God has made to mankind is found in the following verse: "For God so loved the world, that he gave his only begotten Son, that whosoever believeth in him should not perish, but have everlasting life."[195] Jesus made the following bold promise: "And Jesus said unto them, I am the bread of life: he that cometh to me shall never hunger; and he that believeth on me shall never thirst."[196] Because God is faithful, we can trust Him to keep all of His promises.

---

193. *Webster's Third New International Dictionary of the English Language—Unabridged*, p.816.
194. 1,267 biblical promises are listed in *Promises from God's Word*, World Publishing, Inc., Grand Rapids, MI, 1996.
195. John 3:16
196. John 6:35

Here are some passages from the Bible that describe God's faithfulness:

> **God is not a man, that he should lie; neither the son of man, that he should repent: hath he said, and shall he not do it? or hath he spoken, and shall he not make it good?**
>
> —Numbers 23:19

> **Know therefore that the LORD thy God, he is God, the faithful God, which keepeth covenant and mercy with them that love him and keep his commandments to a thousand generations.**
>
> —Deuteronomy 7:9

> **And the LORD, he it is that doth go before thee; he will be with thee, he will not fail thee, neither forsake thee: fear not, neither be dismayed.**
>
> —Deuteronomy 31:8

> **For the word of the LORD is right; and all his works are done in truth.**
>
> —Psalm 33:4

> **For the LORD is good; his mercy is everlasting; and his truth endureth to all generations.**
>
> —Psalm 100:5

> **For his merciful kindness is great toward us: and the truth of the LORD endureth for ever, Praise ye the LORD.**
>
> —Psalm 117:2

> **It is of the LORD'S mercies that we are not consumed, because his compassions fail not. They are new every morning: great is thy faithfulness.**
>
> —Lamentations 3:22–23

For what if some did not believe? shall their unbelief make the faith of God without effect? God forbid: yea, let God be true, but every man a liar; as it is written, That thou mightest be justified in thy sayings, and mightest overcome when thou art judged.

—Romans 3:3–4

God is faithful, by whom ye were called unto the fellowship of his Son Jesus Christ our Lord.

—1 Corinthians 1:9

But the Lord is faithful, who shall stablish you, and keep you from evil.

—2 Thessalonians 3:3

If we believe not, yet he abideth faithful: he cannot deny himself.

—2 Timothy 2:13

If we confess our sins, he is faithful and just to forgive us our sins, and to cleanse us from all unrighteousness.

—1 John 1:9

God is jealous

The word "jealous" means "intolerant of rivalry or unfaithfulness; zealous in guarding (as a possession)."[197] God knows that throughout the history of mankind there are people, false gods, and fallen angels that have wanted to be elevated to a position of equality to or even superiority over His sovereign position. God also knows that there are some people who choose to ignore or even deny that He exists. The attribute of jealousy does not bode well for those who would seek to

197. *Webster's Third New International Dictionary of the English Language—Unabridged*, 1993, p. 1212.

attempt to steal or diminish His sovereignty. God is unwilling to share what is rightfully and morally His.

Here are some passages from the Bible that describe God as jealous:

> **Thou shalt not bow down thyself to them, nor serve them: for I the LORD thy God am a jealous God, visiting the iniquity of the fathers upon the children unto the third and fourth generation of them that hate me.**
>
> —Exodus 20:5

> **When ye have transgressed the covenant of the LORD your God, which he commanded you, and have gone and served other gods, and bowed yourselves to them; then shall the anger of the LORD be kindled against you, and ye shall perish quickly from off the good land which he hath given unto you.**
>
> —Joshua 23:16

> **And Joshua said unto the people, Ye cannot serve the LORD: for he is an holy God; he is a jealous God; he will not forgive your transgressions nor your sins. If ye forsake the LORD, and serve strange gods, then he will turn and do you hurt, and consume you, after that he hath done you good.**
>
> —Joshua 24:19–20

> **I am the LORD: that is my name: and my glory will I not give to another, neither my praise to graven images.**
>
> —Isaiah 42:8

> **Therefore thus saith the Lord GOD; Now will I bring again the captivity of Jacob, and have mercy upon the whole house of Israel, and will be jealous for my holy name.**
>
> —Ezekiel 39:25

> God is jealous, and the LORD revengeth; the LORD revengeth,
> and is furious; the LORD will take vengeance on his adver-
> saries, and he reserveth wrath for his enemies.
>
> —Nahum 1:2

God is personal

The word "personal" means "pertaining to or concerning a particular person; not general or public and relating to, having the qualities of, or constituting a person or persons."[198] The attribute that God is personal allows Almighty God, with His intimidating abilities and characteristics, to be approachable by mere mortals. However, God is much more than approachable. God wants to be our friend.[199]

Here are some passages from the Bible that describe God as being personal:

> And, behold, the LORD stood above it, and said, I am the
> LORD God of Abraham thy father, and the God of Isaac: the
> land whereon thou liest, to thee will I give it, and to thy
> seed.
>
> —Genesis 28:13

> And he said, I will make all my goodness pass before thee,
> and I will proclaim the name of the LORD before thee; and
> will be gracious to whom I will be gracious, and will shew
> mercy on whom I will shew mercy.
>
> —Exodus 33:19

> The LORD doth build up Jerusalem: he gathereth together

---

198. *Funk and Wagnalls Standard Desk Dictionary—Revised Edition,* Funk & Wagnalls Inc. New York, 1977, p. 489.
199. "Ye are my friends, if ye do whatsoever I command you. Henceforth I call you not servants; for the servant knoweth not what his lord doeth: but I have called you friends; for all things that I have heard of my Father I have made known unto you" (John 15:14–15).

the outcasts of Israel. He healeth the broken in heart, and bindeth up their wounds.

—Psalm 147:2–3

I, even I, am he that comforteth you: who art thou, that thou shouldest be afraid of a man that shall die, and of the son of man which shall be made as grass. And forgettest the LORD thy maker, that hath stretched forth the heavens, and laid the foundations of the earth; and hast feared continually every day because of the fury of the oppressor, as if he were ready to destroy? and where is the fury of the oppressor?

—Isaiah 51:12–13

Thou shalt also suck the milk of the Gentiles, and shalt suck the breast of kings: and thou shalt know that I the LORD am thy Saviour and thy Redeemer, the mighty One of Jacob.

—Isaiah 60:16

And Jesus said unto them, I am the bread of life: he that cometh to me shall never hunger; and he that believeth on me shall never thirst.

—John 6:35

Then spake Jesus again unto them, saying, I am the light of the world: he that followeth me shall not walk in darkness, but shall have the light of life.

—John 8:12

I am the door: by me if any man enter in, he shall be saved, and shall go in and out, and find pasture.

—John 10:9

I am the good shepherd, and know my sheep, and am known of mine.

—John 10:14

Jesus said unto her, I am the resurrection, and the life: he that believeth in me, though he were dead, yet shall he live.

—John 11:25

Jesus saith unto him, I am the way, the truth, and the life: no man cometh unto the Father, but by me.

—John 14:6

I am the vine, ye are the branches. He that abideth in me, and I in him, the same bringeth forth much fruit: for without me ye can do nothing.

—John 15:5

As the Father hath loved me, so have I loved you: continue ye in my love.

—John 15:9

These things have I spoken unto you, that my joy might remain in you, and that your joy might be full. This is my commandment, That ye love one another, as I have loved you.

—John 15:11–12

God is Spirit, God is invisible

The word "spirit" has a number of definitions. Appropriate ones are listed here. Spirit means "the vital essence or animating force in living organisms, esp. man, often considered divine in origin." Spirit means "the part of a human being characterized by intelligence, personality, self-consciousness, and will; the mind." Spirit means "the substance or universal aspect of reality, regarded as opposed to matter." In the Bible, Spirit is "the creative, animating power of God."[200] That God is Spirit means God is different in nature from the things He has created.

---

200. *Funk and Wagnalls Standard Desk Dictionary—Revised Edition*, p. 649.

The word "invisible" means "not visible; not capable of being seen and not in sight; concealed."[201] Since God is invisible we have difficulty formulating a "mental image" of His appearance. But the fact that God is Spirit, and the fact that He is invisible, does not detract from His reality.

In 1867 Walter Chalmers Smith wrote the great Christian hymn, "Immortal, Invisible, God only Wise"[202] which helps us appreciate this and others of God's attributes.

Immortal, Invisible, God only Wise[203]

Immortal, invisible, God only wise,
In light inaccessible hid from our eyes,
Most blessed, most glorious, the Ancient of Days,
Almighty, victorious, thy great name we praise.

Unresting, unhasting and silent as light,
Nor wanting, nor wasting, thou rulest in might;
Thy justice like mountains high soaring above
Thy clouds which are fountains of goodness and love.

To all, life thou givest, to both great and small;
In all life thou livest, the true life of all;
We blossom and flourish as leaves on the tree,
And wither and perish, but naught changeth thee.

Great Father of glory; pure Father of light,
Thine angels adore thee, all veiling their sight;
All laud we would render; O help us to see
'Tis only the splendor of light hideth thee!

---

201. Ibid., p. 343.
202. *Immortal, Invisible, God only Wise* is in public domain. 5 January 2008 <www.hymnal.net/>.
203. 4 July 2007 <www.hymnscript.com/g-iig01.html>.

Here are some passages from the Bible that describe God as being a Spirit and God as being invisible:

> And the LORD said, My spirit shall not always strive with man, for that he also is flesh: yet his days shall be an hundred and twenty years.
>
> —Genesis 6:3

> The Spirit of the Lord GOD is upon me; because the LORD hath anointed me to preach good tidings unto the meek; he hath sent me to bind up the brokenhearted, to proclaim liberty to the captives, and the opening of the prison to them that are bound; To proclaim the acceptable year of the LORD, and the day of vengeance of our God; to comfort all that mourn.
>
> —Isaiah 61:1–2

> But they rebelled, and vexed his holy Spirit: therefore he was turned to be their enemy, and he fought against them.
>
> —Isaiah 63:10

> And straightway coming up out of the water, he saw the heavens opened, and the Spirit like a dove descending upon him.
>
> —Mark 1:10

> The Spirit of the Lord is upon me, because he hath anointed me to preach the gospel to the poor; he hath sent me to heal the brokenhearted, to preach deliverance to the captives, and recovering of sight to the blind, to set at liberty them that are bruised, To preach the acceptable year of the Lord.
>
> —Luke 4:18–19

> The wind bloweth where it listeth, and thou hearest the sound thereof, but canst not tell whence it cometh, and

whither it goeth: so is every one that is born of the Spirit.

—John 3:8

God is a Spirit: and they that worship him must worship him in spirit and in truth.

—John 4:24

Even the Spirit of truth; whom the world cannot receive, because it seeth him not, neither knoweth him: but ye know him; for he dwelleth with you, and shall be in you. I will not leave you comfortless: I will come to you.

—John 14:17–18

Howbeit when he, the Spirit of truth, is come, he will guide you into all truth: for he shall not speak of himself; but whatsoever he shall hear, that shall he speak: and he will shew you things to come.

—John 16:13

And suddenly there came a sound from heaven as of a rushing mighty wind, and it filled all the house where they were sitting.

—Acts 2:2

Forasmuch then as we are the offspring of God, we ought not to think that the Godhead is like unto gold, or silver, or stone, graven by art and man's device.

—Acts 17:29

For the invisible things of him from the creation of the world are clearly seen, being understood by the things that are made, even his eternal power and Godhead; so that they are without excuse.

—Romans 1:20

There is therefore now no condemnation to them which are in Christ Jesus, who walk not after the flesh, but after the Spirit.

—Romans 8:1

And grieve not the holy Spirit of God, whereby ye are sealed unto the day of redemption.

—Ephesians 4:30

Who is the image of the invisible God, the firstborn of every creature: For by him were all things created, that are in heaven, and that are in earth, visible and invisible, whether they be thrones, or dominions, or principalities, or powers: all things were created by him, and for him.

—Colossians 1:15–16

But we are bound to give thanks alway to God for you, brethren beloved of the Lord, because God hath from the beginning chosen you to salvation through sanctification of the Spirit and belief of the truth.

—2 Thessalonians 2:13

Now unto the King eternal, immortal, invisible, the only wise God, be honour and glory for ever and ever. Amen.

—1 Timothy 1:17

God is life

The word "life" has a number of meanings. Here are some of the definitions of life that are appropriate to life as the attribute of God: "Life is the form of existence that distinguishes animals and plants from inorganic substances and dead organisms, characterized by metabolism, growth, reproduction, irritability, etc. Life is the characteristic state of an organism that has not died. Life is a spiritual state regarded as a continuation of perfection of animate existence after death: eternal life. Life is the period of an individual's existence between birth and death; also, a specified portion of this period. Life is an energetic force; animation: full of life. Life is also a source of liveliness; animating spirit: the life of the party."[204] Because God is life, God is alive. Since God is alive, He is the energetic force of the universe He created!

Here are some passages from the Bible that describe God as being life:

For thou wilt not leave my soul in hell; neither wilt thou suffer thine Holy One to see corruption. Thou wilt shew me the path of life: in thy presence is fulness of joy; at thy right hand there are pleasures for evermore.

—Psalm 16:10–11

In him was life; and the life was the light of men.

—John 1:4

That whosoever believeth in him should not perish, but have eternal life. For God so loved the world, that he gave his only begotten Son, that whosoever believeth in him should not perish, but have everlasting life.

—John 3:15–16

And Jesus said unto them, I am the bread of life: he that cometh to me shall never hunger; and he that believeth on me shall never thirst.

—John 6:35

Jesus saith unto him, I am the way, the truth, and the life: no man cometh unto the Father, but by me.

—John 14:6

---

204. *Funk and Wagnalls Standard Desk Dictionary—Revised Edition*, p. 374.

Who also hath made us able ministers of the new testament; not of the letter, but of the spirit: for the letter killeth, but the spirit giveth life.

—2 Corinthians 3:6

When Christ, who is our life, shall appear, then shall ye also appear with him in glory.

—Colossians 3:4

God is triune

The word "triune" is an adjective that means "three in one: said of God." As a noun the word triune means "a group of three things that are united; a triad; trinity in unity."[205] The word triune is closely related to the word "trinity," which means "a threefold personality existing in the one divine being or substance; the union in one God of Father, Son, and Holy Spirit."[206] God's being triune is one of the great mysteries of His nature. Jay Rogers[207] made the following statement about the triune God:

He is not only personal, but actually three persons in one God, Father, Son and Holy Spirit. Within the one essence of the Godhead we have to distinguish three "persons" or personalities who are neither three gods, nor three modes, parts or aspects of God, but co-equally and co-eternally one God. The Trinity may seem like a mysterious paradox to us, but it is important to understand God as a personal being in eternal relationship with Himself and with man. He is a God whom we can know personally. To Christians, He is both our Father and Brother, and His Spirit lives within us.[208]

---

205. Ibid., p. 726.
206. Ibid., p. 725.
207. Jay Rogers is the international director for Maranatha Ministries located in Gainesville, Florida.
208. Rogers, Jay, *The Names and Attributes of God*, 19 June 2007 <www.forerunner. com/orthodoxy/X0002_1._Names__Attributes.html>.

Here are some passages that describe God as being Triune or more than a single Being:

> **In the beginning God created the heaven and the earth. And the earth was without form, and void; and darkness was upon the face of the deep. And the Spirit of God moved upon the face of the waters.**
>
> —Genesis 1:1–2

> **And God said, Let us make man in our image, after our likeness: and let them have dominion over the fish of the sea, and over the fowl of the air, and over the cattle, and over all the earth, and over every creeping thing that creepeth upon the earth.**
>
> —Genesis 1:26

> **Thus saith the LORD the King of Israel, and his redeemer the LORD of hosts; I am the first, and I am the last; and beside me there is no God.**
>
> —Isaiah 44:6

> **Come ye near unto me, hear ye this; I have not spoken in secret from the beginning; from the time that it was, there am I: and now the Lord GOD, and His Spirit, hath sent me. Thus saith the LORD, thy Redeemer, the Holy One of Israel; I am the LORD thy God which teacheth thee to profit, which leadeth thee by the way that thou shouldest go.**
>
> —Isaiah 48:16–17

> **And Jesus, when he was baptized, went up straightway out of the water: and, lo, the heavens were opened unto him, and he saw the Spirit of God descending like a dove, and**

lighting upon him: And lo a voice from heaven, saying, This is my beloved Son, in whom I am well pleased.

—Matthew 3:16–17

And Jesus came and spake unto them, saying, All power is given unto me in heaven and in earth. Go ye therefore, and teach all nations, baptizing them in the name of the Father, and of the Son, and of the Holy Ghost.

—Matthew 28:18–19

In the beginning was the Word, and the Word was with God, and the Word was God. The same was in the beginning with God. All things were made by him; and without him was not any thing made that was made. In him was life; and the life was the light of men. And the light shineth in darkness; and the darkness comprehended it not.

—John 1:1–5

For God so loved the world, that he gave his only begotten Son, that whosoever believeth in him should not perish, but have everlasting life. For God sent not his Son into the world to condemn the world; but that the world through him might be saved.

—John 3:16–17

Forasmuch then as we are the offspring of God, we ought not to think that the Godhead is like unto gold, or silver, or stone, graven by art and man's device.

—Acts 17:29

For the invisible things of him from the creation of the world are clearly seen, being understood by the things that

are made, even his eternal power and Godhead; so that they are without excuse.

—Romans 1:20

For through him we both have access by one Spirit unto the Father.

—Ephesians 2:18

That he would grant you, according to the riches of his glory, to be strengthened with might by his Spirit in the inner man.

—Ephesians 3:16

For there are three that bear record in heaven, the Father, the Word, and the Holy Ghost: and these three are one.

—1 John 5:7

Any one of God's many attributes reveal a supernatural being who is beyond human ability to comprehend. By combining all of God's attributes, we are completely overwhelmed by the power, nature, and character of God. All of God's attributes compliment each other and none of His attributes are in conflict with one another.[209] Please take a moment to look at the list of attributes that have been briefly mentioned and consider the magnitude, the memory, the mystery, the morality, the mission, the menace, the mercy, and the majesty of Almighty God. God is:

omniscient ◆ omnipotent ◆ omnipresent ◆ eternal
immutable ◆ incomprehensible ◆ self–existent ◆ self–sufficient
infinite ◆ transcendent ◆ sovereign ◆ holy ◆ gracious
righteous ◆ just ◆ merciful ◆ longsuffering ◆ wise ◆ loving

209. Tozer, A.W., *The Knowledge of the Holy*, p. 88.

good • wrathful • truth/truthful • faithful • jealous
personal • Spirit/invisible • life • triune

When the God of the Holy Bible is compared to any or to all of the idols, the false gods, and the "no gods" that are revered, worshiped, or ignored by many of the earth's inhabitants, there is really no comparison between them.

Chapter 4

What Does God Know?

Dost thou know the balancings of the clouds, the wondrous works of him which is perfect in knowledge?

—Job 37:16

In the last one hundred years there has been an incredible increase in information discovered and dispensed around the earth. Books, newspapers, magazines, journals, and other forms of printed material are visible indicators of the immense amount of "information" available. Perhaps less obvious, but also growing beyond our comprehension, is information available via computers and other electronic devices. Audiotape, videotape, CDs, DVDs, MP3 players, PDAs,[210] cell phones, and the internet are electronic media that both preserve and present amazing quantities of information. These innovative ways to store and transmit information are constantly being made more effective. Music, movies, and messages entertain, enrich, enable, and expand experience. Images from television and words from the radio certainly increase the exposure to information.

Indeed, massive amounts of information are preserved on paper and stored on electronic media. Another vast repository of knowledge is found in the human brain, where thoughts, memories, ideas, and imaginations of human intellect are preserved. Just over fifty percent

---

210. Personal Digital Assistants

of earth's inhabitants live in rural areas.[211] Many of these people possess few if any modern inventions, and those living in truly primitive situations may not possess a written language. Yet people who live "close to the land" have tremendous knowledge of their environment, and they know how to be self–sufficient. Many people who live in rural locations routinely use information that most "city–dwellers" may not even know exists. Most of this knowledge is not documented in a book nor stored on a computer. It is maintained in the minds of men. A few examples of this knowledge would include:

1. The ability of both ancient and modern mariners to build seaworthy craft and navigate oceans without using sophisticated equipment. The expeditions of discovery and colonization of the Pacific Ocean are extraordinary! The explorers possessed seaworthy ships, adequate navigational skills, and meteorological knowledge that enabled them to make accurate landfalls on small islands throughout the Pacific Ocean.[212]

2. The ability of experienced hunters to construct effective weapons using materials found or made in their environment. These hunters track and quickly kill their prey.

3. The ability of fishermen to know where to find and catch fish. These fishermen understand the movement, and to some extent, the motivation of animals that live in or near the water.

4. The abilities of hunters, fishermen, and their families to know how to prepare, cook, and preserve the food and body parts from the animals they claim.

Without a consistent application and oral transmission of this knowl-

---

211. Dabrowa, Michael, ". . . village of 1,000 people," *Atlanta Journal–Constitution*, June 3, 2007, p. B 1.

212. Lewis, David, *We, the Navigators—The Ancient Art of Landfinding in the Pacific*, Second Edition, University of Hawaii Press, Honolulu, 1994, p. 355.

edge from one generation to the next, people and groups without a written language probably would not have survived and thrived as they have for many centuries.

Even in the most remote communities people know how to care for injuries, how to treat illnesses, and even how to deliver babies. Their treatments may include the use of herbs, oils, seeds, plants, leaves, bark from trees, roots of plants, insects, animal parts, and potions. This therapeutic knowledge is preserved in the brains of resourceful and creative people. And, this knowledge is faithfully shared by word of mouth from person to person and from generation to generation.

The oceans of information swirling around mankind certainly can be overwhelming. No human knows everything. In fact, very few humans know a significant amount of information in any given field of study. Thomas Sowell[213] says that the brightest and the very best educated people in the world today know only about one percent of the information currently possessed by all of the peoples of the world.[214]

How does the omniscient God of the Bible handle all of this information? How has the God of the Bible handled and remembered all of the information that has been created and recorded since the beginning of time? What does God know? These are fair questions, and they are questions that should be answered if it is possible. In the next pages we will read some examples of how the Bible answers these questions. We will also identify some statements from the Bible that apply to modern science and may give us a taste of the scope of God's knowledge. God's knowledge is so vast that the individual mind

---

213. Thomas Sowell, born 30 June 1930, A.B. in Economics, magna cum laude, Harvard College 1958, A.M. in Economics, Columbia University 1959, Ph.D. in Economics, University of Chicago 1968, currently Senior Fellow, Hoover Institution, Stanford University, Stanford, California. 16 May 2007 <www.tsowell.com/>.
214. Sowell, Thomas, "Presumptions of the Left,"16 May 2007 <www.townhall.com/columnists/ThomasSowell/2007/05/16/presumptions_of_the_left> p. 1.

cannot even begin to fathom His level of memory, ability, wisdom, and understanding.

What does God know about the universe?

God knows exactly how the universe came into existence because He created the universe. It has been said that the universe contains all matter, space, and time. The beginning of the physical universe is the beginning of matter, material space, and physical time.[215] Since God spoke words[216] and created the universe out of nothing, then He must have caused the beginning of all matter, material space, and physical time. Since God created the physical components of the universe, He was independent of these three things. Since God was independent of matter, He must be non–physical or Spirit, and this is one of God's attributes as revealed in the Bible. Since God was independent of material space, He must be outside of the universe, or transcendent, and this is another of God's attributes revealed in the Bible. Since God was independent of time, He must be unchanging or immutable, always present or omnipresent, and always in existence or eternal. These attributes of God are clearly revealed in the Bible.[217]

God knows the exact composition, the size, the shape, and the age of the universe. The Bible states, "In the beginning God created the heaven and the earth."[218] Have you seriously considered the magnitude of this single sentence? To create all of the galaxies, solar systems, and the earth, the Creator of the universe would have to have knowledge of all of the building blocks or all of the components of the entire universe. To create all of the atoms that make up all of the elements

---

215. Wise, Kurt P., *Faith, Form, and Time—What the Bible teaches and science confirms about creation and the age of the universe*, Broadman & Holman Publishers, Nashville, TN, 2002, p. 86.
216. One example of God speaking and a portion of the universe appearing is found in Genesis 1:3 that reads, "And God said, Let there be light: and there was light."
217. Wise, Kurt P., *Faith, Form, and Time*, p. 86.
218. Genesis 1:1

and all of the molecules in the universe would require God to have infinite knowledge and infinite power. These two attributes of God are described in the Bible: God is omniscient and God is omnipotent.

The first chapter of Genesis states that the Creator created all of the components of the universe by speaking them into existence. The Bible says, "All things were made by him; and without him was not any thing made that was made."[219] The Creator would also need the ability to make all of these components stay together and not fly apart when they are brought into approximation with each other. This holding power is described in another passage from the Bible that says, "For by him were all things created, that are in heaven, and that are in earth, visible and invisible, whether they be thrones, or dominions, or principalities, or powers: all things were created by him, and for him: And he is before all things, and by him all things consist."[220]

The components of the universe include at least all of its subatomic particles, all of its atoms, all of its elements, and all of its molecules. It is quite possible that there are components of the universe that we do not even know exist. The universe contains approximately 100 billion galaxies that are estimated to equal a trillion trillion trillion trillion tons of matter.[221] This tremendous number is a 10 followed with fifty zeroes. The gigantic number looks like this: There are 1,000,000,000, 000,000,000,000,000,000,000,000,000,000,000,000,000 tons of matter in the universe. Note that this is tons of matter, not pounds or kilograms. Try to grasp, if you can, the fact that God created every bit of matter and energy in the entire universe.[222]

The tons of matter in the universe just mentioned are composed of atoms or elementary particles. According to Dr. Richard Swenson,

---

219. John 1:3
220. Colossians 1:16–17
221. Schroeder, Gerald L., *The Science of God: The Convergence of Scientific and Biblical Wisdom*, Broadway Books, New York, 1997, p. 1.
222. "For by him were all things created, that are in heaven, and that are in earth, visible and invisible, whether they be thrones, or dominions, or principalities, or powers: all things were created by him, and for him" (Col. 1:16).

the observable universe contains a hundred million trillion trillion trillion trillion trillion trillion elementary particles (10 followed by eighty zeroes). "Not only does God know precisely where the Earth is, but in fact He also knows precisely where each one of these subatomic particles is located. This might sound ridiculous to us: *There are far too many; they are too small; they move around too fast; and why would God be interested to track them anyway?* My response—stop thinking about God from a human perspective. Go to the dictionary and look up the word *omniscient*. If God is indeed omniscient, then He knows where each of these particles in the universe is located—every second of every day, for the complete duration of eternity."[223]

So how small is an atom? Atoms are incredibly small.

Here are some illustrations demonstrating the incredibly small size of an atom:

1. An atom compares to an orange in the same relative dimensions as the orange compares to the entire earth.
2. To see an atom with human eyes, we would have to shrink down to a billionth of an inch in height.
3. To count the atoms in only one drop of water would require every human on earth counting one atom per second for twenty thousand years.[224]

What are atoms like? It has been said by people who study atoms that an atom is almost scary. Atoms are tiny and are not solid like marbles or the balls used to demonstrate them in chemistry lecture halls and laboratories. An atom is the original hyperactive kid. Everything associated with it is flying around like mad, bumping into things. The electron, for example, circles the nucleus of the atom billions of times in one–millionth of a second. Subatomic particles burst into and then

---

223. Swenson, Richard A., *More Than Meets the Eye—Fascinating Glimpses of God's Power and Design*, Navpress, Colorado Springs, CO, 2000, p. 142-143.
224. Ibid., p. 103.

out of existence in a matter of nanoseconds. A single oxygen molecule, comprised of two bonded atoms, experiences over three billion collisions every second.

It is the rapid movement of the electrons that allows atoms to appear solid. Dimensions at the atomic level—just like dimensions at the astronomical level—are almost all occupied by seemingly empty space. Almost all of an atom's mass (99.9 percent) is located at its diminutive core nucleus. Yet the nucleus only occupies a hundred thousand–billionth of the atom's volume.[225]

Since God is omniscient, He knows the exact locations of all electrons in all atoms at any moment in time. God knows the exact number and precise location of all of the subatomic particles or quarks in all atoms at any moment in time. It has been said that quarks are tiny, really incredibly small, with a diameter of about a billion–billionth of a meter. To do a size comparison, first enlarge an atom until it fills a distance from here to the moon. At that size the nucleus of an atom would be as big as a golf course. A proton would be the size of a football field. And a quark would be the size of a golf ball.[226]

After reviewing the amazingly small size of atoms, let us take a moment to consider a tiny bit of what God knows about the stars in the universe. First, here are some Bible passages that document what God knows about the stars:

> **When I consider thy heavens, the work of thy fingers, the moon and the stars, which thou hast ordained; What is man, that thou art mindful of him? and the son of man, that thou visitest him?**
>
> —Psalm 8:3–4

> **The heavens declare the glory of God; and the firmament sheweth his handywork.**
>
> —Psalm 19:1

225. Ibid., p. 106.
226. Ibid., p. 109.

By the word of the LORD were the heavens made; and all the host of them by the breath of his mouth.

—Psalm 33:6

The heavens are thine, the earth also is thine: as for the world and the fulness thereof, thou hast founded them.

—Psalm 89:11

For all the gods of the nations are idols: but the LORD made the heavens.

—Psalm 96:5

But our God is in the heavens: he hath done whatsoever he hath pleased.

—Psalm 115:3

To him that by wisdom made the heavens: for his mercy endureth for ever. To him that stretched out the earth above the waters: for his mercy endureth for ever. To him that made great lights: for his mercy endureth for ever: The sun to rule by day: for his mercy endureth for ever: The moon and stars to rule by night: for his mercy endureth for ever.

—Psalm 136:5–9

He telleth the number of the stars; he calleth them all by their names.

—Psalm 147:4

Lift up your eyes on high, and behold who hath created these things, that bringeth out their host by number: he calleth

**them all by names by the greatness of his might, for that he
is strong in power; not one faileth.**

—Isaiah 40:26

The Bible says that God has given names to all of the stars in the universe.[227] So how many stars has God named? The answer to this question is a number beyond our comprehension. Here is an idea of how many stars God has named:

> We now realize that an estimated one hundred billion galaxies exist, besides our own, each with an average of one hundred billion stars. This finding fully confirms the biblical teaching that the stars are as numerous as are the grains of sand on the seashore. If you were to name each star known to exist today, and it took just a second to name each one, it would take about 317 trillion years to name them all![228]

After considering this brief description of what God knows about the universe He created, our human minds are totally overwhelmed by His knowledge. This information is very important for us to use to learn more about what God knows.

God Almighty is the author of the Bible. Since God documented the creation of the earth, the celestial bodies, the plants, the animals, and mankind in the Bible, we should carefully consider what God has to say on the subject of origins.

The following is a brief summary of the way God described the origin of the universe:

---

227. Psalm 147:4 and Isaiah 40:26
228. Bergman, Jerry, "The Ancients Knew Little About the Heavens Compared to Today," *Creation Matters*, Creation Research Society, Volume 11, Number 5, September/October 2006, p. 2.

Day	Creative and formative works of God completed during creation week[229]
1	Physical elements of the universe—space, mass/energy, time
2	Atmosphere and hydrosphere—necessary for animal life
3	Lithosphere and biosphere—solid earth and vegetation
4	Celestial bodies—sun, moon, and stars
5	Animals to live in the air and water—birds, whales, and fish
6	Animals to live on the land—cattle, creeping things, beasts, Adam and Eve
7	Creation is complete—God rested and He blessed and sanctified His creation

On the seventh day of creation week, the Bible says that God rested.[230] The Bible does not say that this day of rest was necessary because God was tired. God included this day of rest as an example to humans to take one day out of seven for a time to regain energy. Interestingly, most of the world follows this pattern of work and rest. For thousands of years it has been customary for people to work for six days and then rest on one day during the time frame referred to as a week. It is certainly worth noting that there is no solar and no lunar reason for a seven-day week to be found in the calendars of the civilizations of the world. Since the seven-day work week is a worldwide practice, is it possible that the civilizations of the world are following the pattern of work and rest that was presented to humanity during the seven days of creation week?

What does the theory of evolution say about the universe?

There are a number of well-educated people holding influential and leadership positions in education, business, religion, science, govern-

---

229. Morris, Henry M., *The Defender's Study Bible—King James Version*, p.1503.
230. "And on the seventh day God ended his work which he had made; and he rested on the seventh day from all his work which he had made" (Gen. 2:2).

ment, and the media who do not believe that God created the universe as is documented in the Bible. Some of these people do not even believe that God exists, or if there is a God, He is not relevant to the origin of the universe. The theory of evolution is the dominant paradigm for most people who reject the clear teaching of the Bible on the origin of the universe. Dr. D. James Kennedy said that evolution is not so much a scientific theory as it is a worldview which proposes a way of understanding all of life that entirely excludes God.[231]

Certainly, much has been written and said about the theory of evolution. Individuals who reject the Bible's detailed documentation of the origin of the universe have the daunting and difficult task of explaining the totality of the universe from the perspective of evolutionism.[232] To be both a workable and verifiable theory, evolution[233] should be able to accurately explain the origin of the physical universe, the origin of the first life on the earth, the origin of all plants and animals, and the origin of humans with our unique characteristics of speech, sense of history, common sense, the ability to reason, the ability to learn factual information, the ability to produce and appreciate works of art, and many other human traits. Eugenie Scott[234] says that evolution needs to be defined more narrowly within each of the scientific disciplines because the processes and mechanisms of cosmological, geological, and biological evolution are different.[235] The theory, or in reality the theories, of evolution should also be able to

---

231. DeRosa, Tom, *Evidence for Creation: Intelligent Answers for Open Minds*, Coral Ridge Ministries, Publisher, Fort Lauderdale, FL, 2003, p. 5.
232. Evolutionism is the belief that the physical world organized itself through natural law and process without intervention by a transcendent God. Wise, Kurt P., *Faith, Form, and Time*, p. 279.
233. Evolution in the broad sense is "a cumulative change through time." Scott, Eugenie C., *Evolution vs. Creationism—An Introduction*, University of California Press, Berkeley, CA., 2005, p. 23.
234. Eugenie C. Scott is executive director of the National Center for Science Education, the leading advocacy group for the teaching of evolution in the United States.
235. Scott, Eugenie C., *Evolution vs. Creationism—An Introduction*, p. 23.

explain the origin of the consistent physical forces that are present throughout the universe.

It seems that the theory of evolution is still evolving. Different scientists have their own ideas of origins, and they have developed their own theories of how evolution occurred. In 2003 Dr. Jonathan H. Esensten, a Harvard biochemist, said, "Evolutionary theory is a tumultuous field where many differing views are now competing for dominance."[236] Here are three current theories of biological evolution:

1. Darwinian evolution supports organisms becoming more advanced or complex through slow gradual changes taking place over long periods of time. Charles Darwin[237] wrote that all plants and animals evolved gradually from a single–cell life form that spontaneously sprang into existence in a warm pond.

2. The punctuated equilibrium, or the hopeful monster, concept of evolution promotes the possibility that both significant and major changes in organisms occurred very rapidly during relatively short periods of time. The concept of the hopeful monster was introduced in 1940 by Richard Goldschmidt[238] in his book *The Material Basis for Evolution*. In 1977 Dr. Stephen Jay Gould supported the idea that organic evolution could progress through major advances in the evolutionary process following long periods when little or no change is seen in organisms. Paleontologists Niles Eldredge and Stephen M. Stanley also support the concept of punctuated

236. Esensten, Jonathan H., "Death to intelligent design," *The Harvard Crimson Online Edition*, 31 March 2003, <http://www.thecrimson.com/article.aspx?ref=347206>.

237. Charles Robert Darwin (1809–1882) a British naturalist who became famous for his theories of evolution. He believed all the life on earth evolved (developed gradually) over millions of years from a few common ancestors. 4 July 2007 <www.lucidcafe.com/library/96feb/darwin.html>.

238. Richard Goldschmidt (1878–1958) a University of California Berkeley geneticist who believed that small gradual changes could not bridge a hypothetical divide between microevolution and macroevolution.

equilibrium.[239]

3. Directed panspermia is a method of evolution proposed by Dr. Francis Crick[240] and other scientists. Dr. Crick is a Nobel laureate and understood the incredibly complex and interwoven systems and structures that are involved in the life and reproduction of all cells. He apparently realized that a "simple cell" was far too complex to have formed by "chance" on the earth. So he wrote that life originated somewhere other than on earth. In this idea of organic evolution, living cells or life forms carrying viable DNA[241] and RNA[242] found their way to earth possibly attached to meteors or comets. The life forms that arrived on earth became the "seeds" of life that have produced all the diversity of life now seen on the earth. Directed panspermia discretely removes the challenge of how life originated from non–living chemicals to another location in the universe and provides more time for this extraordinarily unlikely event to have occurred by chance. Leslie Orgel, Chandra Wickramasinghe, and Sir Fred Hoyle have also expressed support for the evolutionary concept of directed panspermia.[243]

The origin of life according to evolution has been discussed earlier, but it is appropriate to revisit this subject at this time so a direct comparison can be made to the origin of life according to God. A very

---

239. 27 June 2007 <http://en.wikipedia.org/wiki/Hopeful_Monster>.
240. Francis Harry Compton Crick (8 June 1916–28 July 2004) was an English molecular biologist who is noted for being one of the co–discoverers of the structure of the DNA molecule in 1953. Dr. Crick shared the 1962 Nobel Prize in Medicine with James D. Watson and Maurice Wilkins.
241. Deoxyribonucleic acid: an extremely long macromolecule that is the main component of chromosomes and is the material that transfers genetic characteristics in all life forms 4 July 2007 <Dictionary.com_Unabridged (v. 1.1)>.
242. Ribonucleic acid: any of a class of single–stranded molecules transcribed from DNA. The composition of the RNA molecule is identical with that of DNA except for the substitution of the sugar ribose for deoxyribose and the substitution of the nucleotide base uracil for thymine. 4 July 2007 <Diction­ary.com_Unabridged (v. 1.1)>.
243. 27 June 2007 <http://en.wikipedia.org/wiki/Panspermia>.

brief summary of the theory of evolution's explanation of origin of the universe says that the universe generally begins with a complex process known as the "big bang." A tremendous explosion caused the formation of lighter elements while heavier elements supposedly came into existence within the energy–rich cores of young stars that formed on their own after the big bang. It is believed most of the elements in the universe were formed over a period of ten to twelve billion years. Then between four to five billion years ago, somehow the earth, our moon, and the other planets with their moons in our solar system formed from the accumulation of matter circling our sun.[244]

Many proponents of the theory of evolution, including some Christians,[245] believe that the earth formed about 4.6 billion years ago as a molten blob of matter. Then after a long cooling process and crust formation on the early earth, water appeared and life created itself from chemicals found on the earth. Through chance, natural selection, and the multiplication and manipulation of both RNA and DNA, life forms were able to produce and reproduce the tremendous variety of life seen around the earth.

History according to proponents of an earth that is about 4.57 billion years old[246]

Time	Events That Have Taken Place by Random Chance
13.7 billion years ago	"Big bang" occurred which started the universe[247]

244. Scott, Eugenie C., *Evolution vs. Creationism—An Introduction*, p. 24.
245. There are some Christians who believe that the earth is in the range of 4.57 billion years old and God used "biologic evolution," with possible supernatural intervention, to create life we now see on the earth. Dr. Hugh Ross and his organization called "Reasons To Believe" <www.reasons.org> is an example.
246. Most of the "deep time" information included in this list is available via the website, 19 December 2007 <www.pbs.org/wgbh/evolution/change/deep-time/index.html>.
247. 6 July 2007 <http://en.wikipedia.org/wiki/Big_bang>.

4.57 billion years ago	Sun of our solar system formed[248]
4.57 billion years ago	Earth formed
4.53 billion years ago	Earth's moon began orbiting[249]
	Planets of our solar system formed out of random matter
	Moons of the solar system's planets formed themselves
	Early earth was molten rock[250]
4.2 billion years ago	Great oceans formed
4.05 billion years ago	Oldest known rocks were formed
3.8 billion years ago	Earth was bombarded by meteors and comets
	Earth developed a major water component
	Earth developed an atmosphere suitable for life
	Earth developed dry land and oceans
	Life spontaneously generated from chemicals[251]
3.7 billion years ago	Photosynthesizing bacteria live in an oxygen–free environment
2.7 billion years ago	First eukaryotes (cells containing a nucleus) existed
2.6 billion years ago	First bacteria appeared on land
1.8 billion years ago	Oldest known eukaryote fossils
1.5 billion years ago	Nucleated one–cell organism somehow came into existence[252]
	The one–cell organism somehow reproduced itself

---

248. 6 July 2007 <http://en.wikipedia.org/wiki/Sun>.
249. 6 July 2007 <http://en.wikipedia.org/wiki/Earth>.
250. The time period from the origin of the earth to 3.8 billion years ago is called "Hadean" or Hell on earth.
251. Scientists are not in agreement on how life formed on the earth.
252. Scott, Eugenie C., *Evolution vs. Creationism—An Introduction*, p. 28.

> The one–cell organism somehow became a two–celled organism
>
> The two–celled organism somehow reproduced itself
>
> The two–celled organism somehow became three–celled
>
> The three–celled organism somehow reproduced itself
>
> The three–celled organism somehow became four–celled

At this point it should be noted that the human body contains between 10 and 100 trillion cells and each cell contains approximately a trillion atoms.[253] For a one–celled organism to become a human being through a random chance process,[254] referred to as evolution, biologic evolution, or naturalistic evolution, it would require an incredibly improbable collection of random, sequential, and beneficial mutations in the DNA that programs an organism's existence. However, this is what people who accept the theory of evolution as fact believe.

1.2 billion years ago	Oldest multicellular algae fossils formed.
1.1 billion years ago	Super continent Rodinia formed.[255]
1 billion years ago	Marine algae evolved—algae became either both plants or animals that developed the ability to reproduce themselves
900 million years ago	Metazoans (smooth worm–like creatures) existed

---

253. Swenson, Richard A., *More Than Meets the Eye*, p. 20.
254. "In bio–evolutionary theory, natural selection chooses from among the best variations available, but the direction of change (to produce variation) is random. Evolution cannot think ahead. It can only work with what is currently available and can only improve it if change just happens to go in the right direction." Wise, Kurt P., *Faith, Form, and Time*, p. 131.
255. 19 December 2007 <http://en.wikipedia.org/wiki/Pangaea>.

543–490 million years ago	The Cambrian explosion of life occurred[256]
500 million years ago	First fish appeared
350 million years ago	First animals and plants appeared on land
270 million years ago	First mammal–like reptiles and coniferous trees appeared
225 million years ago	The super continent Pangaea appeared and was surrounded by a single universal sea, Panthalassa.[257]
220 million years ago	First dinosaurs and mammals appeared
210 million years ago	*Morganucodon oehleri*[258] evolved from some other mammal
206 million years ago	About 50 percent of marine animals went extinct
180 million years ago	Pangaea began to break up to produce today's continents[259]
135 million years ago	First birds and flowering plants and dinosaurs became extinct
100 million years ago	Modern mammals spread and first primates appeared
70 million years ago	*Morganucodon oehleri* moved from holes in the ground to trees, the first stop to its evolving into monkeys, apes, and humans
65 million years ago	60–80 percent of all species went extinct—including dinosaurs

256. DeRosa, Tom, *Evidence for Creation: Intelligent Answers for Open Minds*, Coral Ridge Ministries, Publisher, Fort Lauderdale, FL, 2003, p. 43.
257. 19 December 2007 <www.pangaea.org/continen.htm>.
258. In the Smithsonian Museum of Natural History in Washington, D.C., a sign states that humans, monkeys, and all mammals have descended/evolved from *Morganucodon oehleri*, a 3 to 4" long rat or mouse–like creature that evolved about 210 million years ago. The museum's display model of this creature is twice its normal size. This sign was noted by the author on 31 March 2006.
259. 19 December 2007 <www.pangaea.org/continen.htm>.

50 million years ago	South America separated from South Africa
40 million years ago	Continents neared their present–day positions
35 million years ago	Grazing mammals and first apes appeared with spread of grasses
25 million years ago	Formation of Himalayan–Alpine mountain system
20 million years ago	Great mountain building occurred around the globe
6 million years ago	Chimpanzee and *hominid* lines separated
5.2 million years ago	First *hominids* (human–like ancestors) appeared
2 million years ago	Major ice ages alternating with warmer interglacial periods[260]
1 million years ago	Nearly all mammals and birds over 45 pounds went extinct
1 million years ago	*Homo erectus* appeared
100,000 years ago	*Homo sapiens* and *Homo sapiens neanderthalensis* appeared[261]

The list of events developed by people who believe the earth to be over four billion years old is vastly different from the Holy Bible's account of the creation of the earth. It is very interesting to note in the above listing how many species of animals went extinct. It is also quite significant that this proposed long history records numerous periods of global warming and cooling that had absolutely nothing to do with the current activities of mankind.

Almighty God is the author of the Bible. Since God documented the creation of the earth, the celestial bodies, the plants, the animals,

---

260. Leakey, Richard E. and Lewin, Roger, *Origins—What New Discoveries Reveal About the Emergence of Our Species and Its Possible Future*, E. P. Dutton, New York, 1979, p. 12–15.

261. Ibid., p.85.

and mankind in the Bible, we should carefully consider what God has to say on the subject of origins. God created language and He certainly knows the meaning of the word "day" that He used to describe the time intervals of creation week consisting of seven twenty-four–hour–long days or one hundred sixty–eight hours.

> The Hebrew word for day in the Genesis creation account is used the same way as our English word for day. Whenever this word appears with a numerical word like "first" or "second" as it does in Genesis, it always refers to a literal day. Besides that, there is a different Hebrew word for "age" or "long period of time" which would have been the one to use here if that's what God meant.[262]

Dr. Steven Boyd[263] says there are three approaches generally taken by theologians to interpreting Genesis 1:1–Genesis 2:3, which document the creation of the universe.

1. The passage can be read as an extended poetic metaphor, in which the normal senses of the words do not correspond to reality.
2. The passage can be read as a pre–scientific account that is filled with misinformation and error.
3. The passage can be read as a historical narrative (real history) that accurately reports reality.

The three approaches are very important to our understanding of the messages contained in the Bible. The first approach says that the passage should be read as poetry. However, Dr. Boyd completed a statistical study of Genesis 1:1–Genesis 2:3, after which he came to

---

262. DeWitt, David A., *Can We Believe in Both Evolution and the Bible?*, Search Ministries, Dallas, Texas, no publication date, p. 3.
263. Steven W. Boyd earned his Ph.D. from Hebrew Union College and is a professor of Old Testament and Hebrew at Master's College located in Santa Clarita, CA.

the conclusion that there is less than one chance in ten thousand that this passage is poetry. The second approach says that the passage is filled with error. But if the Bible is to be accepted as totally truthful and the first information presented in its pages is filled with misinformation and error, the credibility and trustworthiness of the rest of the Bible's message has been lost. The third approach says that the passage presents the real history of the early earth and is completely accurate.[264] The first passage in the Bible must be fantasy, filled with error, or totally truthful. If it is fantasy or filled with error, you might as well look somewhere other than the Bible for meaning to your life, because God was apparently unable to accurately communicate how He established the earth. But if the first passage in the Bible conveys the accurate history of the creation of the universe, the message of the entire Bible has extraordinary meaning for all people of all time!

After considering the possible ways to interpret the biblical account of the creation of the earth, the universe, and life on the earth, it would be good to compare the two explanations of origins.

Sequence of events in the origin of components of the universe

Creation according to God
1. Space created
2. Earth created
3. Darkness created
4. Water created on Earth
5. Light created

Evolution according to man
1. No explanation of space's origin
2. No explanation of origin of atoms
3. Natural forces bring elements together
4. Big Bang occurs
5. Evolution of elements

---

264. Vardiman, Larry, *RATE in Review: Reading Genesis As History, Acts and Facts*, Institute for Creation Research, Dallas, TX, November 2007, p. 6.

6. Day and night make day one

6. Elements spread throughout universe

7. Firmament/atmosphere created

7. Stars form from dispersed elements

8. Day two completed

8. Heavier elements form inside of stars

9. Oceans and dry land created

9. Galaxies form from stars

10. Grass, herbs, and trees created

10. Our sun is formed from dispersed elements

11. Day three completed

11. Planets around our sun form from "dust"

12. Sun created

12. Surface of earth is molten rock

13. Earth's moon is created

13. How moons form is not known for sure

14. Day four completed

14. Earth's moon is closer to earth than now

15. Fish, fowl, whales, and all creatures that live in water created

15. Surface of earth cools with comets and meteors possibly bringing water to earth

16. Day five completed

16. Amino acids form on earth by chance

17. Land animals and insects created

17. Primitive living cell forms by chance

18. Adam created out of dust and Eve is created out of a rib

18. Living cells by chance learn to become more complex

19. Day six completed

19. Blue–green algae form by chance

20. Adam and Eve walk with God

20. Sponge spicules, coral, and invertebrates form

21. Adam and Eve rebel against God

21. Mollusks and jawless fishes

22. God curses animals and ground
23. God makes life more difficult
24. God brings death into creation
25. Adam & Eve driven from garden
26. First human baby (Cain) born
27. Abel is born
28. Cain murders Abel
29. Adam died at 930 years of age

form by chance
22. Land plants form by chance
23. Bony fishes and early seed plants form
24. Amphibians and insects form by chance
25. Reptiles and gymnosperms form by chance
26. Mammal–like reptiles and coniferous trees form
27. Mammals and dinosaurs form by chance
28. Birds and flowering plants form by chance
29. Primates, apes, Neanderthals, and humans form

These two lists of events, one originating from God and the other from man, are definitely not compatible. Major differences are found in the sequence of events, including the first appearances of and the death of animals and humans on earth. The Bible says that death did not come into existence until after Adam and Eve rebelled against God. Evolutionists would certainly say that in the process of evolution, billions of animals died during the millions of years that passed before the appearance of humans.

Here are some additional major incompatibilities between what God says in the Bible and what evolutionists say in regard to the appearance of plants and animals:[265]

265. Whitcomb, John C. Jr., *The Early Earth*, Baker Book House, Grand Rapids, MI, 1972, p. 63.

1. Genesis states that all basic types of land plants, including fruit trees, were created on day three of creation week, whereas evolutionary geologists insist that marine creatures came into existence hundreds of millions of years before fruit trees evolved.

2. Genesis says that God made the sun, moon, and stars on day four of creation week, only one day after God created dry land, the seas, and plants.[266] Evolutionists assume that the sun existed before the earth was formed. With the twenty-four–hour–long days described in the Bible, plants would not have any difficulty living without sunlight for one day. But if the days of creation week were millions of years long, plants created on day three would not be able to survive without the energy provided by the sun.

3. Genesis says that all marine creatures and birds were created on day five of creation week. But evolutionists say that birds evolved from either reptiles or dinosaurs that according to Genesis were not created until day six.

4. Genesis says that the creation of insects or "creeping things" occurred on day six, three days after flowering plants were created. This would be impossible if the days of creation week were millions of years long because the propagation of many plants requires pollination provided by specific insects.

The Bible says that on day five God created fish, birds, and aquatic animals, and then on day six God created all of the land animals and all of the insects. The Bible also says that on day six God created Adam from the dust of the ground, and then God created Eve from one of Adam's ribs. Most dinosaurs were land animals, and, according to evolutionary theory, birds evolved from dinosaurs. So, if the sequence of evolution is correct about birds coming into existence after the appearance of dinosaurs, then the Bible's sequence of appearance is wrong, because

---

266. Genesis 1:11–12 describes the plants created on day three of creation week as grass, herb yielding seed after his kind, and the fruit tree yielding fruit after his kind, whose seed is in itself.

the Bible says birds were created before dinosaurs.

Evolutionary theory and methodological naturalism[267] do not allow for Adam to be created from the dust of the ground. Evolutionists say that humans evolved from an unknown creature that gave rise to monkeys, apes, and humans. Also, methodological naturalism does not allow for God to be involved in the formation of the earth, in the appearance of life, or in the development of life. However, the Bible says that God made the sea and formed the dry land.[268] If the theory of evolution is correct and the earth formed by itself through "natural processes," then the Bible is obviously either wrong or deceptive or misleading in its presentation and explanation of the origin of the universe and the order of appearance of plants, animals and humans on the earth.

Theistic evolutionists[269] and progressive creationists[270] believe that the days of creation week were extremely long periods of time and the earth is approximately four billion years old. These individuals have used alternate meanings for some of the Bible's words in order to build a compromise between the ideas of mankind and the message of the Bible. Through their modifications, they believe the biblical account of creation becomes compatible to an earth that is around four billion years old instead of about six thousand years old as the Bible indicates in its text. Below is a short list of contradictions between

---

267. Methodological naturalism says that scientists must do their work as if there is no God and that everything they study must be explained by three things: time, chance, and the laws of nature. Such a methodology for studying the physical world rules out the miraculous and providential works of God in His creation, even before investigation begins. Hodge, Bodie, "Harvard, Yale, Princeton, Oxford—Once Christian?," *Answers Magazine*, Vol. 2 No. 3, July–Sept. 2007, p. 36.

268. "The sea is his, and he made it: and his hands formed the dry land" (Ps. 95:5).

269. Theistic evolution says that God supposedly directed the evolutionary process of millions of years, or God just set up the evolutionary process and let it run its course.

270. Progressive creation says that God supposedly intervened in the process of death and struggle for survival to create millions of species at various times over millions of years.

the order of creation in a six thousand–year–old earth and a four billion–year–old earth.[271]

Biblical account of Creation	Evolutionary/ long-age speculation
Earth before the sun and stars	Stars and sun before the earth
Earth initially covered in water	*Earth initially a molten blob of rock*
Oceans first, then dry land appeared	Dry land first, then oceans appeared
Life first created on the land	*Life started by chance in the oceans*
Plants were created before the sun	Plants came along after the sun
Land animals were created after birds	*Land animals evolved before birds*
Aquatic animals created before land animals	Land animals evolved before whales

In addition, the Bible says:

1. Thorns and thistles appeared as a part of God's curse on the earth after Adam and Eve sinned.[272] But the theory of evolution says that thorns and thistles existed on the earth long before human beings were living on the earth.[273]
2. The death of higher animals[274] possessing *nephesh* or life principle and the death of humans did not occur until after the sin of

---

271. Batten, Don (editor), Ham, Ken, Sarfati, Jonathan, Wieland, Carl, *The Revised & Expanded Answers Book*, Master Books Inc., Green Forest, AR, 2000, p. 51.
272. "Thorns also and thistles shall it bring forth to thee; and thou shalt eat the herb of the field" (Gen. 3:18).
273. Batten, Don (editor), *The Revised & Expanded Answers Book*, p. 43.
274. Animals with *nephesh* would include at least vertebrate land animals, birds, and fish.

Adam and Eve.[275]

3. Adam lived to be nine hundred thirty years old before he died.[276] The Bible also states that some of the descendents of Adam and Eve were very old when they died. Here are examples of long, pre–Genesis flood lifetimes:[277]

Name	Age at death
Seth	912 years
Enos	905 years
Cainan	910 years
Mahalaleel	895 years
Jared	962 years
Methuselah	969 years

These men obviously had a much longer lifespan than people who have lived during the last four thousand years. Adherents to the theories of evolution and methodological naturalism do not accept these long lifespans in humans because the average lifespan of Neanderthals through the Medieval Britain era is in the twenty– to thirty–year range. The current world average lifespan is sixty–seven years, while in 2005 the average in the USA is approximately seventy–seven years.[278]

Since God invented both language and vocabulary, He is certainly capable of using appropriate words to accurately describe the lifespans of people. If the length of these lifespans is not accurate, then the accuracy of all statements found in the Bible is questionable. Inaccurate information in the Bible would be an indication that the Author of the Bible presented information in a less than trustworthy or deceptive manner.

275. Batten, Don (editor), *The Revised & Expanded Answers Book*, p. 42.
276. "And all the days that Adam lived were nine hundred and thirty years: and he died" (Gen. 5:5).
277. Genesis 5:5–27 provides the ages of these pre–flood individuals.
278. "Life expectancy," Wikipedia, 5 January 2008 <http://en.wikipedia.org/wiki/Life_expectancy>.

However, the Bible says that God is trustworthy and that God does not lie:[279] another example that the Bible may be either trusted or not trusted. Since God is trustworthy and since God does not lie, we can trust that all of the information He placed in the Bible is accurate. Therefore we can know that the ages of these men are accurate. Methuselah really did live nine hundred sixty–nine years before he died!

A summary of some of the contradictions between the Bible's history and the theories of mankind

In the Bible, God says on day two of creation week He created the seas, dry land, grass, herbs yielding seed, and fruit trees yielding fruit.[280] Then, on day three, God created the sun and the moon. Plants would have no trouble surviving for less than twenty–four hours without sunlight, but this would be an insurmountable problem if day two was millions of years long as some Bible scholars believe.[281]

The Bible says that the death of animals and the death of humans did not begin until after the rebellion of Adam and Eve in the Garden of Eden. According to the theory of evolution and the concept of an old earth, however, the death of animals has been occurring for millions of years. Note: Genesis chapters six and seven document a flood that covered the entire earth. God sent this flood to "destroy all flesh, wherein is the breath of life, from under heaven; and every thing that is in the earth shall die."[282] This was an extraordinarily great catastrophe! A massive flood that covered the entire earth and killed billions of animals would have produced massive layers of sediment

---

279. "In hope of eternal life, which God, that cannot lie, promised before the world began" (Titus 1:2)

280. "And God called the dry land Earth; and the gathering together of the waters called he Seas: and God saw that it was good. And God said, Let the earth bring forth grass, the herb yielding seed, and the fruit tree yielding fruit after his kind, whose seed is in itself, upon the earth: and it was so" (Gen. 1:10–11).

281. The Day–Age theory states that the six days of creation were actually very long periods of time.

282. Genesis 6:17

containing billions of fossilized animals. The worldwide fossil record is evidence of the rapid death of billions of animals. If the fossil record is the result of the destruction of the worldwide Genesis flood, there is definite agreement with the history recorded in the Bible. If the fossil record is the result of death and sedimentation occurring before the lifetimes of Adam and Eve, the Bible's history is not accurate and is very deceptive.

Some highly educated scholars have attempted to redefine words in the Bible in order to make the Bible's accounts of creation and the history of mankind agree with what some scientists say about the age of the earth and the universe. Generally these compromising redefinitions of words have been an attempt to change the meaning of what the Bible says about the age of the earth. A straightforward reading of the Bible communicates that the earth was created by God about six thousand years ago. The Bible does not mention a "big bang," nor does the Bible suggest that there have been billions of years since the origin of the universe. The idea that the earth and the universe are billions of years old was developed by a few people during the last two hundred years. These ideas of an old earth have been widely distributed through "scientific textbooks," museums, and the media. Attempts to compromise or change the meaning of words in the Bible have caused serious questions to develop about the reliability and the integrity of the Bible in all areas that it addresses.

The God who created the universe by His spoken words is the same God who created language for use by mankind. God created words that have specific meanings, and He used these words in the Bible to communicate His messages to mankind. If God created the universe about 14 billion years ago and created life on the earth through a process of evolution, as is proposed by some scientists and scholars, is it not reasonable that God could have chosen the appropriate words to communicate an accurate message of how life began on a very old earth? God certainly could have chosen the necessary words to communicate that the universe is about 14 billion years old and the earth is about 4.57 billion years old. Is it reasonable that God would intentionally deceive mankind by providing an inaccurate and unreliable explanation for how the universe and the earth came into existence? The answer to this question is absolutely no! God is truthful and God does not deceive or lie.[283]

Almighty God with His supernatural attributes certainly has the ability to create everything in the universe, including everything on the earth, exactly and precisely as He stated in the Bible.

Dr. Kurt Wise has made some concise and profound statements about the age of the earth and the reliability of the Bible:

If the Earth is old, the Bible is wrong.

Old-age chronology and Scripture cannot both be true, and they cannot be reconciled.

The acceptance of humanly devised old–age chronology or any variation of it would require the rejection or modification of divinely inspired Scripture.[284]

These statements make it clear that you cannot have an earth that is billions of years old according to some scientists and scholars while at the same time having an earth that is six thousand years old according to the God of the Bible. If the Bible is wrong in the very first words it records, how can the rest of its message be trusted? The people who have believed the scientists and scholars have undoubtedly lost some degree of confidence and trust in the accuracy of the Bible. The loss of confidence in the complete reliability of the Bible has apparently caused many people to doubt the messages presented in the Bible. Perhaps this loss of confidence in the accuracy of the Bible may be seen in the

---

283. "In hope of eternal life, which God, that cannot lie, promised before the world began" (Titus 1:2).
284. Wise, Kurt P., *Faith, Form, and Time*, p. 54–55.

decreasing number of people attending churches regularly in Europe, Australia, and the United States of America.

So what does God know?

The attribute of omniscience is absolutely awesome! God's having all knowledge is so far beyond human understanding that we cannot even begin to comprehend it. God lovingly tells us that humans do not think like He thinks. One of God's comments on this difference is recorded in Isaiah 55:8, which states, "For my thoughts are not your thoughts, neither are your ways my ways, saith the LORD."

Here are a few illustrations that should help expand our understanding of how much God knows.

1. Trees in a forest

Since God made all of the trees, He should know all that there is to know about all of the trees in the world.[285] It is truly mind boggling for us to consider that God knows *all* there is to know about any and all of the trees on the earth. Consider what God knows about trees in a forest.

Imagine that it is a crystal–clear autumn day blessed with a beautiful blue sky. You are standing with a friend on the top of a tall mountain overlooking a tremendous valley filled with trees that are at their peak of color change. The forest at your feet stretches for miles in every direction. With full sunlight at your back, you can see brilliant reds, oranges, yellows, and browns. It is a magnificent sight! Now, try to count the individual trees that you can see. With your human abilities and limitations, you soon are unable to continue an accurate count of the trees because at a distance they seem to blend together. Just for fun, you look at the closest tree and try to count the number of leaves on that one tree. This is a difficult task, but you try to complete the

---

285. "And God said, Let the earth bring forth grass, the herb yielding seed, and the fruit tree yielding fruit after his kind, whose seed is in itself, upon the earth: and it was so" (Gen. 1:11).

count. You find it necessary to admit to yourself that you are not able to determine the exact number of leaves on the tree.

Now imagine that you have the privilege of asking the omniscient God some questions about the trees in this marvelous forest.

» God, can you count all of the trees in range of sight? Yes.
» God, can you tell how many trees are in this entire forest? Yes.
» God, can you count all of the leaves on all of the trees within sight? Yes.
» God, do you know how many leaves are on all of the trees in this forest? Yes.
» God, can you tell how many cells are in each leaf on all the trees in the forest? Yes.
» God, can you tell how many leaves have fallen off of every tree in this forest? Yes.
» God, can you categorize the different colors on all the leaves? Yes.
» God, can you provide the number of the different kinds of trees in this forest? Yes.
» God, can you tell the names of all of the trees? His response is again, Yes.

In addition God says in case you would like to know. . .

» I can provide all of the common names of the trees, like aspen, birch, maple, oak, etc.
» I can provide all of the Latin names for these trees like the white oak or *Quercus alba*.
» I can provide this information in any language currently spoken in the world.
» I can provide this information in any language that has been used by past civilizations.

Then you ask God some additional questions about the trees in the forest at your feet.

» God, can you tell how many limbs are on each tree in the forest? Yes.
» God, can you tell how many bird nests are in the trees in the forest? Yes.
» God, can you tell the heights of all of the trees that are in this forest? Yes.
» God, can you tell the diameter of the trunks of all the trees in the forest? Yes.
» God, can you tell the depth of the root systems of all of the trees in the forest? Yes.
» God, can you describe the root systems of each tree in the forest? Yes.
» God, can you tell the weight of each tree in the forest? Yes.
» God, can you tell the age of each tree in the forest? Yes.
» God, can you tell the health of each tree in the forest? Yes.
» God, can you provide all of this information for every tree in the world? Yes.
» God, can you provide all of this information in less than a second? Yes.

Certainly this imaginary conversation could go on for much, much longer, but I trust you get the picture with these questions. God knows everything there is to know about the trees in the beautiful forest that we have imagined. God knows all of this information in all of the real forests, too! And, He knows so much more. Since God is omniscient, He can instantly answer all of these questions with complete accuracy.

2. Sparrows in the world

This illustration is presented in the introduction and it is included again for emphasis.

Jesus Christ said that God knows when one sparrow falls on the ground. He also stated that God does not forget a single sparrow. The following two passages tell us some of the information that God knows about sparrows.

Are not two sparrows sold for a farthing? and one of them shall not fall on the ground without your Father. But the very hairs of your head are all numbered. Fear ye not therefore, ye are of more value than many sparrows.

—Matthew 10:29–31

Are not five sparrows sold for two farthings, and not one of them is forgotten before God? But even the very hairs of your head are all numbered. Fear not therefore: ye are of more value than many sparrows.

—Luke 12:6–7

Note again these comments found in the introduction and that are included here for both continuity and emphasis. Dr. Henry M. Morris[286] made the following comment on the verses mentioning sparrows in Matthew and Luke's gospels. In the passage from Matthew the selling price of sparrows is two for a farthing. In Luke, Jesus said that five sparrows are sold for two farthings. Apparently the sparrow merchants of that day had already introduced the sales method of quantity discounts![287]

In case you are not familiar with the term *farthing*, this is the name of a British coin worth one quarter of a penny. Farthings were first minted in England in the thirteenth century and were used as legal

286. Henry M. Morris, 1918–2006, B.S. in Civil Engineering, Rice Univ., M.S. in Hydraulics, and Ph.D. in Hydraulic Engineering, Univ. of Minnesota, assisted in founding Creation Research Society and the Institute for Creation Research, widely regarded as the founder of the modern creationist movement.
287. Morris, Henry M., *The Defender's Study Bible—King James Version*, p. 1021.

tender in England until December 31, 1960.[288]

So what does God know about sparrows?

For God to know when one sparrow falls to the ground anywhere on earth, we must affirm that God has extraordinary—no, supernatural abilities! Consider the magnitude of accomplishing this one task.

» God must know a sparrow from every other bird. God says that He knows "all the fowls of the mountains."[289]

» God must know the number of sparrows in the world at every moment.

» God knows how many kinds of sparrows are in the world at every moment.[290]

» God must know the location of every sparrow in the world at every moment.

» God must know the position of every sparrow in every part of the world at every moment—whether the bird is in an egg, in flight, or is perched on some object.

» God must know the health status and the thoughts of every sparrow at all times. God must know if the sparrow on a perch is planning to fly and God must know if a flying sparrow is thinking about landing.

» God's knowledge about the status of sparrows is for this moment in time, but God's knowledge is also for every previous moment in time going back to the moment when God created the very first sparrows.[291]

» God must truly care about sparrows, and God must truly care about

---

288. 29 December 2006 <http://en.wikipedia.org/wiki/British_Farthing_coin.>.

289. "I know all the fowls of the mountains: and the wild beasts of the field are mine" (Ps. 50:11)

290. Terres, John K., *The Audubon Society Encyclopedia of North American Birds*, Wings Books, a Random House Co., Avenel, New Jersey, 1991 Edition, p. 312–322 lists twenty-nine varieties of sparrows.

291. Genesis 1:21—On the fifth day of creation week God created "every winged fowl after his kind."

all of His creation if He keeps track of what to us may seem to be a very minor and unimportant collection of information.

» If God knows and cares this much about sparrows, it is certainly reasonable to assume that God must also care about albatrosses, bluebirds, cardinals, doves, eagles, finches, great gray owls, hummingbirds, Iceland gulls, jaybirds, king elders, larks, mallards, northern mockingbirds, oilbirds, purple martins, quail, robins, swans, turkey vultures, upland sandpipers, Virginia rails, whippoor-wills, yellow–bellied sapsuckers, zone–tailed hawks, and every other kind of bird in the world. [292]

» Since God tracks, knows, and cares about the movements of sparrows, it would be logical and reasonable to expect that God would extend this same care and knowledge for all birds in the world. God knows as much about all of the other birds as He does about sparrows. As incredible as it seems, God knows when any bird falls to the ground. And, God knows this about every bird since He created birds on day five of creation week.

» God also possesses this knowledge about all of the species of birds that are now extinct.

» May I emphasize that if God cares for humans as He cares for birds, it is certainly reasonable to assume that God must know where every human is in every part of the world at every moment. Is it possible that God cares for humans more than He cares for birds? Jesus said two times,[293] **"Ye are of more value than many sparrows."** Since this is the case, God must also know what every human is doing now and what every human is thinking at every moment.[294] This knowledge would also include the movement and thoughts of every human who has ever lived. Surely, God must also know our health status and our thoughts and intentions at every moment. The Bible has much to say on these last comments, and you should

292. 29 December 2006 <www.birds.cornell.edu/AllAboutBirds/BirdGuide/>.
293. Matthew 10:31 and Luke 12:7
294. Job 42:2 and Psalm 139:1–10

find much more information on what God knows later on in this book. According to the words of Jesus, God has more knowledge than the human mind can even begin to comprehend.[295]

3. The number of hairs on a human head

The Bible says in Matthew 10:30 and in Luke 12:7 that God knows the number of hairs on our heads.

> **But the very hairs of your head are all numbered.**
>
> —Matthew 10:30

> **But even the very hairs of your head are all numbered. Fear not therefore: ye are of more value than many sparrows.**
>
> —Luke 12:7

Certainly, this is astounding information about only one tiny facet of God's knowledge. But let us take a moment to consider the magnitude of the fact that God keeps track of and knows the precise number of hairs on our heads at any point in time.

So what does it mean if God knows the number of hairs on the heads of all humans?

For God to know the exact number of hairs attached to the head of every person living on the earth, we must again affirm that God has supernatural abilities! Consider the magnitude of this one task.

» God must know exactly how many human heads are on the planet at every moment of time. The number of people living on earth at this time is over 6.6 billion. It is surely safe to say that almost all of the people living on earth at this time have heads. So God is obligated to track the number of hairs on the heads of over 6.6 billion people.

» God must have an accurate count of the number of hair strands

---

295. "But the very hairs of your head are all numbered" (Matt. 10:30).

on the head of every person. The first hair follicles begin to form in the skin of a baby only three months after conception.[296] According to Leo Benjamin Jr., of Adrian's Hair Center in Fort Lauderdale, Florida, hair is one of the fastest-growing tissues in the body[297]—second only to bone marrow. The average scalp has one hundred thousand strands.[298] So for God to know the number of hair strands on every head in the world, He must know how many hair strands are on the heads of over 6.6 billion people. At birth a person has all of the hair follicles that he or she will ever have. These hair follicles normally continue to produce hairs for the entire life of an individual. In case you were wondering if God gets a break on tracking the reduced number of hairs on the heads of bald people, consider these comments. Baldness is a condition that replaces normal appearing terminal hairs from the scalp with almost invisible *vellus* hairs. The normal appearing hair of bald people has been replaced with almost invisible hair. Bald people still have hair on their heads.[299] The number of hair strands on human heads that God is tracking at this moment is approximately 6,500,000,000,000,000!

» God must know how many hairs are on the head of every person at every precise moment in time. Leo Benjamin, Jr. says, "A typical person loses 15 to 40 hairs per day" while Richard A. Swenson, M.D. says, "We naturally lose 50 to 125 hairs per day."[300] So for God to keep His word, He must constantly be monitoring the number of hairs that fall from every person's scalp at every moment of time.

» God must know how many hairs have been on the heads of all the

---

296. Menton, David, "The Amazing human hair," *Answers Magazine,* July–September, 2007, p. 81.
297. According to Dr. David Menton, human hair grows about 0.3 mm per day.
298. Marr, Madeleine, "What causes female hair loss," McClatchy Newspapers, *Chattanooga Times Free Press,* 24 April 2007, Section E, Page 4.
299. Menton, David, "The Amazing human hair," *Answers Magazine,* p. 82.
300. Swenson, Richard A., *More Than Meets the Eye,* p. 82.

people who have ever lived since creation. God knows how many hairs were on the head of Adam and how many hairs were on the head of Eve from the time He created them till the time they were laid in their graves.

God must know how many hairs have been on the head of every person who has ever lived at every precise moment in time. The number of people who have lived on earth since Adam and Eve has been estimated to be between 20 billion[301] and 106.5 billion. Using an evolutionary perspective, Carl Haub[302] estimates the total population of the world starting at 50,000 B.C. to A.D. 2002 to be approximately 106.5 billion people.[303] According to biblical history, the 20 billion estimate is surely more accurate.

» Since God is omniscient He has all knowledge. So consider what this means to our brief study of God's knowing the number of hairs on every person's head.
» God knows how long each attached hair strand is for every person in the world.
» God knows how much every hair strand weighs for every person in the world.
» God knows the color of every hair strand for every person in the world.
» God knows the altered color of every hair strand for every person in the world.
» God knows how many hair strands have turned grey for every person in the world.

301. 6 April 2007 <http://www.languagemonitor.com/wst_page7.html>.
302. Carl Haub is a senior demographer at the private, non-advocacy Population Reference Bureau. He is an internationally recognized authority on world population. Since 1980 he has prepared the annual World Population Data Sheet, a widely circulated and up-to-date data source.
303. 7 July 2007 <http://answers.google.com/answers/threadview?id=217634>.

» God knows how long each hair has been attached to every person in the world.

» God knows how many hairs will fall from every head every day.

» God knows the number of cells that are in every hair of every person in the world.

» God knows the number of molecules in every cell of every hair of every person in the world.

» God knows how many atoms are in the molecules that are in the cells that make up the hair of every person in the world.

» God knows how many subatomic particles are in the atoms that are in the molecules that are in the cells that make up the hairs of every person in the world.

» God knows this information for every moment in time for every person who has ever lived.

As exhausting as this illustration is, since God has all knowledge, we should not stop with the consideration of God's only tracking the number of hair strands on people's heads. According to Dr. Swenson, the human scalp has about one hundred thousand hair follicles, and there are a total of about five million hair follicles in the skin of the adult human body. (By the way, hair does not normally grow on the soles of the feet or on the palms of the hands.[304]) So this exercise could honestly be extended to include God's tracking five million hair follicles and strands of hair for every person who is alive now and for every person who has ever lived. Surely you feel as I do at this point when we realize that God has certainly made it clear that He possesses all knowledge when Jesus says in Matthew 10:30, *"**But the very hairs of your head are all numbered.**"*

4. The number of stars in the universe
In Genesis God boldly and clearly states that He created the stars in

---

304. Swenson, Richard A., *More Than Meets the Eye*, p. 82.

the universe.[305] The method God used for this act of creation is also described in the Bible: God spoke, and the stars came into existence.[306] God shares a little more of His knowledge of the stars that He created in the following two Bible verses:

> **He telleth the number of the stars; he calleth them all by their names.**
>
> —Psalm 147:4

> **Lift up your eyes on high, and behold who hath created these things, that bringeth out their host by number: he calleth them all by names by the greatness of his might, for that he is strong in power; not one faileth.**
>
> —Isaiah 40:26

Dr. John F. Hawley[307] has estimated that there are at least one hundred billion billion stars in the universe.[308] The Bible says that God has named every star. The act of naming every star in the universe is an accomplishment that is bewildering to humans. But God has done it. God has named every star!

Certainly naming every star in the universe is an astounding feat. But which is more difficult, giving every star in the universe a name, or creating every star in the universe by speaking so that they all come into existence out of nothing in one day? My vote for the more difficult task is to speak and create all of the stars in the universe out of nothing in only one day.

---

305. "And God made two great lights; the greater light to rule the day, and the lesser light to rule the night: he made the stars also" (Gen. 1:16).
306. "And God said, Let there be lights in the firmament of the heaven . . ." (Gen. 1:14a).
307. John F. Hawley is the chair of the Department of Astronomy at the University of Virginia.
308. 6 July 2007 <www.newton.dep.anl.gov/newton/askasci/1993/astron/AST014.htm>.

5. The number of teeth in every mouth

Since Jesus said, "**But even the very hairs of your head are all numbered**,"[309] is it not reasonable to assume that God knows exactly how many teeth you have in your mouth at this moment? You certainly have fewer teeth than you do hairs. So since God keeps track of the number of hairs on your head, it is logical and reasonable that God would keep track of the number your teeth. The number of teeth in a person's mouth changes during his lifetime.[310] Since God has all knowledge, He knows how many teeth are in the mouth of every person. As with sparrows, God is keeping track of the condition of all teeth. Consider the magnitude of this task:

» God knows at this moment how many teeth you have.

» God knows how many teeth you have had at every moment in your life.

» God knows at this moment how many teeth are in the mouths of all the people in the world.

» God knows how many teeth every person has had in their mouths at every moment in their lives.

» God knows if a child is removing one of his or her baby teeth.

» God knows at any moment if a person is having a tooth or teeth removed by a dentist.

» God knows the condition of all teeth. This means that God knows which teeth have cavities, fillings, caps or crowns, and root canals.

» God remembers the condition of every tooth that has been in every mouth that has ever been in the world since Adam and Eve first used their teeth in Eden.

---

309. "But even the very hairs of your head are all numbered. Fear not therefore: ye are of more value than many sparrows" (Luke 12:7).

310. Children from three to six years old normally have twenty baby teeth. Starting at six years of age, adult teeth usually begin to erupt into the mouth. Adults normally have thirty-two permanent teeth.

» God knows at every moment how many people in the world are wearing partial dentures and how many people are wearing complete dentures.

» God knows how many people in the entire world do not have any teeth at this moment.

» God remembers how many teeth were in the mouth of every person at every moment during his or her entire life.

» God knows how many teeth will be in the mouths of all the people who will live in the future.

» God knows the condition of all of the teeth that will be used by people in the future.

The omniscient God keeps the best dental records imaginable!

6. All human communication

God knows everything that has been thought, spoken, written, or printed by mankind throughout all time. The Bible records a statement that demonstrates this phenomenal ability of God.

> **Let the words of my mouth, and the meditation of my heart, be acceptable in thy sight, O LORD, my strength, and my redeemer.**
>
> —Psalm 19:14

For God to know all my words and thoughts, and then determine if they are acceptable to Him, is quite an accomplishment! Now consider that He remembers all of my words and thoughts since the time I was born. Now consider that God will continue to monitor all of my words and thoughts through the end of my lifetime. Consider that God does the same thing for you. Consider that God does this same thing for every other person who is alive today—over 6.6 billion people. Then consider that God has been doing this same thought and speech analysis for every person who has ever lived—probably well over 20 billion people. Now consider that God will continue this thought and speech analysis for every person who will be born in the future. Is this helping you realize what it means for God to be omniscient?

Here is another example of God's omniscience. Those who read newspapers realize the significant amount of time required to peruse all of the articles and advertisements in only one newspaper. Since God knows everything, we can be assured that He knows every word and every picture in every newspaper in the world. Large libraries may be intimidating because they contain such massive amounts of literature. However, God knows the title, the author, the publisher, the words, and the message of every book that has ever been published. God also knows the content of every website and every blog on the internet. Below is a brief listing of what God knows about human thought and communication in newspapers, publications, and on the internet:

1. God knows all of the words in every paragraph, in every article, on every page, in every section, in every advertisement, in every cartoon, every day of every newspaper that is printed anywhere. God knows this same information for every internet site. God knows every word in every language used in print anywhere in the world. Definitely, God does not limit Himself to speaking and reading only in English, or in any other language for that matter. God is perfectly fluent in every language that has been thought, spoken, written, or printed at any time in the history of mankind.

2. God knows all of this information for all of the newspapers, books, magazines, brochures, pamphlets, and internet that were produced anywhere in the world yesterday, and for every day of history.

3. God knows if any words are misspelled or misused in every publication anywhere on any given day.

4. God knows if the information printed in any publication is accurate or partially accurate, or deceptive, or if the information is totally inaccurate. God knows who wrote every article or advertisement

in every newspaper and publication in the world. God knows if the writer of each article honestly presented the information in the article. God knows if the writer of each article purposefully placed deceptive or inaccurate information into the article.

5. God knows who reads which parts of every newspaper or publication in the world on any given day.

6. God knows the writer of every story that is included in all newspapers and publications on any given day.

7. God knows who is involved in the printing of all the newspapers and publications in the world on any given day.

8. God knows where the paper for each newspaper, book, and magazine came from. He knows where the different inks used for printing were made, how they were delivered to the print shop, when and where the printing took place, who set the type, and who printed each newspaper.

All of this information about newspapers, books, magazines, and the internet is only a very, very small part of what God knows.

7. The human body

Innumerable scrolls and books have been written over the last four thousand years that describe the marvelous design, structure, function, physiology, senses, mental capabilities, repair/healing, and reproduction of the human body. This massive documentation is certainly appropriate, because human beings are truly special! God saved the ultimate creation, man, to be the last. God chose to create men and women in His own image.[311]

Only humans were created in the image of God. Plants possess

---

311. "And God said, Let us make man in our image, after our likeness: and let them have dominion over the fish of the sea, and over the fowl of the air, and over the cattle, and over all the earth, and over every creeping thing that creepeth upon the earth" (Gen. 1:26).

only a body. Animals possess both a body and consciousness. Humans, however, were created to possess a body, consciousness, and the image of God, with an eternal spirit that is capable of personal communion and fellowship with his Creator.[312] The Bible says that on the sixth day of creation week "God formed man of the dust of the ground, and breathed into his nostrils the breath of life; and man became a living soul."[313] Eve, the first woman, was also made on day six of creation week from one of Adam's ribs.[314] This historical event is also noted in the New Testament.[315] Humans are extraordinarily special, regardless of their gender! The Bible does not support the theory of evolution by stating, suggesting, or in any way implying that humans evolved from animals. The theory of evolution is a product of man's wisdom—not God's.

The following passages document a very small but very significant amount of information that God knows about humans. Selected phrases have been italicized to focus on specific information that God has placed in the Bible. Since this is such a large collection of Bible verses, they have been divided into three sections. They are grouped in the following categories:

1. God created mankind and knows everything there is to know about our bodies.
2. God knows all of the thoughts, the motivation, and the deeds of every person who has ever lived. God knows if individuals deserve any rewards.
3. God knows everywhere we will go, all that we have done, all that we will do, and every experience of our lifetime.

---

312. Morris, Henry M., *The Defender's Study Bible—King James Version*, p. 7.
313. Genesis 2:7
314. "And the rib, which the LORD God had taken from man, made he a woman, and brought her unto the man" (Gen. 2:22).
315. "For Adam was first formed, then Eve" (1 Tim. 2:13).

Some of what the Bible says that God knows about human beings

1. **God created mankind and He knows everything there is to know about our bodies.**

So God created man in his own image, in the image of God created he him; male and female created he them.

—Genesis 1:27

And the LORD *God formed man of the dust of the ground, and breathed into his nostrils the breath of life;* **and man became a living soul.**

—Genesis 2:7

Thou hast clothed me with skin and flesh, and hast fenced me with bones and sinews.

—Job 10:11

Who hath put wisdom in the inward parts? or who hath given understanding to the heart?

—Job 38:36

Know ye that the Lord he is God: *it is he that hath made us,* **and not we ourselves; we are his people, and the sheep of his pasture.**

—Psalm 100:3

For *thou hast possessed my reins: thou hast covered me in my* mother's womb. I will **praise thee;** for *I am fearfully and wonderfully made:* **marvellous are thy works; and that my soul knoweth right well.** *My substance was not hid from thee, when I was made in secret, and curiously wrought* **in the lowest parts of the earth.** *Thine eyes did see my substance, yet being unperfect; and in thy book all my members were written,* **which in continuance were fashioned,** *when as yet there was none of* *them. How precious also are thy thoughts unto me, O God! how great is the sum of them! If I should count them, they are more in number than the sand:* **when I awake, I am still with thee.**

—Psalm 139:13–18

The hearing ear, **and** *the seeing eye, the* LORD **hath made even both of them.**

—Proverbs 20:12

The rich and poor meet together: *the* LORD *is the maker of* **them all.**

—Proverbs 22:2

Thus saith the LORD *that made thee, and formed thee from the womb,* **which will help thee; Fear not, O Jacob, my servant; and thou, Jesurun, whom I have chosen.**

—Isaiah 44:2

But now, O LORD, **thou art our father; we are the clay, and thou our potter; and** *we all are the work of thy hand.*

—Isaiah 64:8

I have made the earth, the man and the beast that are upon the ground, **by my great power and by my outstretched arm, and have given it unto whom it seemed meet unto me.**

—Jeremiah 27:5

2. **God knows all of the thoughts, the motivation, and the deeds of every person who has every lived. God knows if individuals deserve any rewards.**

    Then hear thou in heaven thy dwelling place, and forgive, and do, and give to every man according to his ways, *whose* *heart thou knowest; (for thou, even thou only, knowest the hearts of all the children of men.)*

—1 Kings 8:39

And *I have been with thee whithersoever thou hast walked,* and have cut off all thine enemies from before thee, and have made thee a name like the name of the great men that are in the earth.

—1 Chronicles 17:8

Be ye strong therefore, and let not your hands be weak: *for your work shall be rewarded.*

—2 Chronicles 15:7

I know that thou canst do every thing, and that *no thought can be withholden from thee.*

—Job 42:2

Let the words of my mouth, and the meditation of my heart, be acceptable in thy sight, O LORD, my strength, and my redeemer.

—Psalm 19:14

If we have forgotten the name of our God, or stretched out our hands to a strange god; Shall not God search this out? *for he knoweth the secrets of the heart.*

—Psalm 44:20–21

Search me, O God, and know my heart: try me, and know my thoughts: And see if there be any wicked way in me, and lead me in the way everlasting.

—Psalm 139:23–24

The eyes of the LORD *are in every place, beholding the evil and the good.*

—Proverbs 15:3

Hell and destruction are before the LORD: *how much more then the hearts of the children of men?*

—Proverbs 15:11

A false witness shall not be unpunished, and *he that speaketh lies shall perish.*

—Proverbs 19:9

Thou wilt keep him in perfect peace, whose mind is stayed on thee: **because he trusteth in thee.**

—Isaiah 26:3

For *I know their works and their thoughts:* **it shall come, that I will gather all nations and tongues; and they shall come, and see my glory.**

—Isaiah 66:18

And *Jesus knowing their thoughts* **said, Wherefore think ye evil in your hearts?**

—Matthew 9:4

But those things which proceed out of the mouth come forth from the heart; and they defile the man. *For out of the heart proceed evil thoughts, murders, adulteries, fornications, thefts, false witness, blasphemies: These are the things which defile a man:* **but to eat with unwashen hands defileth not a man.**

—Matthew 15:18–20

But when *Jesus perceived their thoughts,* he answering said unto them, What reason ye in your hearts?

—Luke 5:22

But *he knew their thoughts,* and said to the man which had the withered hand, Rise up, and stand forth in the midst. And he arose and stood forth.

—Luke 6:8

But Jesus did not commit himself unto them, because *he knew all men,* And needed not that any should testify of man: for *he knew what was in man.*

—John 2:24–25

He that believeth on the Son hath everlasting life: and *he that believeth not the Son shall not see life;* but the wrath of God abideth on him.

—John 3:36

Verily, verily, I say unto you, *He that heareth my word, and believeth on him that sent me, hath everlasting life, and shall not come into condemnation; but is passed from death unto life.*

—John 5:24

Verily, verily, I say unto you, *He that believeth on me hath everlasting life.*

—John 6:47

Jesus saith unto him, I am the way, the truth, and the life: *no man cometh unto the Father, but by me.*

—John 14:6

And *God, which knoweth the hearts,* bare them witness, giving them the Holy Ghost, even as he did unto us.

—Acts 15:8

Who will render to every man according to his deeds.

—Romans 2:6

For *the word of God* is quick, and powerful, and sharper than any twoedged sword, piercing even to the *dividing asunder of soul and spirit,* and of the joints and marrow, and is a *discerner of the thoughts and intents of the heart. Neither is there any creature that is not manifest in his sight:* but *all things are naked and opened unto the eyes of him* with whom we have to do.

—Hebrews 4:12–13

Marriage is honourable in all, and the bed undefiled: *but whoremongers and adulterers God will judge.*

—Hebrews 13:4

And I will kill her children with death; and all the churches shall know that *I am he which searcheth the reins and hearts: and I will give unto every one of you according to your works.*

—Revelation 2:23

And, behold, *I come quickly; and my reward is with me, to give every man according as his work shall be.*

—Revelation 22:12

3. **God knows everywhere we will go, all that we have done, all that we will do, and every experience of our lifetime.**

Doth not he see my ways, and count all my steps?

—Job 31:4

Behold, *thou hast made my days as an handbreadth;* and mine age is as nothing before thee: verily every man at his best state is altogether vanity. *Selah.*

—Psalm 39:5

Thou tellest my wanderings: put thou my tears into thy bottle: are they not in thy book?

—Psalm 56:8

O LORD, *thou hast searched me, and known me. Thou knowest my downsitting and mine uprising, thou understandest my thought afar off. Thou compassest my path and my lying down,* and *art acquainted with all my ways.* For *there is not a word in my tongue, but, lo, O* LORD, *thou knowest it altogether. Thou hast beset me behind and before,* and *laid thine hand upon me.* Such knowledge is too wonderful for me; it is high, I cannot attain unto it. *Whither shall I go from thy spirit? or whither shall I flee from thy presence? If I ascend up into heaven, thou art there:* if I make my bed in hell, behold, thou art there. *If I take the wings of the morning, and dwell in the uttermost parts of the sea; Even there shall thy hand lead me, and thy right hand shall hold me.*

—Psalm 139:1–10

When my spirit was overwhelmed within me, then *thou knewest my path.* In the way wherein I walked have they privily laid a snare for me.

—Psalm 142:3

He *healeth the broken in heart, and bindeth up their wounds.*

—Psalm 147:3

For *the ways of man are before the eyes of the* LORD, and *he pondereth all his goings.*

—Proverbs 5:21

And even to your old age I am he; and even to hoar hairs will I carry you: *I have made, and I will bear; even I will carry, and will deliver you.*

—Isaiah 46:4

Then the word of the LORD came unto me, saying, *Before I formed thee in the belly I knew thee;* and before thou camest forth out of the womb I sanctified thee, and I ordained thee a prophet unto the nations.

—Jeremiah 1:4–5

Can any hide himself in secret places that I shall not see him? saith the LORD. Do not I fill heaven and earth? saith the LORD.

—Jeremiah 23:24

Behold, I am the LORD, the God of all flesh: *is there any thing too hard for me?*

—Jeremiah 32:27

The LORD God is my strength, and he will make my feet like hinds' feet, and *he will make me to walk upon mine high places.* To the chief singer on my stringed instruments.

—Habakkuk 3:19

Be not ye therefore like unto them: *for your Father knoweth what things ye have need of, before ye ask him.*

—Matthew 6:8

But I say unto you, That *every idle word that men shall speak, they shall give account thereof in the day of judgment.*

—Matthew 12:36

Jesus saith unto her, Go, call thy husband, and come hither. The woman answered and said, I have no husband. Jesus said unto her, Thou hast well said, I have no husband: For *thou hast had five husbands; and he whom thou now hast is not thy husband:* in that saidst thou truly. The woman saith unto him, Sir, I perceive that thou art a prophet.

—John 4:16–19

But *I know you, that ye have not the love of God in you.*

—John 5:42

All that the Father giveth me shall come to me; and *him that cometh to me I will in no wise cast out.*

—John 6:37

No man can come to me, except the Father which hath sent me draw him: and I will raise him up at the last day.

—John 6:44

But there are some of you that believe not. For *Jesus knew from the beginning who they were that believed not, and who should betray him.*

—John 6:64

Peter said unto him, Lord, why cannot I follow thee now? I will lay down my life for thy sake. Jesus answered him, Wilt thou lay down thy life for my sake? Verily, verily, I say unto thee, *The cock shall not crow, till thou hast denied me thrice.*

—John 13:37–38

And *hath made of one blood all nations of men* for to dwell on all the face of the earth, and *hath determined the times before appointed, and the bounds of their habitation.*

—Acts 17:26

What? *know ye not that your body is the temple of the Holy Ghost which is in you, which ye have of God, and ye are not your own?* **For ye are bought with a price:** therefore glorify God in your body, and in your spirit, which are God's.

—1 Corinthians 6:19–20

For now we see through a glass, darkly; but then face to face: now I know in part; but *then shall I know even as also I am known.*

—1 Corinthians 13:12

Be not deceived; God is not mocked: *for whatsoever a man soweth, that shall he also reap.* For he that soweth to his flesh shall of the flesh reap corruption; but he that soweth to the Spirit shall of the Spirit reap life everlasting.

—Galatians 6:7–8

According as *he hath chosen us in him before the foundation of the world,* that we should be holy and without blame before him in love.

—Ephesians 1:4

Nevertheless the foundation of God standeth sure, having this seal, *The Lord knoweth them that are his.* And, Let every one that nameth the name of Christ depart from iniquity.

—2 Timothy 2:19

Neither is there any creature that is not manifest in his sight: but *all things are naked and opened unto the eyes of him* with whom we have to do.

—Hebrews 4:13

For God is not unrighteous to forget your work and labour of love, **which ye have shewed toward his name, in that ye have ministered to the saints, and do minister.**

—Hebrews 6:10

For the eyes of the Lord are over the righteous, and his ears are open unto their prayers: but the face of the Lord is against them that do evil.

—1 Peter 3:12

I know thy works, and thy labour, and thy patience, **and how thou canst not bear them which are evil: and thou hast tried them which say they are apostles, and are not, and hast found them liars.**

—Revelation 2:2

These biblical passages can certainly help us begin to understand what God knows about humans and what God knows about us personally. Consider the following information acquired from biblical passages:

» God knew you before you were formed in your mother's belly.
» God knew all about you while you were being formed within your mother.
» God knows you were formed in His image.
» God knew how, when, where, and why you were born.
» God has given you hope and a motivation to live.
» God has given you a body to use while you live your life.
» God has given you a brain with a conscience and wisdom so you can think, reason, and choose what you will do during your lifetime.
» God has given you senses so you can be aware of the world.
» God knows when you sit down and when you stand up.
» God has given you the ability to communicate.
» God knows what things you need before you ask Him.
» God has given you His comfort and His love.

» God will give you perfect peace when your mind is stayed on Him.
» God gives you air to breathe.
» God knows your motives for everything that you will do during your lifetime.
» God knows everywhere you will go during your lifetime.
» God knows how many steps you will take during your lifetime.
» God knows every thought you will have during your lifetime.
» God knows every word you will speak during your lifetime.
» God knows how many tears you will cry during your lifetime.
» God knows the intensity of your sorrow that caused your tears to form.
» God has given you the ability to know that you have had bad thoughts.
» God has given you the ability to know the difference between right and wrong.
» God has given you the ability to know when you say things that are wrong.
» God has given you the ability to know that you have done things that are wrong.
» God has given you opportunities to ask Him to forgive you for thinking things that are wrong, for saying things that are wrong, and for doing things that are wrong.
» God has given you the opportunity to decide if you will accept or reject His Love.
» God knows if you have asked Him to forgive you of your wrong thoughts and your wrong actions.
» God knows if you will ask Him to forgive your wrong thoughts and your wrong actions.
» God knows if you have made Jesus Christ the Lord of your life.
» God knows if you will make Jesus Christ the Lord of your life.
» God knows how long you will live on this earth.
» God will reward you for the way you live your life.

God's statements make it clear that He knows a mammoth amount of information for every person who has ever lived. However, these passages reveal only a small part of what God knows about us. As an example, since God is omniscient, consider what God knows about the human circulatory system.

The adult human heart contracts or beats about one hundred thousand times, pumping about two thousand gallons of blood, every day. During an average lifetime, the heart will beat about 2.5 billion times and will pump about sixty million gallons of blood. At any moment during your life, God knows exactly how many times your heart has beaten since it started beating only three weeks after you were conceived.[316] At that same moment, God also knows exactly how much blood has been pumped by your heart, and God knows exactly how many more heartbeats remain during your lifetime.

Through a microscope red blood cells, or erythrocytes, look like tiny red donuts. They are a major component of human blood because they carry oxygen from the lungs to the cells throughout the body. A healthy adult human makes over two million red blood cells every second and each red blood cell will live one hundred twenty days before it is recycled by the spleen.[317] As amazing as it seems, at any moment during your life, God knows the exact number of red blood cells in your body and He knows the number of days each blood cell has been floating through your arteries and veins. Dr. Paul Brand[318] provided some amazing information about human blood. He said that a speck of blood the size of this letter "o" contains five million red cells, three hundred thousand platelets, and seven thousand white cells.[319]

---

316. Swenson, Richard A., *More Than Meets the Eye*, p. 23.
317. Ibid., p. 24–26.
318. Dr. Paul Brand (1914–2003) was chief of Rehabilitation Branch of U.S. Public Health Service Hospital in Carville, LA, and a clinical professor of surgery at Louisiana State University Medical School. He is known for his leprosy research in India and attained world recognition as a hand surgeon.
319. Brand, Paul and Yancey, Philip, *In His Image*, Zondervan Publishing House, Grand Rapids, MI, 1984, p. 56.

Every red blood cell carries 280 million hemoglobin molecules.[320] The spleen removes about three hundred billion red blood cells from the circulating blood every day.[321] An average–sized adult male has about six quarts of blood in his circulatory system.[322]

God also knows all about each of the other components in your blood. God knows all about your platelets, which are essential for clotting. Individual platelets survive only a few days, and yet God knows the exact number of platelets that are in your body at any given moment. God knows precisely how many white blood cells are in your body at any moment. You likely have fifty billion white blood cells in circulation that are ready to attack unwelcome bacteria in your body. And if you are healthy, you should have a backup force of a hundred times more white blood cells waiting in your bone marrow to move into action whenever they are needed.[323]

Since He is omniscient, consider what else God knows about your body. God knows the exact number of cells in your body at any moment. Scientists estimate there are from ten to one hundred trillion cells in the human body. God does not have to estimate the number of cells in your body because He knows the exact number. Each cell in your body contains approximately a trillion atoms. The human body is composed of ten thousand trillion trillion atoms—a number greater than the stars in the universe! In each person, more than a trillion of these atoms are replaced every one–millionth of a second.[324] Yes, God knows the exact number of atoms in your body at any moment!

To better appreciate the "mind of God" and His unfathomable knowledge, consider that God knows all of the information on all of the components of our bodies at any moment in time. Then multiply this by all of the people who are living on the earth at this moment.

320. Ibid., p. 171.
321. Ibid., p. 58.
322. 3 August 2007 <www.infoplease.com/ce6/sci/A0807934.htm>.
323. Swenson, Richard A., *More Than Meets the Eye*, p. 27.
324. Ibid., p. 18, 20, and 94.

According to the United States Bureau of Census, the population of the earth was 6.642 billion people on January 5, 2008.[325] In addition, God knows this information for all of the people who have been on the earth from the time of creation until there will no longer be new people being added to the human population. And this knowledge is just for the human beings on the earth. We should realize that Almighty God also knows this same information for all of the animals, rocks, water, and elements on the earth. In addition, God knows the precise number of components in every galaxy in the universe, and He tracks their movements, their location, and their future just as closely as He does for the composition of everything on the earth because He is the omniscient God!

Surely you are asking at this point how God can keep track of all of this information about you. You may also be pondering how God can keep track of all of this information for every person who is living now, and how God has kept track of all of this information for every person who has ever lived. You should also be wondering how God can "keep track" of all of the material in the universe. Certainly, humans are unable to understand how God is capable of knowing and remembering all that He knows. An advertisement on a highway billboard succinctly sums up our situation. It says, "You're only human."[326] However, God has already provided much better answers for your questions about how He remembers information. God's answers are partially revealed in the following verses from the Bible:

> **How precious also are thy thoughts unto me, O God! how great is the sum of them! If I should count them, they are more in number than the sand: when I awake, I am still with thee.**
>
> —Psalm 139:17–18

---

325. 5 January 2008 <www.census.gov/main/www/popclock.html>.
326. The billboard advertised automobile insurance available from the Allstate Insurance Company and was located on Interstate 75 north of Atlanta, Georgia.

Behold, I am the LORD, the God of all flesh: is there any thing too hard for me?

— Jeremiah 32:27

But Jesus beheld them, and said unto them, With men this is impossible; but with God all things are possible.

— Matthew 19:26

And he said, The things which are impossible with men are possible with God.

— Luke 18:27

Now unto him that is able to do exceeding abundantly above all that we ask or think, according to the power that worketh in us.

— Ephesians 3:20

Could it be that *our* God is too small? Do we really appreciate His unfathomable mind? There is no way that any human being can truly appreciate this level of knowledge. Consider again the theories of evolution and the reinterpretation of the Bible's words so as to make the message of the Bible compatible with man's ideas. Is there any reason for the omniscient and omnipotent God to use the clumsy, slow, inefficient, and cruel process of biologic evolution to create humans? There is absolutely no reason that I can imagine as to why Almighty God would choose to create life through any form of evolution. Remember, this is the same God who created Adam from the dust of the ground, who created Eve from one of Adam's ribs, and this is the same God who has a definite purpose for our lives. We are not here by accident, nor are we here by chance. God thinks of us, God knows us inside and out, God cares for us, and God literally holds us together all of the time. Without God's loving "hand" on us, we would not exist!

God is omniscient in the true and complete definition of the word. So how much does God know? **God knows absolutely every-thing!**

Chapter 5

What Has God Done?
What Is God Doing?
What Will God Do?

All things were made by him; and without him was not any thing made that was made. In him was life; and the life was the light of men. And the light shineth in darkness; and the darkness comprehended it not.

—John 1:3–5

The Bible tells us with thousands of words and hundreds of passages what God has done, what God is doing, and what God will do.

What has God done?

God has created a universe and world that provide a pleasant place for humans to live in order that we may fulfill specific purposes that are important to Him. We can see some of God's glory and abilities in His creation. People, plants, animals, gemstones, water, and the celestial bodies are objects we can see. Subatomic particles, atoms, molecules, energy, gravity, air, and darkness are things we cannot see. God also created emotions, talents, and mental abilities that are not usually visible but are commonly used by people. God made it possible for many animals to be able to think, plan, remember, migrate, and communicate in ways that are essentially invisible to human observation.

God gave humans the ability to read, learn, think, remember, forget, laugh, love, speak, sing, sleep, reproduce, and so much more!

What is God doing now?

God is in control of the universe that He created. Jesus told His disciples that He is going to Heaven to prepare a place for all the people who receive His offer of forgiveness.[327] God is observing, evaluating, and remembering all of the motives, thoughts, words, and actions of every person of all time. God has books that record what every person has done during his or her lifetime. These books are described in the last book in the Bible. God says, "He that overcometh, the same shall be clothed in white raiment; and I will not blot out his name out of the book of life, but I will confess his name before my Father, and before his angels."[328] During the great tribulation, there will be people on the earth who will worship the dragon and the beast. The names of these people will not be "written in the book of life of the Lamb slain from the foundation of the world."[329] Also, during the time of judgment at the great white throne, it is recorded, "the books were opened: and another book was opened, which is the book of life: and the dead were judged out of those things which were written in the books, according to their works."[330] So what is God doing now? God is documenting the lives of all people in His books.

What will God do?

At the time of His choosing, God will bring the current period of history to a close. God will evaluate the life of every individual. God will determine if each and every person has at any time during their

327. "In my Father's house are many mansions: if it were not so, I would have told you. I go to prepare a place for you" (John 14:2).
328. Revelation 3:5
329. "And all that dwell upon the earth shall worship him, whose names are not written in the book of life of the Lamb slain from the foundation of the world" (Rev. 13:8).
330. Revelation 20:12b

lifetimes repented of their sin. God will know if each person has asked God to forgive them of their sins. God will reward each person who has received His offer of forgiveness. God will reject everyone who has not turned away from their sin and has not requested God to forgive their sins. The documentation for not receiving God's forgiveness is found in the book of life.[331] Chapter six provides a more detailed look at God's plans for the end of this age.

The best way to answer the questions, "What has God done?" "What is God doing?" and "What will God do?" is to read what is written in the Bible. Below is a sample of biblical references that state what God has done, is doing, and will do. The word "sample" is used because only a very small number of the Bible's passages that document God's activities are included in the following lists. To include all of God's actions would take a volume almost the size of the entire Bible.

The Holy Bible makes it perfectly clear that God is the Creator, the Sustainer, and the Redeemer! These references are categorized in one of these three groups:

1. The Creator section includes verses that describe God's creative activities.
2. The Sustainer section records God's involvement in the universe He created, and His involvement in human activity in order that His purposes will be successful.
3. The Redeemer section shares God's activity in His Plan to rescue rebellious and sinful people from the judgment they deserve. God's redemption allows people to experience His forgiveness and enjoy His blessings.

God is the Creator

In the beginning God created the heaven and the earth.

—Genesis 1:1

---

331. "And whosoever was not found written in the book of life was cast into the lake of fire" (Rev. 20:15).

And God said, Let there be light: and there was light.

—Genesis 1:3

And God said, Let the waters under the heaven be gathered together unto one place, and let the dry land appear: and it was so.

—Genesis 1:9

And God said, Let the earth bring forth grass, the herb yielding seed, and the fruit tree yielding fruit after his kind, whose seed is in itself, upon the earth: and it was so.

—Genesis 1:11

And God made two great lights; the greater light to rule the day, and the lesser light to rule the night: he made the stars also. And God set them in the firmament of the heaven to give light upon the earth.

—Genesis 1:16–17

And God created great whales, and every living creature that moveth, which the waters brought forth abundantly, after their kind, and every winged fowl after his kind: And God saw that it was good.

—Genesis 1:21

And God made the beast of the earth after his kind, and cattle after their kind, and every thing that creepeth upon the earth after his kind: and God saw that it was good.

—Genesis 1:25

So God created man in his own image, in the image of God created he him; male and female created he them.

—Genesis 1:27

And on the seventh day God ended his work which he had made; and he rested on the seventh day from all the work which he had made.

—Genesis 2:2

And the LORD God caused a deep sleep to fall upon Adam, and he slept: and he took one of his ribs, and closed up the flesh instead thereof; And the rib, which the LORD God had taken from man, made he a woman, and brought her unto the man.

—Genesis 2:21–22

For in six days the LORD made heaven and earth, the sea, and all that in them is, and rested the seventh day: wherefore the LORD blessed the sabbath day, and hallowed it.

—Exodus 20:11

Behold, the heaven and the heaven of heavens is the LORD'S thy God, the earth also, with all that therein is.

—Deuteronomy 10:14

For great is the LORD, and greatly to be praised: he also is to be feared above all gods. For all the gods of the people are idols: but the LORD made the heavens.

—1 Chronicles 16:25–26

He divideth the sea with his power, and by his understanding he smiteth through the proud. By his spirit he hath garnished the heavens; his hand formed the crooked serpent.

—Job 26:12–13

When I consider thy heavens, the work of thy fingers, the moon and the stars, which thou hast ordained; What is man, that thou art mindful of him? and the son of man, that thou visitest him? For thou hast made him a little lower than the angels, and hast crowned him with glory and honour. Thou madest him to have dominion over the works of thy hands; thou hast put all things under his feet.

—Psalm 8:3–6

The heavens declare the glory of God; and the firmament sheweth his handywork.

—Psalm19:1

By the word of the LORD were the heavens made; and all the host of them by the breath of his mouth.

—Psalm 33:6

The heavens are thine, the earth also is thine: as for the world and the fulness thereof, thou hast founded them.

—Psalm 89:11

Before the mountains were brought forth, or ever thou hadst formed the earth and the world, even from everlasting to everlasting, thou art God.

—Psalm 90:2

To him that by wisdom made the heavens: for his mercy endureth for ever. To him that stretched out the earth above the waters: for his mercy endureth for ever. To him that made great lights: for his mercy endureth for ever: The sun to rule by day: for his mercy endureth for ever: The moon and stars to rule by night: for his mercy endureth for ever.

—Psalm 136:5–9

Thus saith God the LORD, he that created the heavens, and

stretched them out; he that spread forth the earth, and that which cometh out of it; he that giveth breath unto the people upon it, and spirit to them that walk therein.

—Isaiah 42:5

For thus saith the LORD that created the heavens; God himself that formed the earth and made it; he hath established it, he created it not in vain, he formed it to be inhabited: I am the LORD; and there is none else.

—Isaiah 45:18

I have made the earth, the man and the beast that are upon the ground, by my great power and by my outstretched arm, and have given it unto whom it seemed meet unto me.

—Jeremiah 27:5

For, lo, he that formeth the mountains, and createth the wind, and declareth unto man what is his thought, that maketh the morning darkness, and treadeth upon the high places of the earth, The LORD, The God of hosts, is his name.

—Amos 4:13

And he answered and said unto them, Have ye not read, that he which made them at the beginning made them male and female, And said, For this cause shall a man leave father and mother, and shall cleave to his wife: and they twain shall be one flesh? Wherefore they are no more twain, but one flesh. What therefore God hath joined together, let not man put asunder.

—Matthew 19:4–6

In the beginning was the Word, and the Word was with God, and the Word was God. The same was in the beginning with

God. All things were made by him; and without him was not any thing made that was made. In him was life; and the life was the light of men. And the light shineth in darkness; and the darkness comprehended it not.

—John 1:1–5

He was not that Light, but was sent to bear witness of that Light. That was the true Light, which lighteth every man that cometh into the world. He was in the world, and the world was made by him, and the world knew him not. He came unto his own, and his own received him not. But as many as received him, to them gave he power to become the sons of God, even to them that believe on his name: Which were born, not of blood, nor of the will of the flesh, nor of the will of man, but of God. And the Word was made flesh, and dwelt among us, (and we beheld his glory, the glory as of the only begotten of the Father,) full of grace and truth.

—John 1:8–14

And when they heard that, they lifted up their voice to God with one accord, and said, Lord, thou art God, which hast made heaven, and earth, and the sea, and all that in them is.

—Acts 4:24

Known unto God are all his works from the beginning of the world.

—Acts 15:18

God that made the world and all things therein, seeing that he is Lord of heaven and earth, dwelleth not in temples made with hands.

—Acts 17:24

For the invisible things of him from the creation of the world are clearly seen, being understood by the things that are made, even his eternal power and Godhead; so that they are without excuse.

—Romans 1:20

For by him were all things created, that are in heaven, and that are in earth, visible and invisible, whether they be thrones, or dominions, or principalities, or powers: all things were created by him, and for him: And he is before all things, and by him all things consist.

—Colossians 1:16–17

For Adam was first formed, then Eve.

—1 Timothy 2:13

In hope of eternal life, which God, that cannot lie, promised before the world began.

—Titus 1:2

And, Thou, Lord, in the beginning hast laid the foundation of the earth; and the heavens are the works of thine hands: They shall perish; but thou remainest; and they all shall wax old as doth a garment; And as a vesture shalt thou fold them up, and they shall be changed: but thou art the same, and thy years shall not fail.

—Hebrews 1:10–12

For he spake in a certain place of the seventh day on this wise, And God did rest the seventh day from all his works.

—Hebrews 4:4

Thou art worthy, O Lord, to receive glory and honour and

power: for thou hast created all things, and for thy pleasure
they are and were created.

—Revelation 4:11

And sware by him that liveth for ever and ever, who created heaven, and the things that therein are, and the earth,
and the things that therein are, and the sea, and the things
which are therein, that there should be time no longer.

—Revelation 10:6

God is the Sustainer

And unto Adam he said, Because thou hast hearkened unto
the voice of thy wife, and hast eaten of the tree, of which I
commanded thee, saying, Thou shalt not eat of it: cursed is
the ground for thy sake; in sorrow shalt thou eat of it all the
days of thy life; Thorns also and thistles shall it bring forth
to thee; and thou shalt eat the herb of the field; In the sweat
of thy face shalt thou eat bread, till thou return unto the
ground; for out of it wast thou taken: for dust thou art, and
unto dust shalt thou return.

—Genesis 3:17–19

And I will establish my covenant with you; neither shall all
flesh be cut off any more by the waters of a flood; neither
shall there any more be a flood to destroy the earth.

—Genesis 9:11

And the LORD said, Behold, the people is one, and they have
all one language; and this they begin to do: and now nothing will be restrained from them, which they have imagined
to do. Go to, let us go down, and there confound their language, that they may not understand one another's speech.
So the LORD scattered them abroad from thence upon the
face of all the earth: and they left off to build the city.

—Genesis 11:6–8

But lift thou up thy rod, and stretch out thine hand over the sea, and divide it: and the children of Israel shall go on dry ground through the midst of the sea.

—Exodus 14:16

Behold, I will stand before thee there upon the rock in Horeb; and thou shalt smite the rock, and there shall come water out of it, that the people may drink. And Moses did so in the sight of the elders of Israel.

—Exodus 17:6

For I will have respect unto you, and make you fruitful, and multiply you, and establish my covenant with you.

—Leviticus 26:9

The LORD is longsuffering, and of great mercy, forgiving iniquity and transgression, and by no means clearing the guilty, visiting the iniquity of the fathers upon the children unto the third and fourth generation.

—Numbers 14:18

A land which the LORD thy God careth for: the eyes of the LORD thy God are always upon it, from the beginning of the year even unto the end of the year.

—Deuteronomy 11:12

When the LORD thy God shall cut off the nations from before thee, whither thou goest to possess them, and thou succeedest them, and dwellest in their land.

—Deuteronomy 12:29

For the LORD your God is he that goeth with you, to fight for you against your enemies, to save you.

—Deuteronomy 20:4

Be strong and of a good courage, fear not, nor be afraid of them: for the LORD thy God, he it is that doth go with thee; he will not fail thee, nor forsake thee.

—Deuteronomy 31:6

The eternal God is thy refuge, and underneath are the everlasting arms: and he shall thrust out the enemy from before thee; and shall say, Destroy them.

—Deuteronomy 33:27

Have not I commanded thee? Be strong and of a good courage; be not afraid, neither be thou dismayed: for the LORD thy God is with thee whithersoever thou goest.

—Joshua 1:9

The LORD killeth, and maketh alive: he bringeth down to the grave, and bringeth up. The LORD maketh poor, and maketh rich: he bringeth low, and lifteth up. He raiseth up the poor out of the dust, and lifteth up the beggar from the dunghill, to set them among princes, and to make them inherit the throne of glory: for the pillars of the earth are the LORD'S, and he hath set the world upon them. He will keep the feet of his saints, and the wicked shall be silent in darkness; for by strength shall no man prevail. The adversaries of the LORD shall be broken to pieces; out of heaven shall he thunder upon them: the LORD shall judge the ends of the earth; and he shall give strength unto his king, and exalt the horn of his anointed.

—1 Samuel 2:6–10

So Samuel called unto the LORD; and the LORD sent thunder and rain that day: and all the people greatly feared the LORD and Samuel.

—1 Samuel 12:18

For thou art my lamp, O LORD: and the LORD will lighten my darkness.

—2 Samuel 22:29

So the LORD sent pestilence upon Israel: and there fell of Israel seventy thousand men.

—1 Chronicles 21:14

If I shut up heaven that there be no rain, or if I command the locusts to devour the land, or if I send pestilence among my people; If my people, which are called by my name, shall humble themselves, and pray, and seek my face, and turn from their wicked ways; then will I hear from heaven, and will forgive their sin, and will heal their land.

—2 Chronicles 7:13–14

I know that thou canst do every thing, and that no thought can be withholden from thee.

—Job 42:2

For every beast of the forest is mine, and the cattle upon a thousand hills. I know all the fowls of the mountains: and the wild beasts of the field are mine.

—Psalm 50:10–11

He sendeth the springs into the valleys, which run among the hills. They give drink to every beast of the field: the wild asses quench their thirst. By them shall the fowls of the heaven have their habitation, which sing among the branches. He watereth the hills from his chambers: the earth is satisfied with the fruit of thy works. He causeth the grass to grow for the cattle, and herb for the service of man: that he may bring forth food out of the earth; And wine that maketh glad the heart of man, and oil to make his face to shine, and bread which strengtheneth man's heart.

—Psalm 104:10–15

Behold, he that keepeth Israel shall neither slumber nor sleep.

—Psalm 121:4

O LORD, thou has searched me, and known me. Thou knowest my downsitting and mine uprising, thou understandest my thought afar off. Thou compassest my path and my lying down, and art acquainted with all my ways. For there is not a word in my tongue, but, lo, O LORD, thou knowest it altogether. Thou hast beset me behind and before, and laid thine hand upon me. Such knowledge is too wonderful for me; it is high, I cannot attain unto it. Whither shall I go from thy spirit? or whither shall I flee from thy presence? If I ascend up into heaven, thou are there: if I make my bed in hell, behold, thou art there. If I take the wings of the morning, and dwell in the uttermost parts of the sea; Even there shall thy hand lead me, and thy right hand shall hold me. If I say, Surely the darkness shall cover me; even the night shall be light about me. Yea, the darkness hideth not from thee; but the night shineth as the day: the darkness and the light are both alike to thee. For thou hast possessed my reins: thou hast covered me in my mother's womb. I will praise thee for I am fearfully and wonderfully made: marvelous are thy works; and that my soul knoweth right well. My substance was not hid from thee, when I was made in secret, and curiously wrought in the lowest parts of the earth. Thine eyes did see my substance, yet being unperfect; and in thy book all my members were written, which in continuance were fashioned, when as yet there was none of them.

—Psalm 139:1–16

He healeth the broken in heart, and bindeth up their wounds. He telleth the number of the stars; he calleth them all by their names. Great is our Lord, and of great power: his understanding is infinite.

—Psalm 147:3–5

Who covereth the heaven with clouds, who prepareth rain for the earth, who maketh grass to grow upon the mountains. He giveth to the beast his food, and to the young ravens which cry.

—Psalm 147:8–9

Behold the fowls of the air: for they sow not, neither do they reap, nor gather into barns; yet your heavenly Father feedeth them. Are ye not much better than they?

—Matthew 6:26

Wherefore, if God so clothe the grass of the field, which to day is, and to morrow is cast into the oven, shall he not much more clothe you, O ye of little faith?

—Matthew 6:30

If ye then, being evil, know how to give good gifts unto your children, how much more shall your Father which is in heaven give good things to them that ask him?

—Matthew 7:11

And he saith unto them, Why are you fearful, O ye of little faith? Then he arose, and rebuked the winds and the sea; and there was a great calm.

—Matthew 8:26

Consider the ravens: for they neither sow nor reap; which

neither have storehouse nor barn; and God feedeth them: how much more are ye better than the fowls?

—Luke 12:24

The thief cometh not, but for to steal, and to kill, and to destroy: I am come that they might have life, and that they might have it more abundantly. I am the good shepherd: the good shepherd giveth his life for the sheep.

—John 10:10–11

He that spared not his own Son, but delivered him up for us all, how shall he not with him also freely give us all things?

—Romans 8:32

There hath no temptation taken you but such as is common to man: but God is faithful, who will not suffer you to be tempted above that ye are able; but will with the temptation also make a way to escape, that ye may be able to bear it.

—1 Corinthians 10:13

But my God shall supply all your need according to his riches in glory by Christ Jesus.

—Philippians 4:19

For this is the covenant that I will make with the house of Israel after those days, saith the Lord; I will put my laws into their mind, and write them in their hearts: and I will be to them a God, and they shall be to me a people:

—Hebrews 8:10

God is the Redeemer

And the Lord said, I will destroy man whom I have created from the face of the earth; both man, and beast, and the creeping thing, and the fowls of the air; for it repenteth me that I have made them.

—Genesis 6:7

And, behold, I, even I, do bring a flood of waters upon the earth, to destroy all flesh, wherein is the breath of life, from under heaven; and every thing that is in the earth shall die.

—Genesis 6:17

And they that went in, went in male and female of all flesh, as God had commanded him: and the LORD shut him in.

—Genesis 7:16

And every living substance was destroyed which was upon the face of the ground, both man, and cattle, and the creeping things, and the fowl of the heaven; and they were destroyed from the earth: and Noah only remained alive, and they that were with him in the ark. And the waters prevailed upon the earth an hundred and fifty days.

—Genesis 7:23-24

Then the LORD rained upon Sodom and upon Gomorrah brimstone and fire from the LORD out of heaven; And he overthrew those cities, and all the plain, and all the inhabitants of the cities, and that which grew upon the ground.

—Genesis 19:24-25

And he gave unto Moses, when he had made an end of communing with him upon mount Sinai, two tables of testimony, tables of stone, written with the finger of God.

—Exodus 31:18

And the LORD sent fiery serpents among the people, and they bit the people; and much people of Israel died.

—Numbers 21:6

And the LORD said unto Moses, Make thee a fiery serpent, and set it upon a pole: and it shall come to pass, that every one that is bitten, when he looketh upon it, shall live.

—Numbers 21:8

If ye forsake the LORD, and serve strange gods, then he will turn and do you hurt, and consume you, after that he hath done you good.

—Joshua 24:20

The LORD looked down from heaven upon the children of men, to see if there were any that did understand, and seek God. They are all gone aside, they are all together become filthy: there is none that doeth good, no,. not one.

—Psalm 14:2–3

As far as the east is from the west, so far hath he removed our transgressions from us.

—Psalm 103:12

Search me, O God, and know my heart: try me, and know my thoughts: And see if there be any wicked way in me, and lead me in the way everlasting.

—Psalm 139:23-24

The LORD is nigh unto all them that call upon him, to all that call upon him in truth.

—Psalm 145:18

The eyes of the LORD are in every place, beholding the evil
and the good.

—Proverbs 15:3

A false witness shall not be unpunished, and he that speaketh
lies shall perish.

—Proverbs 19:9

I said in mine heart, God shall judge the righteous and the
wicked: for there is a time there for every purpose and for
every work.

—Ecclesiastes 3:17

For God shall bring every work into judgment, with every
secret thing, whether it be good, or whether it be evil.

—Ecclesiastes 12:14

Therefore the Lord himself shall give you a sign; Behold, a
virgin shall conceive, and bear a son, and shall call his name
Immanuel.

—Isaiah 7:14

Behold, the day of the LORD cometh, cruel both with wrath
and fierce anger, to lay the land desolate: and he shall destroy the sinners thereof out of it. For the stars of heaven
and the constellations thereof shall not give their light: the
sun shall be darkened in his going forth, and the moon shall
not cause her light to shine. And I will punish the world for
their evil, and the wicked for their iniquity; and I will cause
the arrogancy of the proud to cease, and will lay low the
haughtiness of the terrible. I will make a man more precious
than fine gold; even a man than the golden wedge of Ophir.
Therefore I will shake the heavens, and the earth shall re-

move out of her place in the wrath of the LORD of hosts, and in the day of his fierce anger.

—Isaiah 13:9–13

He will swallow up death in victory; and the Lord GOD will wipe away tears from off all faces; and the rebuke of his people shall he take away from off all the earth: for the LORD hath spoken it.

—Isaiah 25:8

For the LORD is our judge, the LORD is our lawgiver, the LORD is our king; he will save us.

—Isaiah 33:22

I, even I, am he that blotteth out thy transgressions for mine own sake, and will not remember thy sins.

—Isaiah 43:25

Surely he hath borne our griefs, and carried our sorrows: yet we did esteem him stricken, smitten of God, and afflicted. But he was wounded for our transgressions, he was bruised for our iniquities: the chastisement of our peace was upon him; and with his stripes we are healed. All we like sheep have gone astray; we have turned every one to his own way; and the LORD hath laid on him the iniquity of us all.

—Isaiah 53:4–6

Behold, the LORD's hand is not shortened, that it cannot save; neither his ear heavy, that it cannot hear: But your iniquities have separated between you and your God, and your sins have hid his face from you, that he will not hear.

—Isaiah 59:1-2

For, behold, I create new heavens and a new earth: and the former shall not be remembered, nor come into mind.

—Isaiah 65:17

The heart is deceitful above all things, and desperately wicked: who can know it? I the LORD search the heart, I try the reins, even to give every man according to his ways, and according to the fruit of his doings.

—Jeremiah 17:9–10

For I have no pleasure in the death of him that dieth, saith the Lord GOD: wherefore turn yourselves, and live ye.

—Ezekiel 18:32

But the LORD sent out a great wind into the sea, and there was a mighty tempest in the sea, so that the ship was like to be broken.

—Jonah 1:4

Now the LORD had prepared a great fish to swallow up Jonah. And Jonah was in the belly of the fish three days and three nights.

—Jonah 1:17

And she shall bring forth a son, and thou shalt call his name JESUS: for he shall save his people from their sins.

—Matthew 1:21

I indeed baptize you with water unto repentance: but he that cometh after me is mightier than I, whose shoes I am not worthy to bear: he shall baptize you with the Holy Ghost, and with fire: Whose fan is in his hand, and he will throughly purge his floor, and gather his wheat into the garner; but he will burn up the chaff with unquenchable fire.

—Matthew 3:11-12

From that time Jesus began to preach, and to say, Repent: for the kingdom of heaven is at hand.

—Matthew 4:17

Not every one that saith unto me, Lord, Lord, shall enter into the kingdom of heaven; but he that doeth the will of my Father which is in heaven.

—Matthew 7:21

Whosoever therefore shall confess me before men, him will I confess also before my Father which is in heaven. But whosoever shall deny me before men, him will I also deny before my Father which is in heaven.

—Matthew 10:32-33

But I say unto you, That every idle word that men shall speak, they shall give account thereof in the day of judgment.

—Matthew 12:36

The Son of man shall send forth his angels, and they shall gather out of his kingdom all things that offend, and them which do iniquity; And shall cast them into a furnace of fire: there shall be wailing and gnashing of teeth.

—Matthew 13:41–42

For the Son of man shall come in the glory of his Father with his angels; and then he shall reward every man according to his works.

—Matthew 16:27

For as the lightning cometh out of the east, and shineth even unto the west; so shall also the coming of the Son of man be.

—Matthew 24:27

Then shall he say also unto them on the left hand, Depart from me, ye cursed, into everlasting fire, prepared for the devil and his angels.

—Matthew 25:41

But that ye may know that the Son of man hath power on earth to forgive sins, (he saith to the sick of the palsy,) I say unto thee, Arise, and take up thy bed, and go thy way into thine house.

—Mark 2:10–11

And then shall they see the Son of man coming in the clouds with great power and glory. And then shall he send his angels, and shall gather together his elect from the four winds, from the uttermost part of the earth to the uttermost part of heaven.

—Mark 13:26–27

For unto you is born this day in the city of David a Saviour, which is Christ the Lord.

—Luke 2:11

And the Holy Ghost descended in a bodily shape like a dove upon him, and a voice came from heaven, which said, Thou art my beloved Son; in thee I am well pleased.

—Luke 3:22

But when Jesus perceived their thoughts, he answering said unto them, What reason ye in your hearts? Whether is easier, to say, Thy sins be forgiven thee; or to say, Rise up and walk? But that ye may know that the Son of man hath power upon earth to forgive sins, (he said unto the sick of the palsy,) I say unto thee, Arise, and take up thy couch, and go into thine house.

—Luke 5:22–24

If I have told you earthly things, and ye believe not, how shall ye believe, if I tell you of heavenly things? And no man hath ascended up to heaven, but he that came down from heaven, even the Son of man which is in heaven. And as Moses lifted up the serpent in the wilderness, even so must the Son of man be lifted up: That whosoever believeth in him should not perish, but have eternal life. For God so loved the world, that he gave his only begotten Son, that whosoever believeth in him should not perish, but have everlasting life. For God sent not his Son into the world to condemn the world; but that the world through him might be saved.

—John 3:12–17

For the Father judgeth no man, but hath committed all judgment unto the Son.

—John 5:22

And this is the will of him that sent me, that every one which seeth the Son, and believeth on him, may have everlasting life: and I will raise him up at the last day.

—John 6:40

For the Lord himself shall descend from heaven with a shout, with the voice of the archangel, and with the trump of God: and the dead in Christ shall rise first.

—1 Thessalonians 4:16

Not by works of righteousness which we have done, but according to his mercy he saved us, by the washing of regeneration, and renewing of the Holy Ghost; Which he shed on us abundantly through Jesus Christ our Saviour.

—Titus 3:5–6

We love him, because he first loved us.

—1 John 4:19

As many as I love, I rebuke and chasten: be zealous therefore, and repent. Behold, I stand at the door, and knock: if any man hear my voice, and open the door, I will come in to him, and will sup with him, and he with me. To him that overcometh will I grant to sit with me in my throne, even as I also overcame, and am set down with my Father in his throne.

—Revelation 3:19–21

And they went up on the breadth of the earth, and compassed the camp of the saints about, and the beloved city: and fire came down from God out of heaven, and devoured them. And the devil that deceived them was cast into the lake of fire and brimstone, where the beast and the false prophet are, and shall be tormented day and night for ever and ever.

—Revelation 20:9–10

And I saw the dead, small and great, stand before God; and the books were opened: and another book was opened, which is the book of life: and the dead were judged out of those things which were written in the books, according to their works. And the sea gave up the dead which were in it; and death and hell delivered up the dead which were in them:

**and they were judged every man according to their works.
And death and hell were cast into the lake of fire. This is the
second death. And whosoever was not found written in the
book of life was cast into the lake of fire.**

—Revelation 20:12–15

**And I heard a great voice out of heaven saying, Behold, the
tabernacle of God is with men, and he will dwell with them,
and they shall be his people, and God himself shall be with
them, and be their God. And God shall wipe away all tears
from their eyes; and there shall be no more death, neither
sorrow, nor crying, neither shall there be any more pain: for
the former things are passed away. And he that sat upon the
throne said, Behold, I make all things new. And he said unto
me, Write: for these words are true and faithful.**

—Revelation 21:3–5

The scriptures just presented are only a sample of the hundreds of
passages in the Bible that document God's supernatural or miraculous
involvement in history. From these and the many other verses we can
know that Almighty God is intimately involved in every facet of human
life—past, present, and future!

What is the God of the Bible doing now?

God is still doing unique and miraculous things for people during our
lifetime. Being able to see the "hand of God" at work in our world
certainly makes reading, seeing, or hearing the daily news much more
interesting. Note: If you only listen to commercial radio, only watch
secular news reports, and only read newspapers and books that have
been produced or written by non–Christians who are either consciously
or unconsciously trying to diminish Christianity's influence on culture,
you will likely miss seeing most of God's activities that have benefited
and changed the lives of individuals around the world.

If you really want to see what God is doing today, you would be wise to read the reports and books written by Christian missionaries. Another great opportunity to witness what God is doing today is to follow the work of Christian mission organizations that are actively sharing the gospel with the people of the world. Some excellent examples of Christian organizations being used by God are listed here.

1. Gospel for Asia

K. P. Yohannan is the founder and president of Gospel for Asia[332], a mission organization involved in evangelism and church planting in the unreached regions of Asia. Gospel for Asia supports over 16,500 church planters in the heart of the 10/40 Window.[333] Gospel for Asia is one of the most effective mission forces in Asia today. The ministry has expanded beyond India to support native missions in Nepal, Myanmar, Cambodia, Laos, Thailand, and other Asian nations.

2. East Gates International

Ned Graham, one of the sons of evangelist Reverend Billy Graham, is the leader of East Gates International.[334] Since 1992 this Christian organization has been working in China to openly share the message of the Bible and the love of Jesus Christ. East Gates was the first Christian organization to negotiate with the China Christian Council to legally print and distribute over three million Bibles. East Gates has established close to two hundred fifty mini–libraries and distribution points in every province in China and Tibet. Through these locations the organization distributes Bibles and a wide variety of Christian literature. "East Gates seeks to equip Christians in China with the tools they need to grow in

---

332. The website for Gospel for Asia is <www.gfa.org>.
333. The 10/40 Window is an area of the world that contains the largest population of non–Christians in the world. The area extends from 10 degrees to 40 degrees north of the equator, and stretches from North Africa to China. 5 January 2008 <http://1040window.org/>.
334. The website for East Gates International is <www.eastgates.org>.

their relationship with God and to reach out with the Good News of Jesus Christ."[335]

3. Mission Aviation Repair Center

In 1964 Roald and Harriett Amundsen founded the Mission Aviation Repair Center[336] (MARC) located in Soldotna, Alaska. Len Wikstrom is the director of this organization. Because much of Alaska does not have roads connecting remote villages with one another, or to Anchorage with its limited road system, many people depend on airplanes to receive their basic needs and to reach out beyond their village. MARC's own three airplanes[337] with its aviation department that services other missionary aircraft are a vital part in getting God's Word to the people in remote Alaskan villages.

4. Answers in Genesis USA

In 1994 Ken Ham, Mark Looy, and Mike Zovath began Creation Science Ministries with a vision of building a creation museum. In 1994, Creation Science Ministries changed its name to Answers in Genesis. Ken Ham is the president of Answers in Genesis USA[338] with its headquarters and state-of-the-art 60,00-square-foot creation museum[339] located in Petersburg, Kentucky. [340] Answers in Genesis is an apologetics ministry dedicated to enabling Christians to defend their faith and proclaim the gospel of Jesus Christ effectively. The ministry focus is on providing answers to questions surrounding the book of Genesis, training in developing a biblical worldview, and exposing the fallacy of evolutionary ideas.

335. *East Gates Connection,* 15th Anniversary Edition, P.O. Box 2010 Sumner, WA, p. 2 and 24.
336. The website for Mission Aviation Repair Center is <www.marcalaska.org>.
337. The three aircraft are twin engine Piper Navajo's with seating for eight people.
338. The website for Answers in Genesis USA is <www.answersingenesis.org>.
339. The museum's purpose is to reach the unsaved with the message of the Gospel and to uphold the truth of God's Word from the very first verse.
340. "Behind the Scenes—A Look Back at God's Faithfulness," *Answers Magazine,* July–Sept. 2007, p. 84.

6. Coral Ridge Ministries

In 1974, D. James Kennedy[341] began Coral Ridge Ministries,[342] a multimedia outreach of Coral Ridge Presbyterian Church in Fort Lauderdale, Florida. In 1978 the Coral Ridge Hour began on two television stations. By 2007 the domestic audience has grown to about three million people and the telecast goes into many nations with a goal to expand to thirty million people by 2012. In addition, Coral Ridge Ministries produces radio programs, sponsors Evangelism Explosion International, Westminster Academy, and Knox Theological Seminary.

So let us return to the question, "What is God doing now?" The Bible says that . . .

1. Jesus is preparing a place for all those who love and obey Him.[343]
2. Jesus is holding everything together.[344]
3. Jesus is forgiving sins.[345]
4. God is keeping track of who knows Him and who is working iniquity.[346]
5. God knows "every idle word that men shall speak."[347]
6. God knows when a sparrow falls to the ground.[348]

---

341. Dr. D. James Kennedy passed away on 5 September 2007.
342. The website for Coral Ridge Ministries is <www.coralridge.org>.
343. "In my Father's house are many mansions: if it were not so, I would have told you. I go to prepare a place for you" (John 14:2).
344. "And he is before all things, and by him all things consist" (Col. 1:17).
345. "But that ye may know that the Son of man hath power on earth to forgive sins . . ." (Mark 2:10a).
346. "And then will I profess unto them, I never knew you: depart from me, ye that work iniquity" (Matt. 7:23).
347. "But I say unto you, That every idle word that men shall speak, they shall give account thereof in the day of judgment" (Matt. 12:36).
348. "Are not five sparrows sold for two farthings, and not one of them is forgotten before God?" (Luke 12:6).

7. God brings rain on the just and the unjust.[349]
8. God is drawing people to Himself.[350]
9. God will be with two or three people that are gathered in His name.[351]

God has all power and can do whatever He wants to do. God is holding His creation together. God is loving. God is watching. God is listening. God is remembering. God is allowing you to decide what you will believe, and God is allowing you to decide how you want to live. God is helping people who ask for His help. God is being very patient with people who have not yet come to the point where they realize their need for His forgiveness, Lordship, and for His salvation and redemption.

God is preparing to bring an end to His earthly exercise of identifying human beings who voluntarily and willingly submit to His dominion. The Bible says that God will visit "the iniquity of the fathers upon the children unto the third and fourth generation of them that hate me."[352] This biblical principle may help explain why some of the world's religions are passed on from generation to generation. When parents reject God's love, their children and grandchildren will undoubtedly be affected by their rebellious decision. It also appears that when leaders of a community or when officials of a government make unwise decisions, the members of that community will reap the consequences of the poor judgment.

---

349. "That ye may be the children of your Father which is in heaven: for he maketh his sun to rise on the evil and on the good, and sendeth rain on the just and on the unjust" (Matt. 5:45).
350. "For the Son of man is come to seek and to save that which was lost" (Luke 19:10).
351. "For where two or three are gathered together in my name, there am I in the midst of them" (Matt. 18:20).
352. "Thou shalt not bow down thyself unto them, nor serve them: for I the LORD thy God am a jealous God, visiting the iniquity of the fathers upon the children unto the third and fourth generation of them that hate me" (Deut. 5:9).

The fact is we can make our own decisions, we can go our own way no matter how it affects others. . . . God allows us that privilege. However, just like Adam and Eve, we have to bear the consequences of our sin. So many other innocent people are hurt because of our sin of trying to be our own boss, just as you and I have been hurt by the decision of Adam and Eve.[353]

Certainly Adam and Eve's decision to disobey God affected their lives. Their sin has also seriously impacted the life of every one of their descendents. All humans now have an inherited "old sin nature" from Adam and Eve's sin. The Bible refers to this nature as "the old man."[354]

God respects people so much that He will allow an individual to reject Him partially or even totally. God will allow you to believe in the "big bang" and in any of the theories of evolution as the explanation for the source of all that we see and experience.[355] God will allow you to believe in, to worship, and to pray to a false god. God will let you be an independent thinker, an intellectual, a free spirit, a pantheist, a New Ager, a member of a cult, a Wiccan, an agnostic, an atheist, a Deist, a Buddhist, a Mormon, a Muslim, a Hindu, a Satanist, a Jew who has not yet found the promised Messiah, a "completed" Jew, a liberal Christian, a conservative Christian, a notional Christian, a nominal Christian, an Anglican, an Apostolic, a Baptist, a Roman Catholic, a Disciple of Christ, a Lutheran, a Methodist, a Pentecostal, a Presbyterian, a Seventh–Day Adventist, or a member of any other

353. Snipes, Felix, "A Personal Knee mail from Felix," New Dimensions Evangelism, Atlanta, GA 30345-2208, June, 2007, p. 1.
354. "Lie not one to another, seeing that ye have put off the old man with his deeds" (Col. 3:9).
355. John D. Morris, president, Institute for Creation Research, El Cajon, CA, said in June 2007, "People choose to believe in evolution, not because of the evidence, but because creation implies a supernatural Creator, one to whom we must give an account of our actions some day, a thought unacceptable to the natural man."

religious or non–religious group. God will allow you to believe that the Holy Bible is a hoax. God will allow you to believe that the Holy Bible is a collection of myths, fables, old interesting stories, helpful maxims, and partially correct history. Or God will allow you to believe that the Bible is the perfectly accurate, non–deceptive, totally truthful, and completely trustworthy Word of God that will last forever.[356] God allows you and me to live and believe as we choose.

Remember . . .

» God knows everything!
» God knows all that we think.
» God knows all that we believe.
» God knows everything we say.
» God knows everything we do.
» God knows why we think the way we do.
» God knows why we believe the way we do.
» God knows why we say the things we say.
» God knows why we do what we do.
» God knows our thoughts.
» God knows our words.
» God knows our actions.
» God loves us so much that He allows us to choose whether or not we want to love Him!

---

356. "Heaven and earth shall pass away, but my words shall not pass away" (Matt. 24:35).

Chapter 6

What Does God Have Planned?

But as it is written, Eye hath not seen, nor ear heard, neither have entered into the heart of man, the things which God hath prepared for them that love him. But God hath revealed them unto us by his Spirit: for the Spirit searcheth all things, yea, the deep things of God.

—1 Corinthians 2:9–10

So what does the God of the Bible have planned for the future? A two-word answer to this question is, "A lot!" However, you deserve more information than only two words.

The Holy Bible records many events that God has planned for the future. Volumes have been written on "the end times," "the last days," "the latter times," etc. as described in the Bible. If this subject interests you, take the advice of former President Ronald Reagan: "Go for it" and read what has been written. But first, to obtain the proper perspective, you should read The Revelation, which is the last book of the Bible, and other related passages in the Bible. If you will do this, there is a real possibility that your heart will be stirred, and you will be blessed and challenged in a unique way as you read some of God's plans to bring this era of human history to an end.

Chapter five of this book contains many passages from the Bible documenting God's actions. These verses report what God has done, is doing now, and will be doing beyond today, yet they reference only a sample of the events that God has planned for the future.

It should be noted that there are significant differences of opinion among Christian groups as to the sequence, the timing, and the nature of future biblical events. Here is a brief overview of these differences.

The Christian millennium is a long period of time where there will be unprecedented peace and righteousness. The millennium is generally considered a period of one thousand years. This time period is closely associated with the second coming of the Lord Jesus Christ. Christians are divided into three positions regarding the millennium.[357]

1. A–millennialists believe the Bible's references to the millennium are only figurative. This position holds that the millennial reign of Jesus Christ occurs in the hearts of His followers. The A–millennial viewpoint believes that in future events there will not be a long period of time called the millennium.
2. Post–millennialists believe that the millennium will occur after the church has completed extraordinarily effective ministry through Spirit–empowered preaching of the gospel. Because God will have changed so many lives, the entire world will become peaceful and people will exhibit godly character and lead righteous lives for a long period of time according to the post–millennial viewpoint. Adherents to this position believe in the inherent goodness of mankind. The two world wars in the twentieth century virtually wiped out the post–millennial position. In 1970 Hal Lindsey said, "No self–respecting scholar who looks at the world conditions and the accelerating decline of Christian influence today is a 'post–millennialist.'"[358] In 2008 there are surely very few people who hold to a post–millennial viewpoint.

357. Weber, Timothy P., *Living in the Shadow of the Second Coming—American Pre-millennialism 1875–1925*, Oxford University Press, Inc., New York & Oxford, 1979, p. 9–11.
358. Lindsey, Hal and Carlson, C. C., The Late Great Planet Earth, Zondervan Publish House, Grand Rapids, MI, 15th printing, 1971, p. 176.

3. Pre–millennialists believe that the Lord Jesus Christ will return to earth before the millennium begins. Jesus Christ will establish the millennium by His might. There are two groups of pre-millennialists.

    A. Historicist pre–millennialists believe the prophetic scriptures give the entire history of the church in symbolic form. They look into church history to find prophetic fulfillments to see where the church is at any point in time in God's prophetic timetable. Historicist pre–millennialists believe the prophecies regarding "end times" are currently being fulfilled.

    B. Futurist pre–millennialists believe that none of the prophecies of the "last days" have been fulfilled in the history of the church. They expect all of the prophecies to come to pass within a short period of time in the future just before the return of Jesus Christ. All futurist pre–millennialists agree on the basic outline of future events. At the end of the present age, human society will grow worse and worse until the Antichrist will gain control of all nations. This will bring the world into a time of terrible terror known as the tribulation. The triumphant return of the Lord Jesus Christ at the Battle of Armageddon will end the reign of the Antichrist and the tribulation. After Jesus Christ has disposed of the Antichrist and his forces and has bound Satan in prison,[359] He will establish His millennial kingdom. The millennium will end after one thousand years when God will allow Satan to "be loosed out of his prison."[360] At this time Satan will deceive many of the people living during the millennium and cause them to revolt against God's earthly kingdom. To bring an end to this revolt, God will send fire from Heaven and devour all of those

---

359. "And he laid hold on the dragon, that old serpent, which is the Devil, and Satan, and bound him a thousand years" (Rev. 20:2).
360. "And when the thousand years are expired, Satan shall be loosed out of his prison" (Rev. 20:7).

involved with this rejection of His leadership.[361] Then God will bring about the resurrection of the dead, the judgment, and the creation of a new heaven and a new earth. Future pre–millennialists do not agree on the exact timing of the rapture of the church.[362] There are three positions on when the rapture of the church will occur that have been taken by future pre–millennialists. Pre–tribulationists believe the church will be raptured before the rise of the Antichrist and before the beginning of the tribulation. Mid–tribulationists believe the church will be raptured during the tribulation after Antichrist's rise to power but before God begins to bring preliminary judgments on the earth. Post–tribulationists believe the church will be on earth during the entire tribulation and the church will be raptured or rescued at the time of the second coming of Jesus Christ.

Future events recorded and described in the Bible

1. Jesus prepares the New Jerusalem
2. The rapture of the church
3. The great tribulation
4. The return of the Lord Jesus Christ
5. The Bema Seat judgment of Christians
6. God ends a satanic revolt
7. The millennial reign of the Lord Jesus Christ
8. The Great White Throne judgment

---

361. "And they went up on the breadth of the earth, and compassed the camp of the saints about, and the beloved city: and fire came down from God out of heaven, and devoured them" (Rev. 20:9).
362. The rapture of the church is the "catching away" of the church to meet Christ in the air. This event is recorded in 1 Thessalonians 4:16–17. "For the Lord himself shall descend from heaven with a shout, with the voice of the archangel, and with the trump of God: and the dead in Christ shall rise first: Then we which are alive and remain shall be caught up together with them in the clouds, to meet the Lord in the air: and so shall we ever be with the Lord."

9. Everything made new
10. Eternity

Information on each of these events is listed below:

1. Jesus prepares the New Jerusalem

The holy city or the New Jerusalem is a huge and marvelous city that God is preparing for all people of all time, including all Christians, who have repented of their sins and have put both their faith and their trust in Him.[363] Jesus Christ said, "Let not your heart be troubled: ye believe in God, believe also in me. In my Father's house are many mansions: if it were not so, I would have told you. I go to prepare a place for you."[364] All Christians should make note of this promise. Jesus Christ said He is preparing a place for you. If you are a Christian, your name may be on the front door of your heavenly home at this very moment.

You must read the majestic description of "the holy city," the "New Jerusalem" found in Revelation 21–22, to understand and visualize what God is building. It is certainly noteworthy that these are the last two chapters in the Bible. The magnitude of the New Jerusalem as revealed in Revelation 21:16 is amazing! Some Bible students believe that the New Jerusalem will have a pyramid shape with a square base, while others believe that the New Jerusalem will be in the shape of a cube.[365] Each side of the cube will be 1,380 miles in length. This means the New Jerusalem will have a "footprint" about the size of the area from Canada to the Gulf of Mexico and from the Atlantic Ocean to Colorado in the United States of America.[366] God has made it perfectly

---

363. "But now they desire a better country, that is, an heavenly: wherefore God is not ashamed to be called their God: for he hath prepared for them a city" (Heb. 11:16).
364. John 14:1–2
365. Lindsey, Hal, *There's a New World Coming—A Prophetic Odyssey*, Vision House Publishers, Santa Ana, CA, 1973, p. 291.
366. Morris, Henry M., *The Revelation Record—A Scientific and Devotional Commentary on the Book of Revelation*, Tyndale House Publishers, Inc. Wheaton, IL and

clear that the New Jerusalem is designed to be the eternal home for all people who have been "redeemed by the blood of the Lamb."[367]

According to the Bible, an individual's faith in the true God coupled with that person's diligently seeking God at some time during his lifetime is critically important to that individual's gaining access to Heaven and the holy city.[368] God has prepared or is preparing Heaven as a supernaturally beautiful place for the people who love Him.[369]

Henry M. Morris estimated the total number of people who have lived on earth from the time of Adam and Eve till 1965 to be approximately 40 billion. Perhaps another billion people have been added to this number during the last forty years. Assuming that people in the New Jerusalem will have the approximate body size of adult humans on earth, Heaven will be so large that it can easily accommodate 20 billion residents. Even with this mammoth population, each person living in the New Jerusalem could have a "block" of space about one-third of a mile in each direction.[370]

Hebrews 11 gives examples of people who lived and practiced their faith in God Almighty during the period of history described in the Old Testament of the Bible. This chapter commends the faith of Abel, Enoch, Noah, Abraham, Sara, Isaac, Jacob, Esau, Joseph, Moses, Rahab, Gideon, Barak, Samson, Jephthae, David, Samuel, and the prophets. Surely, there were millions of people who lived during the Old

---

Creation-Life Publishers, San Diego, CA, 1983, p. 450.

367. "In whom we have redemption through his blood, even the forgiveness of sins" (Col. 1:14). "And, having made peace through the blood of his cross, by him to reconcile all things unto himself; by him, I say, whether they be things in earth, or things in heaven" (Col. 1:20). "Forasmuch as ye know that ye were not redeemed with corruptible things, as silver and gold, from your vain conversation received by tradition from your fathers; But with the precious blood of Christ, as of a lamb without blemish and without spot" (1 Pet. 1:18–19).

368. "But without faith it is impossible to please him: for he that cometh to God must believe that he is, and that he is a rewarder of them that diligently seek him" (Heb. 11:6).

369. 1 Corinthians 2:9

370. Morris, Henry M., *The Revelation Record*, p. 451.

Testament period of history who repented of their sins and placed their faith and trust in God. Jesus Christ said that after He prepares a place and an eternal home for all of the people who choose to love, trust, and obey Him during their time on earth, He "will come again, and receive you unto myself; that where I am, there ye may be also."[371]

2. The rapture of the church

At some unknown time in the future, the Lord Jesus Christ plans to leave Heaven and return to earth for the specific purpose of removing all Christians from the earth. This event is called the "rapture,"[372] translation,[373] or the "catching up."[374] According to Dr. Thomas S. Mc-Call[375] the term "rapture" is derived from *rapere*, the Latin translation of "caught up" in the Vulgate translation of 1 Thessalonians 4:17.[376] The removal process of the church[377] from the earth will occur both suddenly and simultaneously worldwide.[378] The Bible says that it will take place at the sound of His trumpet and in the "twinkling of an eye."[379] The meeting of the Lord Jesus Christ with all Christians will take place

---

371. John 14:3
372. According to *The Funk and Wagnalls Standard Desk Dictionary*, 1977, p. 549 a definition of the word rapture is "the state of being rapt or transported; ecstatic joy; ecstasy."
373. Lindsey, Hal and Carlson, C. C., *The Late Great Planet Earth*, p. 137.
374. Sutton, Hilton, *The Pre-Tribulation Rapture of the Church—A Joyful Looking for His Appearing*, Harrison House, Inc., Tulsa, OK, 1982, p. 8.
375. Thomas S. McCall received his B.A. from the University of Texas, a B.D. and Th.M. from Talbot Theological Seminary, and a Th.D. from Dallas Theological Seminary.
376. Lindsey, Hal, McCall, Thomas, and others, *When Is Jesus Coming Again*, Creation House Publisher, Carol Stream, IL, 1974, p. 33.
377. The term *church* used here refers to born–again believers it Christ. This use of church does not include members of a church who have not personally received Jesus Christ as their Lord and Savior.
378. "And knew not until the flood came, and took them all away; so shall also the coming of the Son of man be" (Matt. 24:39).
379. "Behold, I shew you a mystery; We shall not all sleep, but we shall all be changed, In a moment, in the twinkling of an eye, at the last trump: for the trumpet shall sound, and the dead shall be raised incorruptible, and we shall be changed" (1 Cor. 15:51–52).

in the air above the surface of the earth.[380] The rapture of the church is a different event from the second coming of Jesus Christ.[381] Jesus is coming back for His "own"![382] Think of what a strange world earth will be one minute after the rapture occurs. There will be no Christians anywhere on the surface of the earth! Two verses that describe this event are provided here.

> **For the Lord himself shall descend from heaven with a shout, with the voice of the archangel, and with the trump of God: and the dead in Christ shall rise first: Then we which are alive and remain shall be caught up together with them in the clouds, to meet the Lord in the air: and so shall we ever be with the Lord.**
>
> —1 Thessalonians 4:16–17

A sequence of events in the rapture of the church is documented in this passage.

» First, the Lord Jesus Christ will descend from Heaven with three mighty sounds:
  › A shout,
  › The voice of the archangel,
  › A blast from the trumpet of God.
» Second, the dead in Christ shall rise first.[383]
» Third, the Christians that are alive at that moment in time will be caught up in the air
» Fourth, "and so shall we ever be with the Lord."[384]

---

380. 1 Thessalonians 4:17c
381. Zechariah 14:1–11 records an excellent view of the second coming of Jesus Christ.
382. "And if I go and prepare a place for you, I will come again, and receive you unto myself; that where I am, there ye may be also" (John 14:3).
383. The bodies of the Christians who have died will arise, be transformed, re-united with their souls, and taken to Christ's side in the air.
384. *What Can We Know About the Endtimes?*, Radio Bible Class, Grand Rapids,

Now consider the magnitude of God's knowledge put into action during the rapture of the church. If the rapture should take place this year, when the world's population is approximately 6.6 billion people, God must know who in this massive number are Christians and who are not. The Bible says that the rapture will occur very rapidly. When the time for the rapture occurs, God will know exactly who He will snatch away from the earth and who He will leave behind. [385] In the parable of the good shepherd, Jesus said, "To him the porter openeth; and the sheep hear his voice: and he calleth his own sheep by name, and leadeth them out."[386] It is possible that at the rapture of the church, God may call each believer by name as he or she is caught up from the surface of the earth.

A biblical case for the calling of each believer's name at the time of the rapture could be made by looking at how God addressed people in the Bible . . . He often called people by their name. A few examples are given here: God called Moses by name out of the midst of the burning bush.[387] God called the child Samuel by name when he ministered to the LORD before Eli.[388] Immediately before Jesus was betrayed in Gethsemane, Jesus called Peter by name.[389] Jesus called Simon by name when He told him that "Satan hath desired to have you, that he may sift you as wheat: But I have prayed for thee, that thy faith fail not."[390] After Lazarus had been dead for four days, Jesus "cried with a loud voice, Lazarus, come forth. And he that was dead came

---

Michigan, 1986, p. 6–7.

385. "When the Son of man shall come in his glory, and all the holy angels with him, then shall he sit upon the throne of his glory: And before him shall be gathered all nations: and he shall separate them one from another, as a shepherd divideth his sheep from the goats: And he shall set the sheep on his right hand, but the goats on the left" (Matt. 25:31–33).

386. John 10:3

387. Exodus 3:4b

388. 1 Samuel 3:1, 3:4, 3:6, and 3:8

389. Mark 14:37

390. Luke 22:31b–32a

forth,"[391] However, after the young daughter of the ruler of the synagogue had died, Jesus took her by the hand and said, "Maid, arise."[392] The statement, "the dead in Christ shall rise first,"[393] makes it clear that God knows the identity of all believers who have passed away since the creation of Adam and Eve! We cannot be positive that God will call all believers by their names at the rapture, but it does seem possible. However, you can be sure that God will neither mistakenly leave a believer behind nor mistakenly snatch away anyone who is not a believer at the rapture of the church. God's knowledge of His people also extends to every person who has repented of his or her sins and turned to Him for forgiveness and salvation.[394]

The word "rapture" is not used in the King James Version of the Holy Bible.[395] However, rapture is a word that is used to describe one of the most extraordinary events in history, an event that will take place precisely when God chooses. Here are some additional biblical passages that describe or refer to the rapture of the church.

Then shall two be in the field; the one shall be taken, and the other left. Two women shall be grinding at the mill; the one shall be taken, and the other left. Watch therefore: for ye know not what hour your Lord doth come.

—Matthew 24:40–42

Therefore be ye also ready: for in such an hour as ye think not the Son of man cometh.

—Matthew 24:44

---

391. John 11:43b–44a
392. Luke 8:54
393. 1 Thessalonians 4:16c
394. God knows the name of every person who has repented of his or her sins and has properly sought His forgiveness for his or her sins since the time of Adam and Eve.
395. *The New Strong's Concordance of the Bible, Concise Edition*, Thomas Nelson Publishers, Nashville, TN, 1985, p. 504, does not document the use of the word "rapture" in the King James Version of the Bible.

Watch ye therefore, and pray always, that ye may be accounted worthy to escape all these things that shall come to pass, and to stand before the Son of man.

—Luke 21:36

And if I go and prepare a place for you, I will come again, and receive you unto myself; that where I am, there ye may be also.

—John 14:3

Behold, I shew you a mystery; We shall not all sleep, but we shall all be changed, In a moment, in the twinkling of an eye, at the last trump: for the trumpet shall sound, and the dead shall be raised incorruptible, and we shall be changed.

—1 Corinthians 15:51–52

Now we beseech you, brethren, by the coming of our Lord Jesus Christ, and by our gathering together unto him.

—2 Thessalonians 2:1

It should be noted that there are at least five differing views among authorities on the Bible as to when and how the rapture will occur and when Jesus will return to the earth.[396] These will be briefly mentioned for your consideration:

A. Pre–tribulation rapture—All true believers in Christ will suddenly be caught up in the air to go with the Lord to Heaven. This rapture will include all believers throughout the Church age.[397] A strong support for a pre–tribulation rapture is found in Jesus' statement, "I also will keep thee from the hour of temptation, which shall come upon all the world, to try them that dwell upon

---

396. Lindsey, Hal and McCall, Thomas S., *When is Jesus Coming Again?*, p. 3.
397. Ibid., p. 34.

the earth."[398] The seven-year tribulation period will begin immediately after the rapture of the church.[399] The seven-year tribulation period will end when the Lord Jesus Christ stands on the Mount of Olives adjacent to Jerusalem.[400]

B. Partial rapture—Only spiritual believers in Christ will be caught up before the tribulation. Carnal believers will have to suffer through all of the terrible tribulation along with the rest of the world.[401]

C. Mid-tribulation rapture—At the mid-point, or three and one-half years into the tribulation, all Christians will suddenly be caught up in the air to go with the Lord to Heaven.[402]

D. Post-tribulation rapture—The rapture of all Christians will occur just before the triumphant return of the Lord Jesus Christ. In this view Jesus Christ meets the saints in the air and the Lord proceeds to earth and brings an end to the tribulation. Following the defeat of the armies of the world and their leaders, Jesus immediately establishes His millennial reign on the earth. The raptured believers do not go immediately to Heaven.[403]

E. Past-tribulation rapture—In this view of the rapture, Jesus Christ could come back to earth today and immediately set up His millennial kingdom. The period known as the great tribulation will have already occurred during the Church age.[404]

Regardless of which of the preceding viewpoints is correct, Christians should never terminate fellowship with another Christian because of a Bible-based difference on interpretation over the time of the rap-

398. Revelation 3:10b
399. Dalton, Hollis L., *The Consummation of the Ages—A Countdown to the End of Time*, self-published, 101 Cayle Ave., Longwood, FL 32750, 1977, p. 10.
400. Zechariah 14:2–4
401. Lindsey, Hal and McCall, Thomas S., *When is Jesus Coming Again*, p. 35.
402. Ibid., p. 43.
403. Ibid., p. 56.
404. Ibid., p. 70.

ture and the time of the great tribulation.[405] In John 14:3b, the Lord Jesus Christ said, "I will come again, and receive you unto myself; that where I am, there ye may be also will." God has promised that He will return to earth.

3. The Great Tribulation

The great tribulation is described in many passages from both the Old and the New Testaments of the Bible.[406] God will send the great tribulation upon the earth to accomplish His purposes. It will be a time of extraordinarily great suffering and affliction. There is disagreement between some Bible students on whether the great tribulation will precede or follow the millennial reign of the Lord Jesus Christ, while some believe that it may come just before the ushering in of the new heavens and the new earth.[407] The historicist pre–millennialist point of view of the great tribulation adds the possibility that it occurred when the Roman legions destroyed Jerusalem in A.D. 70, while other scholars believe it may be continuing for the Jewish people through the last two thousand years.[408]

Certainly significant tribulation has been, and is being, experienced by many Christians. Some Christians in the future will surely experience major tribulation and serious persecution. However, the great tribulation is generally believed to be a specific period of time that will last seven years. Pre–tribulationists generally believe the seven-year period will begin at the time of the rapture of the church.[409]

Many Bible scholars believe that during the first three and a half years of the great tribulation, the Antichrist and the False Prophet will take control of the world's government. They will promise peace

---

405. Ibid., p. 73.
406. Daniel 12:1, Matthew 24:21, and Revelation 7:14
407. Knight, George W. and Ray, Rayburn W., *The Illustrated Bible Dictionary*, Barbour Publishing, Inc. Uhrichsville, Ohio, 2005, p. 337.
408. 4 January 2008 <http://en.wikipedia.org/wiki/Tribulation> p. 1.
409. Rogers, Adrian, *Countdown in the Holy Land*, Love Worth Finding Ministries, Memphis, TN, (date of publication not provided), p. 19.

and safety[410] for all those who follow their leadership. But the world's government system led by the Antichrist will cause great hardship for all people who do not comply with their demands.[411] At the mid-point of the great tribulation, the Antichrist will sustain and survive a deadly wound and he will cause fire to come down from heaven in the sight of men.[412] The Antichrist will then proclaim himself to be God[413] and will cause an image to be created of himself.[414] All of the world's population who do not have their names written in the book of life of the Lamb will worship the Antichrist as their god.[415]

At some point during the first half of the great tribulation, the Jewish people of Israel will build a third temple in Jerusalem.[416] The first Jewish temple was built over three thousand years ago in Jerusalem by King Solomon.[417] The first temple was destroyed by the armies of King Nebuchadnezzar, the king of Babylon.[418] Following the seventy-year exile of the Jewish people in Babylon, a smaller second Jewish temple was rebuilt in Jerusalem over twenty-four hundred years ago.[419] The second Jewish temple was magnificently restored by King Herod about two thousand years ago, but it lacked the Ark of the Covenant. The restored second temple was the edifice that was being used by the Jewish people when Jesus Christ was crucified.[420] After a two-year-long siege of Jerusalem, Titus and the Roman legions under his command destroyed the second Jewish temple in A.D. 70.

---

410. 1 Thessalonians 5:3
411. Revelation 13:5-7
412. Revelation 13:12-13
413. 2 Thessalonians 2:4
414. Revelation 13:14
415. Revelation 13:8
416. Revelation 11:1-2
417. 1 Kings 6:1
418. 2 Kings 25:8-9
419. Ezra 3:10-13
420. Edersheim, Alfred, *The Temple, Its Ministry and Services as they were at the time of Christ*, Wm. B. Eerdmans Publishing Co. Grand Rapids, MI, July 1972, p. 61.

Also during the first three and a half years of the tribulation, God will allow a false religion to grow to the point that it will dominate the world.[421] The seven seal judgments[422] and the seven trumpet judgments[423] described in the Revelation will fall upon the nations bringing indescribable horror, causing the death of millions of people. Incredibly, most surviving men and women on the earth will continue to curse the true Creator God of the universe. However there will be a great multitude of Gentiles who will turn to God during the tribulation.[424] Sadly, many of these "tribulation Christians" will be martyred for their decision to trust in Jesus Christ as their Lord and Savior. In Revelation 7:9, John refers to these tribulation Christians as "a great multitude, which no man could number, of all nations, and kindreds, and people, and tongues."

As terrible as the first half of the tribulation will be, the second half of the tribulation will be immensely worse. Seven angels carrying seven vials filled with the wrath of God will pour them out on the earth.[425] Even in the midst of these horrific worldwide plagues, people will not repent of their sin.[426] The city of Babylon will be destroyed in one day.[427] The great tribulation will come to an end at the conclusion of the Battle of Armageddon,[428] when the Lord Jesus Christ will appear in the sky riding a white horse[429] followed by the armies of Heaven all mounted on white horses.[430] He will have on His clothing the following

---

421. Revelation 17 provides a description of the impact of a worldwide, non-Christian religion.
422. The seven seal judgments are described in Revelation 6:1–17 and Revelation 8:1–6.
423. The seven trumpet judgments are described in Revelation 8:6–9:21 and Revelation 11:15–19.
424. *What Can We Know About the Endtimes?*, Radio Bible Class, p. 12–13.
425. Revelation 15:1–16:21
426. Revelation 16:9
427. Revelation 18:8
428. Revelation 16:16
429. Revelation 19:11
430. Revelation 19:14

titles, "KING OF KINGS, AND LORD OF LORDS."[431] The Lord Jesus will destroy all of the armies of the world and capture the beast and the False Prophet.[432] A description is given in Zechariah 14:12 of God's terrible judgment on all the people who have rebelled against God. This passage says, "Their flesh shall consume away while they stand upon their feet, and their eyes shall consume away in their holes, and their tongue shall consume away in their mouth." God's fiery judgment will be horrendous on all of His enemies!

The great tribulation will accomplish the following two purposes: First, it will bring tremendous judgment and punishment upon all of the nations that have rejected God's love and leadership and that have oppressed His people.[433] Second, it will bring the nation of Israel to the place where she can be restored to the position of spiritual favor that she once possessed in God's eyes. Israel will suffer with the other nations, but only more intensely.[434] The suffering of Israel during the great tribulation has been described as the time of Jacob's trouble.[435]

4. The return of the Lord Jesus Christ

The highly visible return of the Lord Jesus Christ was mentioned in the earlier section about the great tribulation. When Jesus Christ returns to earth, He will come back in a similar manner to His departure. Consider the following passages which concern this return.

And when he had spoken these things, while they beheld, he was taken up; and a cloud received him out of their sight. And while they looked stedfastly toward heaven as he went up, behold, two men stood by them in white apparel; Which also said, Ye men of Galilee, why stand ye gazing up into

---

431. Revelation 19:16
432. Revelation 19:18–21
433. Lindsey, Hal, McCall, Thomas, and others, *When Is Jesus Coming Again*, p. 39.
434. *What Can We Know About the Endtimes?*, Radio Bible Class, p. 13.
435. "Alas! for that day is great, so that none is like it: it is even the time of Jacob's trouble; but he shall be saved out of it" (Jer. 30:7).

heaven? **this same Jesus, which is taken up from you into heaven, shall so come in like manner as ye have seen him go into heaven. Then returned they unto Jerusalem from the mount called Olivet, which is from Jerusalem a sabbath day's journey.**

—Acts 1:9–12

And Enoch also, the seventh from Adam, prophesied of these, saying, Behold, the Lord cometh with ten thousands of his saints, To execute judgment upon all, and to convince all that are ungodly among them of all their ungodly deeds which they have ungodly committed, and of all their hard speeches which ungodly sinners have spoken against him.

—Jude 14–15

Matthew 24:15–31 also documents the return of the Lord Jesus Christ. One of the key verses in this passage is Matthew 24:27, which states, **"For as the lightning cometh out of the east, and shineth even unto the west; so shall also the coming of the Son of man be."** Yes, the entire earth will witness the Lord's return. The visible return of the Lord Jesus Christ to earth may well be the most spectacular event of all time!

5. The millennial reign of the Lord Jesus Christ

Different interpretations of the millennium were shared at the beginning of this chapter. I myself believe that the Scriptures teach that the millennium will be an actual period in future history that will last for one thousand years. During this time, the Lord Jesus Christ will literally and physically reign over or govern the entire earth from Jerusalem.[436]

---

436. "And many people shall go and say, Come ye, and let us go up to the mountain of the LORD, to the house of the God of Jacob; and he will teach us of his ways, and we will walk in his paths: for out of Zion shall go forth the law, and the word of the LORD from Jerusalem" (Isa. 2:3).

Because of the Lord Jesus Christ's leadership and blessing, both the climate and civilization around the earth will be pleasant and peaceful.[437] The following passage describes this unique era in the history of the world.

> **But in the last days it shall come to pass, that the mountain of the house of the LORD shall be established in the top of the mountains, and it shall be exalted above the hills; and people shall flow unto it. And many nations shall come, and say, Come, and let us go up to the mountain of the LORD, and to the house of the God of Jacob; and he will teach us of his ways, and we will walk in his paths: for the law shall go forth of Zion, and the word of the LORD from Jerusalem. And he shall judge among many people, and rebuke strong nations afar off; and they shall beat their swords into plowshares, and their spears into pruninghooks: nation shall not lift up a sword against nation, neither shall they learn war any more. But they shall sit every man under his vine and under his fig tree; and none shall make them afraid: for the mouth of the LORD of hosts hath spoken it. For the people will walk every one in the name of his god, and we will walk in the name of the LORD our God for ever and ever.**
>
> —Micah 4:1–5

In the millennium there will be a radical change in the behavior of animals. Fierce and dangerous animals will no longer attempt to kill and eat their prey. The following passage describes animal behavior during the millennium:

---

437. "Then shall he give the rain of thy seed, that thou shalt sow the ground withal; and bread of the increase of the earth, and it shall be fat and plenteous: in that day shall thy cattle feed in large pastures. The oxen likewise and the young asses that ear the ground shall eat clean provender, which hath been winnowed with the shovel and with the fan" (Isa. 30:23–24).

> **The wolf also shall dwell with the lamb, and the leopard shall lie down with the kid; and the calf and the young lion and the fatling together; and a little child shall lead them. And the cow and the bear shall feed; their young ones shall lie down together: and the lion shall eat straw like the ox. And the sucking child shall play on the hole of the asp, and the weaned child shall put his hand on the cockatrice' den. They shall not hurt nor destroy in all my holy mountain: for the earth shall be full of the knowledge of the LORD, as the waters cover the sea.**
>
> —Isaiah 11:6–9

God plans to construct a place of worship for people living during the millennium. The following passage describes this event:

> **In that day will I raise up the tabernacle of David that is fallen, and close up the breaches thereof; and I will raise up his ruins, and I will build it as in the days of old.**
>
> —Amos 9:11

The "tabernacle of David" described by Amos may be the same tabernacle that Moses and Aaron constructed following the plans given by God on Mt. Sinai.[438]

The millennium will be God's demonstration of what human rulers throughout the history of the world have promised, but never provided. For one thousand years,[439] God will show how His government can promote and provide true peace, prosperity, and security for all people at the same time!

---

438. Exodus 25–30 provides a detailed description of the Tabernacle.
439. "And they lived and reigned with Christ a thousand years. But the rest of the dead lived not again until the thousand years were finished. This is the first resurrection. Blessed and holy is he that hath part in the first resurrection: on such the second death hath no power, but they shall be priests of God and of Christ, and shall reign with him a thousand years" (Rev. 20:4c–6).

6. God ends a satanic revolt

At the conclusion of the peaceful millennium God will allow Satan to have one last opportunity to deceive the nations. The following passage describes this "last battle":

> **And when the thousand years are expired, Satan shall be loosed out of his prison, And shall go out to deceive the nations which are in the four quarters of the earth, Gog and Magog, to gather them together to battle: the number of whom is as the sand of the sea. And they went up on the breadth of the earth, and compassed the camp of the saints about, and the beloved city: and fire came down from God out of heaven, and devoured them. And the devil that deceived them was cast into the lake of fire and brimstone, where the beast and the false prophet are, and shall be tormented day and night for ever and ever.**
>
> —Revelation 20:7–10

God will give all the people living at the end of the millennium one last opportunity to demonstrate their acceptance or rejection of His sovereign lordship. At the beginning of the millennium all of the people living on the earth will have chosen to honor and obey the Lord Jesus Christ. Sadly, some of the children and descendents of the families that began the millennium will have chosen not to accept the lordship of Jesus Christ. These people will not be believers and will not be faithful to the Lord. God will know who these people are and He will allow them to show their "true colors" in this "last battle."[440] These nonbelievers will be deceived by Satan, and they will organize themselves for battle against Jesus Christ and His followers. However, their defeat will be swift and complete, as God will send fire

---

440. Lindsey, Hal and Carlson, C. C., *The Late Great Planet Earth*, p. 177.

from Heaven to devour them.[441] This last satanic revolt will be quickly terminated by Almighty God.

7. The judgment seat of Christ

The following passages describe the event known as the judgment seat of Christ.

> But why dost thou judge thy brother? or why dost thou set at nought thy brother? for we shall all stand before the judgment seat of Christ. For it is written, As I live, saith the Lord, every knee shall bow to me, and every tongue shall confess to God. So then every one of us shall give account of himself to God.
>
> —Romans 14:10–12

> For we are labourers together with God: ye are God's husbandry, ye are God's building. According to the grace of God which is given unto me, as a wise masterbuilder, I have laid the foundation, and another buildeth thereon. But let every man take heed how he buildeth thereupon. For other foundation can no man lay than that is laid, which is Jesus Christ. Now if any man build upon this foundation gold, silver, precious stones, wood, hay, stubble; Every man's work shall be made manifest: for the day shall declare it, because it shall be revealed by fire; and the fire shall try every man's work of what sort it is. If any man's work abide which he hath built thereupon, he shall receive a reward. If any man's work shall be burned, he shall suffer loss: but he himself shall be saved; yet so as by fire. Know ye not that ye are the temple of God, and that the Spirit of God dwelleth in you?
>
> —1 Corinthians 3:9–16

---

441. Revelation 20:9

**For we must all appear before the judgment seat of Christ;
that every one may receive the things done in his body, according to that he hath done, whether it be good or bad.**

—2 Corinthians 5:10

The judgment seat of Christ will be a time when the works of all believers of all ages will be evaluated and judged by the Lord Jesus Christ.[442] This specific time of judgment is only for believers. Non–believers will have their time of judgment during a different event known as the Great White Throne judgment. This is discussed in the next section. The judgment seat of Christ is not a time to determine if an individual is a believer. God has previously made this determination for every person present at the judgment seat of Christ.[443]

The judgment seat of Christ is also called the Bema[444] seat judgment. The name of the Bema seat comes from the ancient Olympic games held in Greece. At the finish line of the Olympic race course, a judge was seated on a Bema seat. It was from this position that the first, second, and third place winners in the athletic event were identified. Following the event, the judge seated on the Bema would present the appropriate awards to those who competed in the contest.

Some Bible scholars believe that the judgment seat of Christ will occur individually for every believer at the moment of his or her death. Others believe that the judgment seat of Christ will occur for all believers at the same time at some time during the end times. God knows precisely at what time the judgment seat of Christ will take

---

442. "I said in mine heart, God shall judge the righteous and the wicked: for there is a time there for every purpose and for every work" (Eccl. 3:17).
443. "For God so loved the world, that he gave his only begotten Son, that whosoever believeth in him should not perish, but have everlasting life" (John 3:16) and "That if thou shalt confess with thy mouth the Lord Jesus, and shalt believe in thine heart that God hath raised him from the dead, thou shalt be saved" (Rom. 10:9).
444. The word "Bema" is not found in the King James Version of the Bible according to *The New Strong's Concordance of the Bible, Concise Edition.*

place, and it is extremely important that every believer be ready for this perfect, personal, and penetrating evaluation of his or her life. At the judgment seat of Christ, the life of every believer will be individually evaluated by how faithfully he or she served, obeyed, and followed Jesus Christ.[445] God said, through one of His prophets, Azariah, "your work shall be rewarded."[446]

First Corinthians 3 provides a wealth of information about how God will judge our lives. We should understand that the life of every Christian is built on the foundation of Jesus Christ.[447] Using the metaphor of a building or temple constructed by the individual Christian to represent his or her life is an extraordinarily effective way to demonstrate what is important to God.[448] God is looking for building construction utilizing His ordained building materials—gold, silver, and precious stones. However, inferior and undesirable building materials—wood, hay, and stubble—will also be used by Christians in the construction of their "life building."[449] God plans to judge every Christian's "life building" or temple by fire to visually demonstrate what sorts of construction materials have been used.[450] The undesirable materials will be burned by God's fire and will be a loss for the believer.[451] The desirable building materials will not be burned up and their survival will bring glory to God and will also earn the Christian

445. "All about God, Bema seat—what is it and when is it?" 4 January 2008 <www.allaboutgod.com/bema-seat.htm>.
446. "Be ye strong therefore, and let not your hands be weak: for your work shall be rewarded" (2 Chron. 15:7).
447. "For other foundation can no man lay than that is laid, which is Jesus Christ" (1 Cor. 3:11).
448. "Know ye not that ye are the temple of God, and that the Spirit of God dwelleth in you?" (1 Cor. 3:16).
449. "Now if any man build upon this foundation gold, silver, precious stones, wood, hay, stubble" (1 Cor. 3:12).
450. "Every man's work shall be made manifest: for the day shall declare it, because it shall be revealed by fire; and the fire shall try every man's work of what sort it is" (1 Cor. 3:13).
451. "If any man's work shall be burned, he shall suffer loss: but he himself shall be saved; yet so as by fire" (1 Cor. 3:15).

a reward from Jesus Christ.[452]

The Bible reveals that God plans to reward all Christians who were faithful to Him or whose lives were "well-lived" with one or more crowns.[453] Since the judgment seat or the Bema seat of Christ will be a time for believers to give an account of the way they have lived their lives, this would be a logical and an appropriate time for the Lord Jesus Christ to reward believers with their crowns. The following is a list of crowns that God may be presenting at the Judgment Seat of Christ.[454]

Name of crown	Scripture reference
Incorruptible crown	1 Corinthians 9:25; 2 Timothy 2:5
Crown of rejoicing	1 Thessalonians 2:19[455]
Crown of righteousness	2 Timothy 4:8[456]
Crown of life	James 1:12[457]; Revelation 2:10[458]
Crown of glory	1 Peter 5:4[459]

452. "If any man's work abide which he hath built thereupon, he shall receive a reward" (1 Cor. 3:14).
453. "Know ye not that they which run in a race run all, but one receiveth the prize? So run, that ye may obtain. And every man that striveth for the mastery is temperate in all things. Now they do it to obtain a corruptible crown; but we an incorruptible" (1 Cor. 9:24–25) and "And if a man also strive for masteries, yet is he not crowned, except he strive lawfully" (2 Tim. 2:5).
454. Morris, Henry M., *The Defender's Study Bible—King James Version*, p. 1331.
455. "For what is our hope, or joy, or crown of rejoicing? Are not even ye in the presence of our Lord Jesus Christ at his coming?" (1 Thess. 2:19).
456. "Henceforth there is laid up for me a crown of righteousness, which the Lord, the righteous judge, shall give me at that day: and not to me only, but unto all them also that love his appearing" (2 Tim. 4:8).
457. "Blessed is the man that endureth temptation: for when he is tried, he shall receive the crown of life, which the Lord hath promised to them that love him" (Jam. 1:12).
458. "Fear none of those things which thou shalt suffer: behold, the devil shall cast some of you into prison, that ye may be tried; and ye shall have tribulation ten days: be thou faithful unto death, and I will give thee a crown of life" (Rev. 2:10).
459. "And when the chief Shepherd shall appear, ye shall receive a crown of glory that fadeth not away" (1 Pet. 5:4).

The judgment seat of Christ will be a time when God will demonstrate his omniscience to every Christian. God's total and complete knowledge will recall and reveal all of the thoughts, motives, attitudes, words, works, and actions generated by the individual throughout his or her lifetime. God will show us how and when we wasted our time, and how and when we followed His leadership, and accomplished work that brought glory and honor to Him. God will surely show the effect that an individual's attitudes, thoughts, words, works, and actions had on the individual, and how they influenced and impacted the lives of others. We cannot change what we have already done with our lives. However, Christians can start today living a life that will bring honor and glory to their Lord and Savior. How we live the remainder of our lives is our decision and it will be evaluated thoroughly at the judgment seat of Christ.

8. The Great White Throne judgment

At the Great White Throne, God will judge all of the people who have rejected His love, all of the people who have not repented of their sins, and all of the people who have died without having their sins forgiven by Almighty God.[460] Sadly, this will be a very large group of people. The people present at the Great White Throne judgment will include unbelievers of Old Testament days, the Church age, the tribulation, and the millennium.[461] No Christians will be present and no Christians will be judged at the Great White Throne.[462] For our own benefit and to make this portion of the book crystal clear, a passage of scripture that describes what is surely the saddest event of all time is shared here.

> **And I saw a great white throne, and him that sat on it, from whose face the earth and the heaven fled away; and there**

---

460. "I said in mine heart, God shall judge the righteous and the wicked: for there is a time there for every purpose and for every work" (Eccl. 3:17).
461. *What Can We Know About the Endtimes?—Future: Coming Events*, Radio Bible Class, p. 21.
462. Lindsey, Hal, *There's a New World Coming—A Prophetic Odyssey*, Vision House Publishers, Santa Ana, CA, 1973, 282.

was found no place for them. And I saw the dead, small and great, stand before God; and the books were opened: and another book was opened, which is the book of life: and the dead were judged out of those things which were written in the books, according to their works. And the sea gave up the dead which were in it; and death and hell delivered up the dead which were in them: and they were judged every man according to their works. And death and hell were cast into the lake of fire. This is the second death. And whosoever was not found written in the book of life was cast into the lake of fire.

—Revelation 20:11–15

The Lord Jesus Christ's judgment on all of the individuals present at the Great White Throne will be personal, and it will be permanent! The length of time required for each "case" to be tried in this Supreme Court will be adequate and sufficient to demonstrate the fact that the individual rejected God's love throughout his or her lifetime. The evidence will be clear and complete. Almighty God will, of course, have access to His total knowledge of every individual. God will surely identify each person who stands before Him by name and perhaps by lineage, by time of life on earth, by place of birth, and by place of death. God will carefully review the thoughts, motives, words, works, and impact of the individual's actions on others. God will give His final verdict to each individual. The Lord Jesus Christ's closing comment to an individual may be something like, "Depart from me, ye cursed, into everlasting fire."[463] Or the Lord may say, "I never knew you: depart from me, ye that work iniquity."[464] The individual's name will be announced and his or her sentence will be declared. The lost individual

---

463. "Then shall he say also unto them on the left hand, Depart from me, ye cursed, into everlasting fire, prepared for the devil and his angels" (Matt. 25:41).
464. Matthew 7:23

will be cast into the lake of fire, which is the second death.[465] This is surely the saddest event of all time because all of the individuals who rejected God's love and who did not ask for God's mercy during their earthly lifetime will leave the presence of Almighty God forever.[466] After the individual leaves the presence of God at the Great White Throne judgment, he or she will be cast into Hell with its everlasting fire that was prepared for the devil and his angels.[467]

This is certainly an extremely depressing documentation of a future event! But, fortunately, everyone reading these words can escape being present for God's judgment at the Great White Throne. Chapter eight presents a way for you to have all of your sins forgiven, and it shares how you can establish an eternal relationship with Almighty God. Please make sure *now* that you will not stand before God at the Great White Throne.

9. Everything made new

God will make everything in the universe "new again." This monumental renewal project will take place after the millennium and after the Great White Throne judgment. However, it appears that before God commences to make all things new again, He will have committed all of the evil angels and all of sinful mankind to their eternal punishment and to their eternal dispensation in Hell. Making all things new again is comparable to God's initial creation of the universe. This extraordinary event is described in the following verses:

For, behold, I create new heavens and a new earth: and the former shall not be remembered, nor come into mind.

—Isaiah 65:17

---

465. "And death and hell were cast into the lake of fire. This is the second death. And whosoever was not found written in the book of life was cast into the lake of fire" (Rev. 20:14–15).
466. "And these shall go away into everlasting punishment: but the righteous into life eternal" (Matt. 25:46).
467. Matthew 25:41b

And he shall send Jesus Christ, which before was preached unto you: Whom the heaven must receive until the times of restitution of all things, which God hath spoken by the mouth of all his holy prophets since the world began.

—Acts 3:20–21

But the heavens and the earth, which are now, by the same word are kept in store, reserved unto the fire against the day of judgment and perdition of ungodly men.

—2 Peter 3:7

But the day of the Lord will come as a thief in the night; in the which the heavens shall pass away with a great noise, and the elements shall melt with fervent heat, the earth also and the works that are therein shall be burned up. Seeing then that all these things shall be dissolved, what manner of persons ought ye to be in all holy conversation and godliness.

—2 Peter 3:10–11

And I saw a new heaven and a new earth: for the first heaven and the first earth were passed away; and there was no more sea.

—Revelation 21:1

And he that sat upon the throne said, Behold, I make all things new. And he said unto me, Write: for these words are true and faithful.

—Revelation 21:5

The new heaven and the new earth will come into existence only after the complete destruction and the total disintegration of the old heaven and the old earth. It is so fitting that before God makes the earth new,

He will destroy in an instant all of the vast reserves of natural gas and crude oil or petroleum[468] that have been so important to modern mankind for the operation of their engines and machines of transportation and industry. Certainly God will provide a new and unlimited source of energy that will be used throughout eternity.

Since God is in complete control of all of the elements in the universe, He may totally remake every molecule, every atom, every proton, every neutron, every electron, and every subatomic particle. We can be sure that whatever process God uses to make the new heaven and the new earth, it will be thorough, complete, and will perfectly prepare the new earth and the new universe for the eternal occupation and enjoyment of all of His redeemed people. God's remaking of the heavens and the earth will definitely be the most spectacular, dramatic, and awesome display of His power witnessed by people up to this point in history.

10. Eternity

It is beyond human comprehension to understand the magnitude of a perpetual and everlasting time period. Eternity has no end. Eternity is intimately and completely intertwined with the New Jerusalem, the new heavens, and the new earth. The new earth is the restoration of the Garden of Eden and the perfect universe that God created during the six days of creation week. Eden was paradise on earth before Adam and Eve rebelled against God's command. In eternity, God plans to have eternal fellowship with all of the people who expressed and demonstrated their love for Him during their lifetime on earth. The following passages from the Bible provide some descriptions of what will take place during eternity. You should note that God has not told us all that He is planning for eternity. But we do know that God's mercy

---

468. Petroleum is called a fossil fuel because it is formed from the remains of plants and animals. 30 December 2007 <http://lsa.colorado.edu/summarystreet/texts/petroleum.htm>.

will be present in eternity.[469] God has some marvelous surprises awaiting the redeemed people who enter into eternity with Him!

He hath made every thing beautiful in his time: also he hath set the world in their heart, so that no man can find out the work that God maketh from the beginning to the end.

—Ecclesiastes 3:11

For since the beginning of the world men have not heard, nor perceived by the ear, neither hath the eye seen, O God, beside thee, what he hath prepared for him that waiteth for him.

—Isaiah 64:4

For, behold, I create new heavens and a new earth: and the former shall not be remembered, nor come into mind. But be ye glad and rejoice for ever in that which I create: for, behold, I create Jerusalem a rejoicing, and her people a joy. And I will rejoice in Jerusalem, and joy in my people: and the voice of weeping shall be no more heard in her, nor the voice of crying.

—Isaiah 65:17–19

But as it is written, Eye hath not seen, nor ear heard, neither have entered into the heart of man, the things which God hath prepared for them that love him.

—1 Corinthians 2:9

Keep yourselves in the love of God, looking for the mercy of our Lord Jesus Christ unto eternal life.

—Jude 21

---

469. "O give thanks unto the LORD; for he is good; for his mercy endureth for ever" (1 Chron. 16:34).

And there shall in no wise enter into it any thing that defileth, neither whatsoever worketh abomination, or maketh a lie: but they which are written in the Lamb's book of life.

—Revelation 21:27

And there shall be no more curse: but the throne of God and of the Lamb shall be in it; and his servants shall serve him: And they shall see his face; and his name shall be in their foreheads. And there shall be no night there; and they need no candle, neither light of the sun; for the Lord God giveth them light: and they shall reign for ever and ever.

—Revelation 22:3–5

God's Word,[470] the Holy Bible, will be in eternity.[471] What a blessing it will be to all of the redeemed saints to read and fully understand the original manuscripts as they were first penned. This ability will make it possible for all of the saints to study God's biblical message[472] in every way possible. It seems likely that God's people will memorize all sixty–six books of the Bible, and they will use this storehouse of knowledge as a central part of their worship and their work.

God has so many plans for His redeemed people that a literal eternity will be needed to accomplish them. Eternity will be a time of fellowship between God and each individual.[473] In eternity there will be times for the saints to worship God and to serve God. A biblical example of this relationship and a foreshadowing of activity in eternity is found in the second chapter of Genesis. Before Adam and Eve

---

470. "For ever, O LORD, thy word is settled in heaven" (Ps. 119:89).
471. "But the word of the Lord endureth for ever. And this is the word which by the gospel is preached unto you" (1 Pet. 1:25).
472. "Heaven and earth shall pass away, but my words shall not pass away" (Matt. 24:35).
473. "Then we which are alive and remain shall be caught up together with them in the clouds, to meet the Lord in the air: and so shall we ever be with the Lord" (1 Thess. 4:17).

sinned, God put Adam in the Garden of Eden to dress it and keep it.[474] It is also strongly indicated that, in the cool of the day, God would walk and talk with Adam and Eve.[475]

If an individual Christian in Heaven is part of a family and family line of Christians, there will be joyous reunions with brothers and sisters, cousins, aunts, uncles, spouses, parents, grandparents, great-grandparents, and on through all generations of mankind. Undoubtedly, there will be hugs and holy kisses[476] beyond our imagination. Surely there will be opportunities to meet and to become friends with every other redeemed saint of all time. Imagine the opportunities to get to know as many as ten or twenty billion people as individuals. Imagine that all of these individuals are your best friends and you have all the time in eternity to do enjoyable, meaningful, and rewarding things together. Surely, we will be able to remember the names of every one of these eternal friends.[477] We will know where they live and what they like to do.

Astronomers tell us there may be one hundred billion galaxies in the universe. There also may be one hundred billion suns and solar systems in every galaxy. Henry Morris suggested that in eternity perhaps God will assign each person an entire galaxy to explore and develop for the glory of God.[478] There is a strong hint found in the parable of the talents[479] that God will reward His most faithful servants by making them rulers over "many things."[480] In the Old Testament

---

474. Genesis 2:15
475. Genesis 3:8
476. "Salute one another with an holy kiss. The churches of Christ salute you" (Rom. 16:16).
477. "But I trust I shall shortly see thee, and we shall speak face to face. Peace be to thee. Our friends salute thee. Greet the friends by name" (3 John 14).
478. Morris, Henry M., *The Revelation Record*, Tyndale House Publishers, Inc., Wheaton, IL & Creation-Life Publishers, San Diego, CA, 1983, p. 468.
479. Matthew 25:14–30
480. "His lord said unto him, Well done, thou good and faithful servant: thou hast been faithful over a few things, I will make thee ruler over many things: enter thou into the joy of thy lord. He also that had received two talents came and

God said that our works would be rewarded.[481]

When God remakes the heavens, He can create precisely what He wants His saints to have. In a galaxy–filled universe, God could certainly customize each galaxy as a reward that is appropriate for the saint that will be responsible for its care and maintenance. The new heaven could be ten times or ten thousand times the size of the universe that now surrounds our planet earth. If God chooses, He could even create multiple universes.

What we call space travel now is really quite limited. "Modern" space travel requires expensive and complex equipment to escape the earth's gravity for travel just to the earth's moon. Surely in eternity, it could be commonplace for each person to move from earth, where the New Jerusalem will be located, to any galaxy in the universe. Each redeemed saint will have a home in the New Jerusalem and, likely, each redeemed saint will have places to live throughout the universe. If Morris is accurate in his imagination, each saint may have a galaxy to rule, to maintain, and to make available to other saints and to God. It is possible that angels may assist each saint as he or she works to cultivate the flora and fauna on all of the planets in their galaxy. Eternal friends may assist each other as they work on developing and maintaining their galaxies. Do all of these possibilities stretch your mind? And since we can't imagine it . . . they should.

We do not know all of what God has in store for us in eternity.[482] But these thoughts and other passages from the Bible can give us a starting point of things to consider.

---

said, Lord, thou deliveredst unto me two talents: behold, I have gained two other talents beside them. His lord said unto him, Well done, good and faithful servant; thou hast been faithful over a few things, I will make thee ruler over many things: enter thou into the joy of thy lord" (Matt. 25:21–23).

481. "Be ye strong therefore, and let not your hands be weak: for your work shall be rewarded" (2 Chron. 15:7).

482. "But as it is written, Eye hath not seen, nor ear heard, neither have entered into the heart of man, the things which God hath prepared for them that love him" (1 Cor. 2:9).

Chapter 7

So What?

Unto thee it was shewed, that thou mightest know that the LORD he is God; there is none else beside him.

—Deuteronomy 4:35

That all the people of the earth may know that the LORD is God, and there is none else.

—1 Kings 8:60

I am the LORD, and there is none else, there is no God beside me. . . .

—Isaiah 45:5a

"So what?" was one of the favorite questions asked by Dr. Walter Martin[483] when he taught the Bible and presented statements made by the Lord Jesus Christ. The question "So what?" does not "beat around the bush" but goes straight to the point—straight to the heart of the issue. So what difference does it make if the God of the Bible has twenty–eight or more inexhaustible attributes that reveal a unique, eternal, and incomprehensible Being? The Scriptures reveal that the God of the Bible is

---

483. Rev. Walter Martin (10 September 1928–26 June 1989) was a Christian apologist and an authority on religions originating in the United States. He earned a Masters degree from New York University and a Ph.D. from California Western University. 22 November 2007 <www.waltermartin.org/about.html>.

1. Omniscient
2. Omnipotent
3. Omnipresent
4. Eternal
5. Immutable
6. Incomprehensible
7. Self–existent
8. Self–sufficient
9. Infinite
10. Transcendent
11. Sovereign
12. Holy
13. Gracious
14. Righteous
15. Just
16. Merciful
17. Longsuffering
18. Wise
19. Loving
20. Good
21. Wrathful
22. Truth/Truthful
23. Faithful
24. Jealous
25. Personal
26. Spirit/Invisible
27. Life
28. Triune

I have attempted to document more than a mere introduction to the nature of Almighty God. But certainly the faithful and broad description of God presented in this book is still completely inadequate to communicate the total nature of the Creator God. Hopefully, the

Scripture verses, the illustrations describing a portion of the character of Almighty God, and the presentation of a few things that He has done begin to reveal His unique nature and awesome attributes and actions. Even with this book's limited description of the attributes, the knowledge, and the power of Almighty God it should be possible for the reader to understand that the God of the Holy Bible has the ability to do anything He chooses to do.

God is the author of the Holy Bible, and He is therefore responsible for every word and every fact that it contains.[484] We read in the Bible that

» God says that He has always existed, and that He created the entire universe by speaking words that caused every atom in the universe to come into existence.

» God says He holds everything in the universe together.

» God says He knows the number of stars in the universe and that He calls them all by their names.[485]

» God says that He loves all of the people He created.[486]

» God reveals that He knows everything there is to know about the bodies of every person.

» God says He knows all of the thoughts, words, and actions of every person.

» God states that because of the sin of Adam and Eve, every person is under the curse of sin.

» God sent his Son, the Lord Jesus Christ, to make a way for every person to receive forgiveness for every sin that they commit during their lifetime.

---

484. It is possible that some translations of the Holy Bible have accidentally or purposefully altered the message contained in the original manuscripts.

485. "He telleth the number of the stars; he calleth them all by their names" (Ps. 147:4).

486. "For God so loved the world, that he gave his only begotten Son, that whosoever believeth in him should not perish, but have everlasting life" (John 3:16).

Statements containing this information and many others communicating the knowledge of the Holy God are clearly and continually made throughout the Bible.

Throughout history there have been forces, movements, philosophies, nations, religions, and individuals that have rejected God or that have twisted the statements made by God. As a result, billions of people have been deceived and have not trusted what God has stated in Scripture. Sadly, many people have been deceived into believing that the God of the Bible is not who He says He is.

But consider that God, who possesses the attributes which are described in the Holy Bible and only briefly mentioned in this book, has enormous abilities that are completely beyond human comprehension.[487] Remember, God documented in the Bible His creation of the earth and the universe in six days. Below is a brief summary of the events of creation week:

1. On day one of creation week, God spoke and the earth was created with water, darkness, light, time, gravity, night, and day.
2. On day two of creation week, God spoke and there was a firmament and an atmosphere.
3. On day three of creation week, God spoke and dry land, seas, and plants were created.
4. On day four of creation week, God spoke and lights in the firmament of heaven appeared to divide the day from the night and for seasons and the keeping of time. God says He made the sun, the moon, and the stars on this day.
5. On day five of creation week, God spoke and created all of the animals that live in the water and all of the birds that fly above the earth.
6. On day six of creation week, God spoke and created all of the land

---

487. The complete nature of God is unfathomable to any human who has ever lived.

animals. On this day God also records that He made the first man, Adam, from the dust of the ground, and He made the first woman, Eve, from one of Adam's ribs. God says that both Adam and Eve were created in His own image.[488] In all of the things God created, He only made humans to possess His own image. At the end of day six of creation week, God says that He saw everything that He had made and described it as being very good. In six days, God created the earth to be a self–sustaining situation that provided a perfect environment for life.

God definitely had no need to use any process of evolution to accomplish all of these incredibly complex tasks. The God who has all knowledge and who has all power certainly did not need to use billions of years of chance mutations, natural selection, and trial and error to populate the earth with plants and animals living in a perfect environment for life and a self–sustaining situation.

In addition, if God used some form of evolution to fill the earth with plants, animals, and humans, He certainly misled readers of the Bible by His description of the origin of mankind. It is beyond belief that the God who created thoughts, ideas, words, language, and all forms of communication could not accurately describe the manner in which He brought all forms of natural laws, energy, material, and life into existence.

Moving from creation week to the Genesis flood, described in Genesis 6–8, the Bible continues to describe God's involvement with His creation. God directed male and female representatives from all of the land animals that He created during creation week to board Noah's ark so they could survive the flood.[489] Many of the descendants of those

---

488. Genesis 1:27
489. "They, and every beast after his kind, and all the cattle after their kind, and every creeping thing that creepeth upon the earth after his kind, and every fowl after his kind, every bird of every sort. And they went in unto Noah into the ark, two and two of all flesh, wherein is the breath of life. And they that went in, went in male and female of all flesh, as God had commanded him:

animals are living today. Modern scientific studies are revealing some of the unique abilities that these animals possess. God's marvelous provision for these animals is programmed into their DNA. God made it possible for many of His creatures to adapt to severe and to changing environments. God made it possible for some of His creatures to migrate extremely long distances with information encoded into their DNA. God made it possible for animals to protect themselves from attack with special devices. This is possible through the information found in their DNA.

A few examples of animals with extraordinary genetic programming are shared here:

1. The wood frog (*Rana sylvatica*) is able to survive being frozen into a frog–shaped piece of ice for months during winter in Alaska and other places. When the frog is frozen, its heart stops beating, its blood stops flowing, and it cannot move. But when spring arrives with warm temperatures, the frog's body thaws and in only a few hours the frog returns to normal life. To restart all of the wood frog's systems after they have been frozen requires extremely complex genetic programming that God created in its DNA.[490]

2. The oilbird or Guacharo (*Steatomis caripensis*) has a wing–span of about forty inches and lives in caves in northern South America. It is the only nocturnal, fruit–eating bird in the world. The nests of oilbirds are located on ledges in pitch black caves and it is here that they are born and learn to fly with dolphin–like sonar[491] and bat–like radar[492] navigation skills. They have extraordinarily keen eyesight in very dark situations. At night oilbirds leave their caves and may fly as much as one hundred fifty miles to find their food by smell. They can hover like a kingfisher. The unique abilities of

---

and the LORD shut him in" (Gen. 7:14–16).

490. Schroeder, Lawson, "Frozen Frogs" *Creation* 30(1) December 2007–February 2008, p. 42.
491. Sonar means SOund NAvigation and Ranging
492. Radar means RAdio Detection And Ranging.

oilbirds were designed by God, and He programmed their DNA with the information needed to do exactly what they do.[493]

3. The monarch butterfly is about and inch and a half long and weighs about half a gram. Some monarch butterflies migrate as much as three thousand miles from Nova Scotia, Canada, to the mountains west of Mexico City. These butterflies make this journey flying in calm air at a speed of up to thirty miles per hour. They usually fly close to the ground but have been seen as high as twelve thousand feet. They have been known to fly for more than three hundred seventy–five miles over water in sixteen hours without stopping. If they are blown off course, they are still able to find their way to their destination. These butterflies normally find their way back to the same tree visited by their ancestors even when they have never made this trip before. All of this is done by a small insect with a brain no larger than a pin head. God programmed this butterfly to accomplish this amazing migration.[494]

God has been intimately involved with human history. Below are a few examples of how God has interacted with humans and the earth:

1. God walked and talked with Adam and Eve in the Garden of Eden.[495]

2. God brought judgment on Adam and Eve and the universe because of sin.[496]

3. God told Noah to build the ark so life could be preserved during the worldwide flood.[497]

---

493. Bell, Philip, "The Super–Senses of Oilbirds—Bizarre birds elude an evolutionary explanation," *Creation* 28(1) December 2005–February 2006, p. 38–41.

494. Poirier, Jules, "The magnificent migrating monarch," *Creation* 20(1) December 1997, p. 28–31.

495. "And they heard the voice of the LORD God walking in the garden in the cool of the day: and Adam and his wife hid themselves from the presence of the LORD God amongst the trees of the garden" (Gen. 3:8).

496. Genesis 3:14–19 records God's judgment on the sin of Adam and Eve.

497. "Make thee an ark of gopher wood; rooms shalt thou make in the ark, and

4. God closed the door to the ark just before the flood commenced.[498]

5. God made a covenant with Abram.[499]

6. God allowed Moses to give a glimpse of His power to the pharaoh of Egypt.[500]

7. God parted the waters of the Red Sea to allow for the children of Israel to escape from Egyptian slavery. God destroyed the Egyptian army by covering the soldiers with the waters of the parted Red Sea.[501]

8. Israel was victorious in battle while Moses held his hands and staff in the air.[502]

9. God made the walls of Jericho fall at a precise moment.[503]

10. God made the sun and the moon stand still.[504]

11. God arranged for a giant fish to swallow Jonah.[505]

---

shalt pitch it within and without with pitch" (Gen. 6:14).

498. "And they that went in, went in male and female of all flesh, as God had commanded him: and the LORD shut him in" (Gen. 7:16).

499. "In the same day the LORD made a covenant with Abram, saying, Unto thy seed have I given this land, from the river of Egypt unto the great river, the river Euphrates" (Gen. 15:18). There are six references in Genesis were God makes or confirms His covenant with Abram. They are found in Genesis 12:1–3, 7; 13:14–18; 15:4, 5, 13–18; 17:1–8; 18:17–19; and 22:15–18.

500. The plagues God brought upon the people of Egypt prior to the Exodus of the children of Israel are described in Exodus 7:14–11:10 and Exodus 12:29–30.

501. The parting and closing of the waters of Red Sea is documented in Exodus 14:13–30.

502. "And it came to pass, when Moses held up his hand, that Israel prevailed: and when he let down his hand, Amalek prevailed" (Exod. 17:11).

503. ". . . And it came to pass, when the people heard the sound of the trumpet, and the people shouted with a great shout, that the wall fell down flat, so that the people went up into the city, every man straight before him, and they took the city" (Josh. 6:20b).

504. "And the sun stood still, and the moon stayed, until the people had avenged themselves upon their enemies. Is not this written in the book of Jasher? So the sun stood still in the midst of heaven, and hasted not to go down about a whole day. And there was no day like that before it or after it, that the LORD hearkened unto the voice of a man: for the LORD fought for Israel" (Josh. 10:13–14).

505. "Now the LORD had prepared a great fish to swallow up Jonah. And Jonah

12. God made many prophecies of the coming of Messiah.[506]
13. God sent Jesus Christ into human history in the body of a baby born to Mary without the normal process of a human father.
14. Jesus Christ died on a Roman cross as payment for the sin debt owed by all mankind.
15. Jesus Christ defeated death through His resurrection.
16. Jesus Christ ascended into Heaven.

God created the human body to be a very special collection of unbelievably complex components that include, but are certainly not limited to, systems, organs, sensory devices, and an incredible brain. These components may appear to act independently, but they are connected to and support each other with nerves, vessels, and chemicals that continually communicate information. Here are a few examples of God's creative handiwork in the human body:

1. The function of the eyes
2. The function of the ears
3. The function of the digestive system
4. The function of the lymphatic system
5. The function of the heart
6. The ability to smell
7. The ability to taste
8. The ability of blood to clot
9. The function of the reproductive system
10. The function of the brain

All of these examples demonstrate supernatural understanding, knowledge, wisdom, design, power, and ability on the part of the Cre-

---

was in the belly of the fish three days and three nights" (Jon. 1:17).

506. According to 4 January 2008 <www.messiahrevealed.org> there are over three hundred prophecies from the Hebrew Scriptures that reveal Messiah. One of these states that Messiah's hands and feet would be pierced (Ps. 22:16c) and this was fulfilled when Jesus Christ was crucified (Matt. 27:38).

ator who has revealed Himself in the Holy Bible. There are thousands more examples that could be added to these brief lists. The interested reader can easily and quickly identify a multitude of additional examples that reveal exceptional abilities and irreducible complexity in living organisms.

In addition, all of these examples defy gradual evolutionary modifications through chance mutations in the DNA with subsequent natural selection of plants or animals. Some people believe that occasional chance mutations make organisms better adapted to their environment and thus better able to survive. As these better adapted organisms survive, the less adapted organisms "die out," leaving only the stronger or better equipped organisms to continue the evolutionary process. This idea of the evolution of plants and animals is not taught in the Bible. The theory of the evolution of organisms is an invention of humans. Evolution is not the method God used to create the world and the universe.

The real issue at the heart of the creation by God or the evolution by chance explanation for the origin of life and the universe is centered on trust. Where should our trust be placed? Should the Author of the Holy Bible receive our trust, or should some scientists and textbook authors of the modern age be the recipient of our trust?

A proverb from the Bible provides excellent guidance on whom to trust:

Trust in the LORD with all thine heart; and lean not unto thine own understanding. In all thy ways acknowledge him, and he shall direct thy paths.

—Proverbs 3:5–6

Evolution is hopeless. But the God of the Bible gives hope, purpose, forgiveness, salvation, security, peace, and especially love to all those who choose to accept Him on His terms. The Creator God as revealed in the Bible is the greatest Being in the universe, with total authority, total power, total knowledge, and total truth. If the God of the Bible is not who He says He is, then He is not the greatest Being in the universe and He does not possess total authority, total power, total knowledge, and total truth. If the God of the Bible is not who He says He is, then there is no need to believe the message in the book He provided. There is no middle ground. The God of the Bible cannot be a weak God. God is either exactly who He says He is or He is nothing.[507] The Holy Bible that God has authored and provided for mankind is either accurate or it is worthless. Any individual who rejects the authority and the message of the Holy Bible makes a terrible mistake, as this decision is a denial of the integrity of the Sovereign God of the universe.

On the other hand, if the God of the Bible is who He says He is, then He deserves our complete trust. The God of the Bible says He loves every person He created. The God of the Bible has the answer to all problems and to all questions. The God of the Bible has a plan for every human. The God of the Bible wants every human to have fellowship with Him. Yes, the complete nature of the God of the Bible is light years beyond our comprehension, but He has made it possible for humans to have a personal relationship and fellowship with Him. Dr. Richard Dawkins is an atheist and one of the most respected and well-known scientists in the world. He made an extremely insightful comment about the unfathomable nature of God during a discussion with Dr. Francis Collins, a Christian geneticist, recorded in *Time* magazine.[508] In essence, Dr. Dawkins said that if there is a God, He will be bigger and He will be more incomprehensible than any God that has been described by the leaders of any of the world's religions. Dr. Dawkins indeed made a profound statement. The Creator God of the Bible is absolutely beyond human comprehension. As this book has attempted to demonstrate, the knowledge of God is complete, which is

507. Anderson, Kevin, *Postmodern Creationists?*, *Creation Research Society Quarterly*, Vol. 44(2), Fall 2007, p. 74.
508. Biema, David Van, "God vs. Science," *Time* magazine, November 13, 2006, Vol. 168, Issue 20, p.48.

why the Bible describes God as being omniscient. And this omniscience is only one of the twenty–eight attributes that have been mentioned in this book about the nature of God. Unfortunately, the religions of the world do not accept the God of the Bible as their God, so they fail to comprehend God's attributes. And sadly, it appears that there are many leaders in the Christian faith that do not understand, or at least do not communicate, the unfathomable nature of Almighty God. But, when the Bible is read with complete trust in its Author, the Bible's description of God clearly reveals the Ultimate Being.

Blaise Pascal[509] proposed that there are only two choices for humans to make about the existence of God.[510] One choice is that God exists. The other choice is that God does not exist. Pascal presented these two choices as a way to determine how a person can choose to live his or her life. According to Pascal, these are the four options available to humans:[511]

1. If God does not exist, and you live as though He does not exist, you lose nothing.
2. If God does not exist, and you live as though He does exist, you lose nothing but gain the advantages of a better life.
3. If God does exist, and you live as though He does not exist, you lose everything.
4. If God does exist, and you live as though He does exist, you lose nothing and gain everything.

The decision to trust and believe the God of the Bible is an individual choice that makes an eternal difference in the life and death of an individual. If you would like to learn how to trust and believe the God of the Bible, you will find assistance in the following chapter.

If your God is not the Ultimate Being, your God is too small.

---

509. Blaise Pascal was a 17th century scientist and Christian.
510. This choice presented by Blaise Pascal is referred to as Pascal's Wager.
511. Steyne, Russell, "Pascal's Wager," *Creation*, 30(1) December 2007–February 2008, p. 49.

Chapter 8

The Four "Rs" That Return Us to God

For God so loved the world, that he gave his only begotten Son, that whosoever believeth in him should not perish, but have everlasting life.

—John 3:16

God has made it perfectly clear in the Bible that He loves every individual.[512] When God created human beings, He demonstrated His perfect love and His respect for all people by giving every person the right to choose whom he or she will love, trust, and obey. This was a bold step by God, as it gave every man and every woman who would live throughout history a "free will" with the right to choose to reject or to receive Jesus Christ as their Lord and Savior. God made every individual an independent agent. Simply stated, God does not force people to love Him. He sincerely desires the love and the fellowship of the humans He created. Through God's plan of redemption, He has made it possible during the lifetime of every individual for that person to voluntarily choose to believe in the Lord Jesus Christ and to receive Him as his or her Lord and Savior.

Since the rebellion and sin of Adam and Eve in the Garden of Eden, all of mankind must now make the choice to reject or to receive the Lord Jesus Christ. The Bible states that every person has "gone

---

512. "For God so loved the world, that he gave his only begotten Son, that whosoever believeth in him should not perish, but have everlasting life" (John 3:16).

astray"[513] or has sinned against God.[514] An individual's sin or rebellion against God and his or her rejection of God that continues throughout the person's entire lifetime is a failure to believe in the Lord Jesus Christ. This is a very serious matter![515] Failure to believe in the Lord Jesus Christ separates that person from God. The Bible says that people who do not believe in the Lord Jesus Christ are condemned already.[516] Ultimately, what a person believes about the Lord Jesus Christ will determine where that individual will spend eternity. There are only two choices. The first choice is that he or she will believe in the Lord Jesus Christ and will spend a glorious eternity in Heaven with Him.[517] The second choice is that he or she will choose not to believe in the Lord Jesus Christ and will spend a miserable eternity in Hell[518] separated from Him.

The Bible documents an actual event in history where a jailer, who was a lost person, is saved, giving us a biblical example of how a sinner becomes a Christian. This event is recorded in the following passage where the Philippian jailer believes in the Lord Jesus Christ:

---

513. "All we like sheep have gone astray; we have turned every one to his own way; and the LORD hath laid on him the iniquity of us all" (Isa. 53:6).
514. "What then? are we better than they? No, in no wise: for we have before proved both Jews and Gentiles, that they are all under sin; As it is written, There is none righteous, no, not one: There is none that understandeth, there is none that seeketh after God" (Rom. 3:9–11).
515. "For the wages of sin is death; but the gift of God is eternal life through Jesus Christ our Lord" (Rom. 6:23).
516. "He that believeth on him is not condemned: but he that believeth not is condemned already, because he hath not believed in the name of the only begotten Son of God" (John 3:18).
517. "And I heard a great voice out of heaven saying, Behold, the tabernacle of God is with men, and he will dwell with them, and they shall be his people, and God himself shall be with them, and be their God. And God shall wipe away all tears from their eyes; and there shall be no more death, neither sorrow, nor crying, neither shall there be any more pain: for the former things are passed away" (Rev. 21:3–4).
518. "And in hell he lift up his eyes, being in torments, and seeth Abraham afar off, and Lazarus in his bosom. And he cried and said, Father Abraham, have mercy on me, and send Lazarus, that he may dip the tip of his finger in water, and cool my tongue; for I am tormented in this flame" (Luke 16:23–24).

And when they had laid many stripes upon them, they cast them into prison, charging the jailor to keep them safely: Who, having received such a charge, thrust them into the inner prison, and made their feet fast in the stocks. And at midnight Paul and Silas prayed, and sang praises unto God: and the prisoners heard them. And suddenly there was a great earthquake, so that the foundations of the prison were shaken: and immediately all the doors were opened, and every one's bands were loosed. And the keeper of the prison awaking out of his sleep, and seeing the prison doors open, he drew out his sword, and would have killed himself, supposing that the prisoners had been fled. But Paul cried with a loud voice, saying, Do thyself no harm: for we are all here. Then he called for a light, and sprang in, and came trembling, and fell down before Paul and Silas, And brought them out, and said, Sirs, *what must I do to be saved? And they said, Believe on the Lord Jesus Christ, and thou shalt be saved,* and thy house. And they spake unto him the word of the Lord, and to all that were in his house. And he took them the same hour of the night, and washed their stripes; and was baptized, he and all his, straightway. And when he had brought them into his house, he set meat before them, and rejoiced, believing in God with all his house.

—Acts 16:23–34

This passage describes a responsible government employee, a good person, who was preparing to kill himself because he believed he had failed to do the job that he was given by the leaders of his community. However, before he could take his own life, he was surprised by a human voice coming from his dark prison with its doors standing open; "But Paul cried with a loud voice, saying, Do thyself no harm: for we are all here." This night was the defining moment in the jailer's life, because he was introduced to the Lord Jesus Christ, and he believed on and personally received Him.

The Philippian jailer believed on the Lord Jesus Christ. The word "believe" is very much a part of God's plan of redemption. It should be noted how Paul and Silas answered the Philippian jailer's question, "What must I do to be saved?" Paul and Silas said, "Believe on the Lord Jesus Christ, and thou shalt be saved, and thy house." Their response included the extremely significant word "Lord." For the Philippian jailer to be saved, he must make Jesus Christ his **Lord.** The word "believe" used in Paul and Silas' response means much more than just acknowledging who Jesus Christ is. You can be sure that all of the demons and even the devil himself believe that Jesus Christ exists and that Jesus Christ is the Son of God and that Jesus Christ is God. Certainly, there is much more to the word *believe* than just acknowledging who Jesus Christ is because otherwise the demons and the devil would be redeemed. There are no Bible passages that I know of that give any indication that the demons or the devil himself will ever be redeemed or forgiven of their rebellion against God. The Bible says that Hell, with its everlasting fire, has been prepared for the devil and his demons.[519]

Believe

These passages from the Bible use the word "believe" in the context of redemption and salvation.

> **But as many as received him, to them gave he power to become the sons of God, even to them that believe on his name.**
>
> —John 1:12

> **And as Moses lifted up the serpent in the wilderness, even so must the Son of man be lifted up: That whosoever believeth**

---

519. "Then shall he say also unto them on the left hand, Depart from me, ye cursed, into everlasting fire, prepared for the devil and his angels" (Matt. 25:41).

in him should not perish, but have eternal life. For God so loved the world, that he gave his only begotten Son, that whosoever believeth in him should not perish, but have everlasting life.

—John 3:14–16

He that believeth on him is not condemned: but he that believeth not is condemned already, because he hath not believed in the name of the only begotten Son of God.

—John 3:18

He that believeth on the Son hath everlasting life: and he that believeth not the Son shall not see life; but the wrath of God abideth on him.

—John 3:36

Verily, verily, I say unto you, He that heareth my word, and believeth on him that sent me, hath everlasting life, and shall not come into condemnation; but is passed from death unto life.

—John 5:24

And this is the will of him that sent me, that every one which seeth the Son, and believeth on him, may have everlasting life: and I will raise him up at the last day.

—John 6:40

Verily, verily, I say unto you, He that believeth on me hath everlasting life.

—John 6:47

To him give all the prophets witness, that through his name whosoever believeth in him shall receive remission of sins.

—Acts 10:43

And by him all that believe are justified from all things, from which ye could not be justified by the law of Moses.

—Acts 13:39

And [he] brought them out, and said, Sirs, what must I do to be saved? And they said, Believe on the Lord Jesus Christ, and thou shalt be saved, and thy house.

—Acts 16:30–31

The following is a summary of the steps that the Philippian jailer took to believe on the Lord Jesus Christ. These steps may help us to understand what it means to "believe on the Lord Jesus Christ."

How you may have your sins forgiven and become a Christian:

1. Realize that God exists and that you have broken His laws.
2. Repent of your sins.
3. Request God to forgive your sins.
4. Receive Jesus Christ as your Lord and your Savior.

The following biblical passages explain these four "Rs."

Realize

Realize that the God of the Bible exists and that you have broken some of His laws.[520] Realize that you have committed wrong thoughts and wrong actions or sins. Realize that these sins have caused you to be separated from God. The realization of a sinful condition and the realization of a need for forgiveness are only brought about by the working of the Holy Spirit of God.

In the beginning God created the heaven and the earth.

—Genesis 1:1

---

520. "For whosoever shall keep the whole law, and yet offend in one point, he is guilty of all" (Jam. 2:10).

No man can come to me, except the Father which hath sent me draw him: and I will raise him up at the last day.

—John 6:44

They are all gone out of the way, they are together become unprofitable; there is none that doeth good, no, not one.

—Romans 3:12

For all have sinned, and come short of the glory of God.

—Romans 3:23

For the wages of sin is death; but the gift of God is eternal life through Jesus Christ our Lord.

—Romans 6:23

So then faith cometh by hearing, and hearing by the word of God.

—Romans 10:17

Repent

To repent means to turn away from contemplating wrong thoughts and engaging in wrong actions or sins. Repentance means to have a change of mind or attitude toward God and toward sin. When repentance occurs the individual will turn from his or her sins and will earnestly and solely trust in the Lord Jesus Christ for salvation. The following are passages from the Bible that speak on the subject of repentance:

In those days came John the Baptist, preaching in the wilderness of Judaea, And saying, Repent ye: for the kingdom of heaven is at hand.

—Matthew 3:1–2

I tell you, Nay: but, except ye repent, ye shall all likewise perish.

—Luke 13:3

Then Peter said unto them, Repent, and be baptized every one of you in the name of Jesus Christ for the remission of sins, and ye shall receive the gift of the Holy Ghost.

—Acts 2:38

Repent ye therefore, and be converted, that your sins may be blotted out, when the times of refreshing shall come from the presence of the Lord; And he shall send Jesus Christ, which before was preached unto you.

—Acts 3:19–20

That if thou shalt confess with thy mouth the Lord Jesus, and shalt believe in thine heart that God hath raised him from the dead, thou shalt be saved. For with the heart man believeth unto righteousness; and with the mouth confession is made unto salvation.

—Romans 10:9–10

But if we walk in the light, as he is in the light, we have fellowship one with another, and the blood of Jesus Christ his Son cleanseth us from all sin. If we say that we have no sin, we deceive ourselves, and the truth is not in us. If we confess our sins, he is faithful and just to forgive us our sins, and to cleanse us from all unrighteousness. If we say that we have not sinned, we make him a liar, and his word is not in us.

—1 John 1:7–10

Request

Request that the Lord Jesus Christ forgive you of your wrong thoughts and your wrong actions or sins. Request the Lord Jesus Christ to become your Lord and Savior.

Ask, and it shall be given you; seek, and ye shall find; knock,

and it shall be opened unto you: For every one that asketh receiveth; and he that seeketh findeth; and to him that knocketh it shall be opened.

—Matthew 7:7–8

And all things, whatsoever ye shall ask in prayer, believing, ye shall receive.

—Matthew 21:22

For whosoever shall call upon the name of the Lord shall be saved. How then shall they call on him in whom they have not believed? and how shall they believe in him of whom they have not heard? and how shall they hear without a preacher?

—Romans 10:13–14

Be careful for nothing; but in every thing by prayer and supplication with thanksgiving let your requests be made known unto God. And the peace of God, which passeth all understanding, shall keep your hearts and minds through Christ Jesus.

—Philippians 4:6–7

Receive

Receive God's forgiveness that has been made possible by the Lord Jesus Christ through His perfect life, His sacrificial death[521] on the cross,[522] and His defeat of death through His resurrection. Receive

---

521. "How much more shall the blood of Christ, who through the eternal Spirit offered himself without spot to God, purge your conscience from dead works to serve the living God?" (Heb. 9:14). "And almost all things are by the law purged with blood; and without shedding of blood is no remission" (Heb. 9:22).
522. The sacrificial death of Jesus Christ on the cross includes the blood sacrifice that He made by shedding his blood for the remission and forgiveness of all

the Lordship of Jesus Christ. Receive God's gift of forgiveness as the total payment for all of the sins that you have committed and all of the sins that you will commit during your entire lifetime.

> **Whosoever shall receive one of such children in my name, receiveth me: and whosoever shall receive me, receiveth not me, but him that sent me.**
>
> —Mark 9:37

> **Verily I say unto you, Whosoever shall not receive the kingdom of God as a little child, he shall not enter therein.**
>
> —Mark 10:15

> **And Jesus, perceiving the thought of their heart, took a child, and set him by him, And said unto them, Whosoever shall receive this child in my name receiveth me: and whosoever shall receive me receiveth him that sent me: for he that is least among you all, the same shall be great.**
>
> —Luke 9:47–48

> **Verily I say unto you, Whosoever shall not receive the kingdom of God as a little child shall in no wise enter therein.**
>
> —Luke 18:17

After reading the hundreds of verses from the Bible that are presented in this book, I hope you now have a better understanding of the unfathomable attributes of the God who created both the universe and you. God's Holy Spirit may have been speaking to you as you have considered the truly awesome nature of Almighty God. Hopefully, you realize that God knows you and loves you beyond your ability to comprehend. Do you understand that God loves you so much that He

---

of the sins that have been or will be committed by all humans.

gave his only Son, the Lord Jesus Christ, to provide the necessary perfect sacrifice, through his voluntary death on the cross, to pay for the sin debt that you and I both owe? When we believe in the Lord Jesus Christ and consciously chose to make Him our Lord we receive God's gift of forgiveness for all of our sins. When we make Jesus Christ our Lord we also receive the privilege of being allowed to spend eternity in close fellowship with the Creator God of the universe.[523]

Is your God too small? Do you want to trust your eternal existence to a weak and limited god, or do you want to believe in the Lord Jesus Christ? Do you want to trust, obey, and love the God who has all power and all knowledge, and who created the universe and has offered you total forgiveness and complete eternal redemption? The decision is yours, and the decision you make will determine where you will spend eternity. Choose wisely.

---

523. "For I am persuaded, that neither death, nor life, nor angels, nor principalities, nor powers, nor things present, nor things to come, Nor height, nor depth, nor any other creature, shall be able to separate us from the love of God, which is in Christ Jesus our Lord" (Rom. 8:38–39).

Selected resources for additional information

This section provides sources for information that can assist the reader in learning more about God and the world He has created. The list is only a small sample of the material that is available. However, it will give you a starting point for a rewarding and an enriching journey to learn more about the God of the Bible.

Answers in Genesis
P.O. Box 510
Hebron, KY 41048
www.answersingenesis.org

Christian Answers.Net
www.christiananswers.net

Creation Research, Science Education Foundation
P.O. Box 62702
Cincinnati, Ohio 45262
www.worldbydesign.org

Creation Science Movement
P.O. Box 888
Portsmouth
England PO6 2YD
UK
www.csm.org.uk

Creation Studies Institute
5554 North Federal Highway
Fort Lauderdale, FL 33308
www.creationstudies.org

Institute for Creation Research
1806 Royal Lane
Dallas, TX 75229
www.icr.org

Creation Research Society
P.O. Box 8263
St. Joseph, MO 64508-8263
www.creationresearch.org

Creation Ministries International
P.O. Box 4545
Eight Mile Plains
Queensland 4113 Australia
www.CreationOnTheWeb.com

Southwest Radio Ministries
P.O. Box 100
Bethany, OK 73008
www.swrc.com

Summit Ministries
P.O. Box 207
Manitou Springs, CO 80829
www.summit.org

Who Is Your Creator
P.O. Box 1736
Minnetonka, MN 55345
www.WhoIsYourCreator.com

World of the Bible Ministries, Inc.
P.O. Box 827
San Marcos, TX 78667-0827
www.worldofthebible.com

"Yes Lord" Ministries
P.O. Box 22397
Chattanooga, TN 37422
www.Biblestudies.net